SUPER
WEALTH

SUPER
WEALTH

WHY WE SHOULD STOP WORRYING ABOUT
THE "GAP" BETWEEN RICH AND POOR

MAX BORDERS

THRONE
PUBLISHING GROUP

Throne Publishing Group
220 S. Phillips Ave.
Sioux Falls, SD 57104

For Sid

Table of Contents

Fame and Fortune

Let's get something out of the way: I want to get rich with this book. Not super wealthy, but comfortable. I wouldn't turn away bestseller success, but if *Superwealth* keeps me writing books, I'll be happy.

Right now, I'm sneaking out of bed at night to write this book while working a day job. When you have finished reading, I hope you like it enough to buy a copy for your friends and family for their birthdays. Maybe you'll start a book club about *Superwealth* and talk about it with your closest friends. Perhaps you'll buy a box of copies to give away at the Rotary Club meeting. Pretty shameless, huh? Maybe.

You see, I'm of the belief that if you like this book enough to share it, then I have created something of value. In return for the cover price (or digital download), I have given you something you value *more* than the money you handed over for the book. To repeat: You valued it *more* than what you gave for it. That is not just the nature of this exchange between you and me—it's the nature of exchange.

It is possible that in fifty pages you could have buyer's remorse. But at the time you let go of the money, you valued the book more than the foregone resources. At least in browsing the book prior to purchase, you thought it looked pretty good. I'll try not to let you down.

So, if a lot of readers just like you make me a wealthy man, am I justified in keeping the wealth? Are third parties justified in interfering with our agreement and skimming some off the top for various causes championed by politicians at various levels of government? This is a big question. But if you and a lot of other people push me up into the "one percent," will that change be just?

Keep in mind, as I type these words I'm not rich yet. But if I'm entrepreneurial enough, savvy enough, write well enough, and get some good help marketing this book, I could make a decent amount of money from people who—for one reason or another—found this volume in their hands.

Why did *you* pick up *Superwealth?* What motivated *you* to read a book that purports to argue people should stop worrying about the gap between rich and poor? I suspect you're reading this for one of five reasons:

1. You lack the 'envy gene' and you want to know what all this income inequality fuss is about;

2. You have a sneaking suspicion that we should stop picking on rich people because, after all, they make our lives better;

3. You're a rabid, free-market conservative or libertarian and want to reinforce your perspective;

4. You're a rabid, left-leaning liberal and someone told you to read this book because they think you can be turned to the dark side; or,

5. You're a wealthy person who wants to articulate why you shouldn't have to keep apologizing for your wealth.

Whatever your motivations for reading *Superwealth*,[i] I'm happy for you to come on this journey with me.

If by this point you're thinking, *This guy's out of his mind to write a book like this,* you'd be right. But that's beside the point. I have put together a strong set of independent reasons for urging you to ignore the rich-poor gap and focus on more important things. I'm just a useful conduit for those reasons, and if I'm especially useful as a conduit, then I will be rewarded.

Usefulness to you, reward for me: This pairing is more or less the nature of entrepreneurship. I have to keep that in mind as I write this. I am an entrepreneur. How do I know? Because I know that *if* I don't please you, dear customer, you'll chuck this book and tell your friends not to bother. Unlike an IRS agent, I can't point a gun at you or withhold money from your paycheck. I have to create value for you. And Lord knows I might fail.

Like many writers, I am used to failure. I have failed in many ventures, in fact, not just writing. Maybe that's why I make no bones about my admiration for successful people.

FAMILIARITY WITH FAILURE

My first entrepreneurship story starts in early 2000. The tech bubble had not yet burst. I was a grunt at Andersen Consulting

---

i Entrepreneurs are the ones who make the pie. Investors are the ones who bake the pie. Consumers are the ones who buy the pie. Then there are those who use the state to take the pie. (They help themselves.) Once we learn to tell the difference among these groups, we can better help those who have a hard time earning a crust. The rest of the book is commentary.

(now Accenture), a Big Four consulting firm in the Chicagoland area. My job was to write columns about emerging technologies and startups in order to keep consultants on the cutting edge. The world was drunk on "irrational exuberance." IPO was America's favorite three-letter word. I was no exception, but I was a chump—a washed-up philosopher unable to break 500 on the math portion of the GRE. I was lucky to make an entry-level salary and, as I would later learn, I have no follow-through when it comes to starting a business. Still, I had ideas—lots of them.

One of my friends and fellow technology writers Adam Knapp and I were riding a bus one day to our corporate headquarters in Northbrook, Illinois, outside of Chicago. We often read business and technology magazines on the way in, which was a way for a couple of liberal arts guys to stay plugged in to an industry we half understood. I remember reading an article about eBay, which was already starting to revolutionize exchange. Then I opened a different magazine and I started reading some dry article about the economy. One of the more interesting points in that otherwise dry article was that, for the first time, half of U.S. economic activity comprised services. Not goods—Elvis memorabilia, lawnmowers, and chickens—but services—washing cars, fixing teeth, and writing software code. So it came to me like a lightning strike. I felt the blood drain out of my face as my heart became sanguine. Remember, those were the days when companies started on the backs of napkins.

I looked up at Adam.

"What?" he said.

"Why is there no eBay for services?"

"Oh my God," he said. "I don't know." He got it immediately.

Adam was the editor of an internal Andersen newsletter about start-up companies. He'd been out to Silicon Valley scores of times to interview CEOs of these baby firms (many of which would soon perish), so he was enough of an authority to see why I'd gone pale.

We talked more. It was like a flood. I explained that such a site would have to make life simple for people to buy a service with easy-to-navigate categories. We agreed that in order for it not to be just another Craigslist it would have to help people on both the price *and* quality dimensions. A reverse auction would be important, as well as some sort of reputation engine. We envisioned a sliding value bar that you—the buyer of a service—could move back and forth to arrange the offers by price or reputation. And, of course, we were thrilled by the idea of offering access to work opportunities for free agents and unemployed people. Before we got off the bus, we had decided to start a company.

"Want your house cleaned? Your dog washed? Your driveway paved? There are people out there who want to clean your house, wash your dog, and pave your driveway. We just have to get you all together."

We flirted with a couple of names and bought a few URLs. Finally, Adam and I settled on OddjobsX.com, where the "X" stands for your service need. (Not wild about the name now, but whatever...)

We knew this website would have to be geographically oriented. We also decided that we would not yet focus on professional services, but start with small, simple things such as lawn care, window cleaning, and babysitting. Accounting and graphic design could come later. This online service would be a disruptive innovation a la Harvard Business School guru Clayton Christensen.

Adam and I soon began to collaborate cross country. Conveniently, he'd been transferred out to the Bay Area. We soon got ourselves incorporated. He'd found a 'Frisco techie named Moses Ma with an auction code he'd already written in Java. He agreed to be our chief engineer. Adam also made contacts with some venture capitalists who, at the time, were walking around with jeans, sports jackets and Palm Vs. We worked for months, high on the idea. That is, until the tech bubble burst.

As quickly as these millionaires were minted, the capital dried up. And that capital flight meant these Steve Jobs lookalikes were running around not with brainstorming napkins, but with their tails between their legs. Nobody had any stomach for tech after that. It was bad timing. Neither Adam nor I were coders. Our chief engineer went into filmmaking and Adam and I went into a blue funk. At that point we should have dug down deep—perhaps we could have found some out-of-luck coder—but we didn't.

Thomas Edison said genius is 1 percent inspiration and 99 percent perspiration. It's in all the perspiration that success happens. And he's right. If one breaks down perspiration into its composite parts, it includes persistence, patience, and perseverance. I guess Adam and I didn't have enough of these P's, because eventually we gave up on the idea. I started putting my energy back into writing a fiction book that would never get published and into a relationship with a woman that would eventually dissolve.

Entrepreneurship is hard. Being a one-man idea incubator is one thing; and, you better believe I have cool ideas (CEO-types: call me.) But being able to locate resources—human and financial—and then put them all together to make a solvent organization requires a special sort of person. It's not just about noticing the arbitrage opportunity, finding the market niche, or having the spark to create a new thing. It's about starting up and staying up. It's about sustaining the organization for survival while making good things happen—one customer at a time—all in an environment where competitors, regulators, and lawyers are swirling around you, red in tooth and claw. I guess you could say I admire entrepreneurs because I failed at being one.

I flirted with trying to start OddjobsX again in 2008 with my friend Jason Turner, but that flirtation fizzled, too. I had lost the fire for the idea both because I'd held on to it for so long and, to mix metaphors, been burned by it already.

Then, one day recently, my wife sent me an email which read simply (and I quote): "NOOOO! IT'S ODDJOBS!!!!" Below that email was attached a newsletter ad for HelloHandy.com. "Compare prices and schedule local pros for any home project or service," the website read. I knew this day would come.

Who knows if HelloHandy.com will make its founder the next Pierre Omidyar. They have a long way to go to become the eBay of services, but they have a good idea. It will all depend on a lot of factors: a good management team, marketing, and making sure all the customers (the buyers and sellers of services) have a good experience using the site. I wish them luck, because if they succeed I will feel somehow vindicated.

But what if Adam and I had succeeded in getting the company off the ground? What if we'd sold it for $50 million? We would have become wealthy beyond our wildest dreams. We'd have worked our proverbials off and become rich men—the "one percent." Yet we did not.

Persistence and Patience

I won't stop trying. As I said, this book is just another kind of venture. But I know I'm a better writer than a CEO. So I'm going to keep 'doing what I do best and trade for the rest.' I might fail, yet again, at publishing and selling this book.

Back in 2005 I wrote a book called *Complexity Politics*. I had an agent, but she might have been one of five people in the world who would have enjoyed that book. It was smart, but I was still green. She shopped the proposal around to a number of editors, but they all thought the book was too esoteric. They were right: I had written 300 pages of something few would ever read. And while I'm a better writer today for having done it, it was a failure.

I want to start this book with a rather counterintuitive point: Failure is vital. It is essential. It is the very stuff of entrepreneurship. It is what made the late Steve Jobs so great. As one of my mentors Nick Schulz writes:

> Everyone today thinks of Jobs as the genius who gave us the iPod, MacBooks, the iTunes store, the iPhone, the iPad, and so on. Yes, he transformed personal computing and multimedia. But let's not forget what else Jobs did.
>
> Jobs (along with Steve Wozniak) brought us the Apple I and Apple II computers, early iterations of which sold in the mere hundreds and were complete failures. Not until the floppy disk was introduced and sufficient RAM added did the Apple II take off as a successful product.
>
> Jobs was the architect of Lisa, introduced in the early 1980s. You remember Lisa, don't you? Of course you don't. But this computer — which cost tens of millions of dollars to develop — was another epic fail. Shortly after Lisa, Apple had a success with its Macintosh computer. But

Jobs was out of a job by then, having been tossed aside thanks to the Lisa fiasco.

Jobs went on to found NeXT Computer, which was a big nothing-burger of a company. Its greatest success was that it was purchased by Apple — paving the way for the serial failure Jobs to return to his natural home. Jobs's greatest successes were to come later—iPod, iTunes, iPhone, iPad, and more.[1]

If success is yin, failure is yang. "Capitalism without failure is like religion without sin," quips economist Allen Meltzer. "It doesn't work well."

So what does all this have to do with the rich-poor gap?

For one thing, we have to understand that a lot of people get rich because they have something special about them. They make our lives better, yes, but they are able to make our lives better because they are not afraid to fail—often over and over again. Among Silicon Valley venture capitalists and startup CEOs this is not new. Indeed, it's a mantra. But I want to start with the appreciation of failure because success is rare and wonderful. And the rewards of success make other successes more likely, which means the world gets better and better—the "gap" notwithstanding. *Superwealth* is my effort to break this case down. I want to make it not just by arguing against the most vocal gap fetishists, but by telling stories of real people who are both excellent and improve the world.

So please, enjoy. And don't forget: if you enjoy it, buy a copy for a friend. I'm ready to occupy the one percent.

1

The Richest Poor Man In History

The Southerner's primary approach to his world was not through the idea of class. He never really got around in his subconsciousness to thinking of himself as being, before all else, a member of a caste, with interests and purposes in conflict with the interests and purposes of other castes. […] Rather, he saw with essentially naïve, direct, and personal eyes. Rather, his world, as he beheld it, remained always, in its basic aspect, a simple aggregation of human units, of self-continued and self-sufficient entities, whose grouping along class lines, though it might and would count tremendously in many ways, was yet not a first thing.

–W. J. Cash, from The Mind of the South (1941)

Addie Waterson Borders lived to be 104. That means I had more than 30 years to know the woman I call Mama Borders. I got to stand at her hip when she made brown sugar toast. She told me the secret to making livermush when I was older and I got to introduce her to my new wife when I was grown. However you look at it, I'm lucky.

When I was in high school, Mama Borders was already old. I'd been assigned a class project to interview someone who had lived during the Great Depression. A no-brainer: I chose my great grandmother who—during the worst of it—would have been about my age today. Because she never suffered from dementia, the only trouble I ever had getting information out of her was when her ears were clogged and I had to repeat a question. She would sometimes squint in her determined way to mine a deep, deep memory. Otherwise, she was sharp.

So, with recorder rolling, I asked about her experience during the Great Depression:

"We didn't know thar was hard times a-goin' on," she said. "It was all the same to us."

Like many rural Southerners, Mama Borders and my Granddaddy, Garland, were farmers. You could say they were the original purveyors of "organic and locally grown" fare. The fellow natives of Cleveland County, North Carolina, used to envy Mama Borders because her vegetables would come up so sweet and they could never figure out her secret. (She raised all sorts of delicious items well into her nineties, so I got to experience enviable tomatoes, cucumbers, and turnips by the plateful.) But her agrarian lifestyle was shielded from the exogenous shocks of the Smoot-Hawley tariff of 1930, the stock market crash, and the subsequent run on the banks. Mama and Garland lived in a different world. There had been no dust bowl in North Carolina. They had heard about the Doughboys going off to war the first time, and later, their son went off to Germany in the Second World War. But what happened in between was something the grandchildren would read about later in history books or via Steinbeck.

Before that interview with Mama Borders, I had romanticized their way of life. I used to walk around their gardens and wonder at the detritus of their former lives: dried up gourds and rusty implements, barns housing decaying farm machinery. This was the kind of tableau you might read about in the less-macabre passages of a Cormac McCarthy novel. To Mama Borders, these were the relics of a harsher, more austere era. Don't get me wrong, I still get goose bumps when I think about Mama and Granddaddy slaughtering a hog at first frost; tobacco barns on rolling foothills; and sweet corn rows tended by stout folks with a cheek full of chaw or a nose full of snuff. I look back on these times with the luxury of nostalgia, not least because I never had to pull a plow. For Mama Borders, the only good thing about the "good ole days" is that they went.

A DAY IN THE LIFE OF ADDIE BORDERS

Mama's day began well before the cock crowed. If she was going to make breakfast, she had to get the cook stove going with kindling and firewood. She made bacon, biscuits with butter (which she churned herself), and bubbling grits. She would serve preserves, marmalade, or scupperdine[i] jam for the biscuits, all of which she would have found time to prepare and can. After setting out break-fast and eating a square meal before work, she cleaned the dishes by hand. After drying the plates and putting them away, she pulled on her galoshes to meet Garland down at the milk barn.

They let the cows in to feed and locked them into place. She cleaned and sanitized the cows' teats. Early on, she would have milked the cows by hand, just like in the movies. If a cow found a patch of wild onions, she could smell it and she would save that batch for home use. She kept the sweetest milk (from cows eating clover and lick feed) aside for sale. With the cows milked, Mama Borders would lower the full milk cans into an icebox until the milk truck came around. Once the milking was complete, she'd wash and disinfect everything top to bottom, stem to stern. She washed out

---

i   A scupperdine is a kind of grape that grows in North Carolina. It is probably a cross between the muscadine and the scuppernong – both natural N.C. grape varieties.

the empty bottles in a tin tub with water from the well. (On the way, she'd sometimes get stung by bees from a hive nearby.) She had to be sure to clean the manure from the milking area every day, which may have had something to do with the sweetness of her vegetables.

After that, it was on to tending the fields and the garden. Before tractors came onto the scene, Mama and Garland tended the fields with a mule. They grew alfalfa for hay, cotton, corn, oats, and sugar cane for lick feed (molasses made the cows' milk extra sweet). There was almost always something in the ground. She would hitch the mule to the plow and go into the field to clean the rows, which meant cutting under the weeds and pulling between the good plants with a hoe. When it got hot, they carried iced tea with them, slung over their shoulders. She worked in the field until it was time to make lunch.

Before midday, she might make ham sandwiches, creamed corn, and fresh cantaloupe. There were always pies—peach, berry, persimmon, apple, you name it. After lunch, she cleaned the dishes again and prepared for the second half of the work day.

Garland would pull the plow in the garden himself, sometimes, and Mama would work the plow. The mule couldn't go in the garden, as it risked damaging those tender plants, so the two of them plowed it together. As with the fields, dragging the hoe to pull weeds was a Sisyphean but necessary task. Once the mule had done his part, they'd return him to the stable. Then it was time to tie up the plants and dust the tomato and cabbage for worms. Depending on the time of year, they might be tending beans, peas, watermelon, cantaloupe, squash, or gourds. I'm only scratching the surface of what they brought out of the earth.

On laundry days, Mama put lye soap into a cook pot. She'd stir that soapy concoction with a big wooden stick, which started the process of cleaning the clothes. Once this stage was complete, she'd transfer the clothes into a foot tub with a scrubbing board. Once fully scrubbed—cleaned of all sweat, red-clay clods, and humus— she'd transfer the clothes to the rinse water to commence "bluing." This agent, which Mama added to the rinse water, made the whites look extra white. After bluing, rinsing, and considerable wringing, she draped the clothes on the bushes or over a clothesline. Luckily, laundry didn't have to be done every day.

Mama's and Garland's small house lay between eight majestic water oaks. She rued the day she ever planted them. As pretty as they were, there was always something falling from them. She often said time spent cleaning up after the oaks might have been better spent elsewhere. Recall that in those days a "pretty" yard was swept, not cut. Green grasses and lawn tractors didn't come around until later.

Once she'd watered and fed the animals, and taken down the dry clothes, Mama would head inside to prepare chicken 'n' dumplings, fresh cantaloupe, and a pie for dessert. By this time it was dark, and Garland would have had his feet up. Not Mama. After she'd finished cooking and eating supper, she still had to clean the dishes. Once she was done, it was time to do all the little extra things she needed to do. Whether she had to do the sewing, let the milk clabber, or set aside sweet cream for churning, there were still things to be done before bed. After cleaning herself up with soap and a hot washcloth, she'd finally get to sleep around nine o'clock.

A Hard Life Gives Way to Progress and Prosperity

Despite the gothic histories of Southern racism, black and white tenant farmers shared a rugged communitarianism that defies most stereotypes of the Old South. It may be difficult for us to believe in the here and now, but it happened. Black and white people roamed the red clay more together than apart. In the days before they lined up at the Department of Social Services, people had to depend on each other.

Once, a black neighbor came over and asked Garland to help him euthanize his rabid son. The boy's disease had progressed beyond the medicine of that time and place. The two men had to put the boy between two corn-shuck tick mattresses and suffocate him. It may be hard for us to understand the ethic of that time, but these two men, separated pretty much only by color, were united that day in a gruesome rite of mercy killing. Had it been Garland's son—my grandfather—who had been afflicted, the black neighbor would have done the same thing for him. That's just the way things were.

But with prosperity and progress came inoculations and vaccines. Rabies became treatable. Tractors began pulling plows. Cool boxes gave way to refrigerator/freezers. Labor-saving devices abounded. Colonoscopies found cancers. In the quarter-century between 1947 and 1970, they'd come to have electric milkers (the cows got electricity six months before the humans did), an electric pump for water, cars, tractors, a hay bailer, a lawnmower, indoor plumbing (no more outhouse), lights, a bulk cooler, a 'fridge/freezer, and a clothes washer.[ii] Mama Borders never looked back.

She had no regrets. Her life was a natural progression, a co-evolution between modern conveniences and an old soul willing to work from the pre-dawn dark into the moonlit night if necessary. As she got older, things got easier. There might have been some lag

---

ii   Much like the one described by Hans Rosling in "The Magic Washing Machine" video for TED.

time for Mama and Garland compared to the big shots in town, but good things eventually came from capitalism's abundance.

BOURGEOIS INDIGNITIES

Having known Addie Borders, it's difficult to connect with passages such as this one from class warrior Barbara Ehrenreich. In her 2001 novel Nickel and Dimed, Ehrenreich writes about traveling the country posing as a working-class person (here as a maid):

> Self-restraint becomes more of a challenge when the owner of a million-dollar condo … who is … an acquaintance of the real Barbara Bush takes me into the master bathroom to explain the difficulties she's been having with the shower stall. Seems its marble walls have been "bleeding" onto the brass fixtures, and can I scrub the grouting extra hard? That's not your marble bleeding, I want to tell her, it's the world-wide working class—the people who quarried the marble, wove your Persian rugs until they went blind, harvested the apples in your lovely fall-themed dining room centerpiece, smelted the steel for the nails, drove the trucks, put up this building, and now bend and squat and sweat to clean it.

The working class. In a way, she's talking about Mama Borders. Or Bryan Borders: Addie's son, a farmer and a truck driver. Or my dad: her grandson, a truck driver. Or my dad's wife—any number of people without a Ph.D. in cellular biology who see with "essentially naïve, direct, and personal eyes" and who would view Ehrenreich's laundry list above as a list of opportunities rather than offenses. As W. J. Cash notes, people such as those in my family "never felt even the premonitory twinges of class awareness in the full sense – of that state in which the concept of society as divided into rigid layers and orders burrows into the very tissues of the brain and becomes the irresistible magnetic pole for one's deepest loyalties and hates, the all-potent determiner of one's whole ideological and emotional pattern."[2] My mother's side of the family, though better off, is similarly blind to class distinctions.

Ehrenreich's sensational prose is not meant for working-class people; it's meant for guilt-ridden rich ones. In fact, my working-class family members would find little value in her critique because they find dignity in an honest day's work, even if it involves scrubbing someone else's grout, driving a truck, or harvesting apples. If they knew someone like Ehrenreich pitied them from her perch in the ivory tower—or worse, perhaps, play-acted their workaday lives—they'd be insulted, not edified.

Because people such as Barbara Ehrenreich's father could earn fortunes through copper mining, and the Maytag family could get rich making better-faster-cheaper washers, and Sam Walton could get rich building a better retail system, Mama Borders' quality of life steadily improved.

I remember Mama Borders telling my father and me about how she pulled up the hem of her dress and tucked it into the waist of her apron so she could run like the boys to lay eyes on the first Model-T Ford. Of course, the changes brought about by the automobile have been nothing short of miraculous. (By the time she died, Mama Borders rode to the hairdresser in cars with airbags, air conditioning, and more than 150,000 miles on the odometer.) These changes made Henry Ford rich. Is that a bad thing?

"That is the economic system that has transformed our society in the past century and more," said Milton Friedman in 1980, continuing:

That is what gave the Henry Fords, the Thomas Alva Edisons, the Christiaan Barnards, the incentives to produce the miracles that have benefitted us all. It's what gave other people the incentive to provide them with the finance for their ventures. Of course, there were lots of losers along the way. We don't remember their names, but … they went in with their eyes open; they knew what they were doing; and win or lose, we [as a] society benefitted from their willingness to take a chance.

If no nation in the world had been the exception—a nation that let people be as entrepreneurial as they might, and get rich or fail trying—Mama Borders would have died well before 2006 in the same penury in which she started.

A COMFORTABLE SLOTH?

In 2011, George Mason University economist Tyler Cowen caused quite a stir with his Great Stagnation thesis. Cowen argues that the seismic changes in American quality of life started in 1947 (when Addie's son came home from Germany) and ended around 1973 (when her great grandson was born). So while Mama Borders witnessed the effects of an exploding cornucopia of capitalism, she spent her golden years watching America settle into a kind of comfortable sloth. At least that's more or less how Cowen describes it. In economic terms, in the post-war period up to 1973, median household income doubled. Since 1973, it's leveled off with real family income growing by only 22 percent.[3]

But the changes in quality of life depend on your perspective. The biggest changes that have come about in my lifetime have actually been, quite literally, small changes. Microprocessing, viral biology, psychopharmacology, gene sequencing, and so on, all have changed the American landscape. While Mama got to see the first generation Model-T, the polio vaccine, radio, and television, I've been living in a world in which information is ubiquitous, there are pills to control cholesterol, and murderers are convicted with DNA evidence. These may seem like small advances by comparison, but they represent a million little improvements that add up to make our quality of life much, much better. (My mother-in-law, for example, just informed me she would be foregoing barbaric knee replacement surgery in favor of stem-cell injections.)

And there may yet be more "low-hanging fruit," as Cowen calls transformative developments. These won't come from open land or cheap oil, but from medical technologies that can radically extend people's lifespans and the process of Moore's Law—the latter idea being that processing power (or storage, or whatever) doubles about every 18 months. Advances made both at the micro level (genetics, proteomics, nanotechnology, neural interfaces) and changes to social technologies at the macro level (new institutional forms, Internetworking, and organization theory) have the potential to hasten the next great leap in human progress.

Allow me to linger on that last point by appealing to the work of Stephen Johnson in *Where Good Ideas Come From*:

> Watching the ideas spark on [...] different scales reveals patterns that single-scale observations easily miss or undervalue.
>
> I call that vantage point the long zoom. It can be imagined as a kind of hourglass. As you descend toward the center of the glass, the biological scales contract. From the global, deep time of evolution to the microscopic changes of neurons or DNA. At the center of the glass, the perspective shifts from nature to culture, and the scales widen: from individual thoughts and private workspaces to immense cities and global information networks. When we look at innovation from the vantage point of the

long zoom, what we find is that unusually generative environments display similar patterns of creativity at multiple scales simultaneously.

Seen from the long zoom, maybe the period that began with Generation X – my generation – hasn't been so stagnant. Between 1973 and today, the world has seen some remarkable changes. For example, how much labor does it take to get the things we want and need today as opposed to when I was a tot?

Back in 2006, economist Donald Boudreaux of George Mason University reissued a delightful "1975 Sears Catalogue," a set of labor-hour comparisons. According to Boudreaux, in 1975 it took 7.5 labor hours to buy an automatic coffeemaker at a price of $151.03 (in 2006 inflation-adjusted dollars). In 2006, you could buy one for $23.69, which would cost you only 1.2 hours of your labor. In 1979, you could get a cathode-ray TV that took up more than half your living room for about $3,100, or 154 labor hours. In 2006, you could buy a flat-panel plasma or LCD TV for $239, or 12.6 labor hours. As I write this, we're already six years beyond, so some things might have gotten even less expensive if it weren't for Federal Reserve policy. Things are already better, faster, cheaper, and more energy-efficient than they were only five years ago.

"Other than the style differences," adds Boudreaux:

The fact most noticeable from the contents of this catalog's 1,491 pages is what the catalog doesn't contain. The Sears customer in 1975 found no CD players for either home or car; no DVD or VHS players; no cell phones; no televisions with remote controls or flat-screens; no personal computers or video games; no food processors; no digital cameras or camcorders; no spandex clothing; no down comforters (only comforters filled with polyester).

Again, Boudreaux wrote this passage in 2006—about a month before Mama Borders died. Whatever one thinks of the Great Stagnation, Addie Borders witnessed incredible human advancement in her 104 years of life. In some way, she lived the long zoom and things are still getting better, despite the dead weight of the political class and its supplicants.

THE RICHEST POOR

The poor person in America today enjoys more goods, services, and greater quality of life than any poor person ever has in human history. The inequality of outcomes makes that possible. As business professors Ronald Schmidt and Janice Willett write:

> [E]conomic inequality is another term for incentives that encourage investment in education—or, for that matter, starting a new business. Of course, most new start-ups fail, so there's a lot of risk involved. But taxing the successful ones will not make failures less likely—and it will discourage the risky investments that are the engine of economic growth. Just ask your local lottery retailer if more tickets are sold when the prizes are large or when they are small.[4]

Indeed, compared to most of the rest of the world, the American poor have it made. Many can afford lottery tickets and in the United States the poor live longer and better lives than any 18th-century nobleman.

"But people do not experience life as an interesting moment in the evolution of human societies," retorts Timothy Noah in his 2010 Slate series on inequality. "They experience it in the present and weigh their own experience against that of the living."

It's a funny thing, but I haven't noticed the poor tearing at the gilded gates of the rich. As I write, crime is down—way down. A great swath of the working poor are prepared to turn the worst of the redistributionists out on their ears despite their relative poverty. By the time you read this, they might already have. False consciousness?

Despite the economic fallout after the recession of 2008–2009, maybe life just isn't that bad for America's poor. If they're "weighing their experience against the living," they're weighing it against that of their neighbors—many of whom the government pays to do nothing. If they're angry about anything, it's not about a rich person making an honest dollar, but about people getting rich at their expense, thanks to politicians colluding with cronies.

Still, by historical and international standards, the American poor are in fine shape. In Bourgeois Virtues, economic philosopher Dierdre McCloskey reminds us that the "amount of goods and services produced and consumed by the average person on the planet has risen since 1800 by a factor of about eight and a half." Think about that: People consume eight-and-a-half times more food, clothing, housing, and education worldwide. And most of those gains have been made after Mama Borders' birth in just one-third of the world—the third that more or less allows those who create value in society to get rich. And that's a global measurement. If we made a similar calculation for just the United States, we'd be looking at even more staggering increases in living standards.

The most breathtaking explanation for the benefits of human advancement by way of free market capitalism is the polymath zoologist Matt Ridley's beautiful book, *The Rational Optimist*:

> The Sun King has dinner each night alone. He chose from forty dishes, served on gold and silver plates. It took a staggering 498 people to prepare each meal. He was rich because he consumed the work of other

people, mainly in the form of their services. He was rich because other people did things for him. At that time, the average French family would have prepared and consumed its own meals as well as paid tax to support his servants in the palace. So it is not hard to conclude that Louis XIV was rich because others were poor.

But what about today? Consider that you are an average person, say a woman of 35, living in, for the sake of argument, Paris and earning the median wage, with a working husband and two children. You are far from poor, but in relative terms, you are immeasurably poorer than Louis was. Where he was the richest of the rich in the world's richest city, you have no servants, no palace, no carriage, no kingdom. As you toil home from work on the crowded Metro, stopping at the shop on the way to buy a ready meal for four, you might be thinking that Louis XIV's dining arrangements were way beyond your reach. And yet consider this. The cornucopia that greets you as you enter the supermarket dwarfs anything that Louis XIV ever experienced (and is probably less likely to contain Salmonella). You can buy a fresh, frozen, tinned, smoked or pre-prepared meal made with beef, chicken, pork, lamb, fish, prawns, scallops, eggs, potatoes, beans, carrots, cabbage, aubergine, kumquats, celeriac, okra, seven kinds of lettuce, cooked in olive, walnut, sunflower or peanut oil and flavoured with cilantro, turmeric, basil or rosemary ... You may have no chefs, but you can decide on a whim to choose between scores of nearby bistros, or Italian, Chinese, Japanese or Indian restaurants, in each of which a team of skilled chefs is waiting to serve your family at less than an hour's notice. Think of this: never before this generation has the average person been able to afford to have somebody else prepare his meals.

You could say something very similar about America's poor.

OK, poor people are not as likely to buy aubergine (eggplant *en Americain*). Weirdly, an unprecedented symptom of American poverty today is obesity. I know, I know, the most recent anti-capitalist narrative is that the poor can only afford unhealthy food. This "crisis" is as much sociological as economic, but can we at least admit that, in either historical or international perspective, obesity looks like a hell of a nice problem to have?

Even in comparison to Matt Ridley's Parisian *supermarché*, Mama Borders' homegrown fare was uniquely delicious and beautiful. To this day, my memories are alive with the flavors she brought to the table, and I'm still a sucker for a farmer's market, despite the higher cost and inconsistent quality. But Mama Borders toiled away every day in those fields to produce only a fraction of what my family can get on a trip to any of five nearby grocery stores. Today, being a locavore is something of a bourgeois luxury, but thanks to those stores, farmers in Chile, Mexico, and California can make a living.

And despite all the fretting about what constitutes a living wage, we cannot ignore the gains the American poor have made. I'm heartened by the idea that their lives will continue to get better—as long as we don't completely abandon the system that got them to this place.

MOBILE PHONES AND S-CURVES

Two things Mama never owned in her life were a dishwasher and a mobile phone. She could have, of course, but she never lost the habit of cleaning plates herself. And once you're in your nineties, it's pretty easy for people to find you at home. Still, the ubiquity of the mobile phone is an object lesson in the degree of access the poor have to the fruits of (relatively) free enterprise. What's also interesting is how this process happens: It's not immediate and, for better or worse, it usually starts with the rich. Then, if you'll forgive the term, there really is a kind of "trickle-down" effect.

After a new innovation comes to market, the wealthy buy it first. They're often the first adopters, because the first prices are high and they've got the money. The first version of something is usually the worst version of something, but to a wealthy person it's better than not having that thing at all. Recall Gordon Gecko with that clunky box of a cell phone, which was about 10 times the size (and price) of our sleek, modern mobile devices. At the close of 2010, however, more than 91 percent of the U.S. population[5] had a mobile phone, up from 82 percent in 2007. By the time you read these words, more than 95 percent of the American people will likely have mobile phones.[iii] How did this happen? And how did so many of these mobile devices become computers, cameras, and game platforms since the glory days of Gordon Gekko and the fabulously fat cell phone?

To economists and business wonks, the diffusion of innovation is a familiar pattern. They call it an "S-curve." Population growth, the spread of cancer in a body, and the adoption of new technologies all seem to follow certain patterns. The mobile phone, for example, began with slow acceptance, followed by explosive growth, only to level off before "hitting the wall." The mobile device, after a slow initial acceptance by Gordon Gekko and his cohorts, can be imagined moving fast through established (though narrow) channels into the marketplace. This is the steep upslope of the "S." As this technology matures and its penetration slows, any growth, or "flow," moves outward from the initial penetration channels in a shorter and slower way.

---

iii   But that's still 15.5 million Americans without mobile devices. Oh the humanity! Many of these Americans will, like Mama Borders, have little use for mobile telephony or smart devices. Others, often the poor, will make due sharing a phone with family members. Some will opt for even less expensive options, such as internet telephony on a home computer. There will be only a very small percentage of Americans for whom mobile phones are inaccessible.

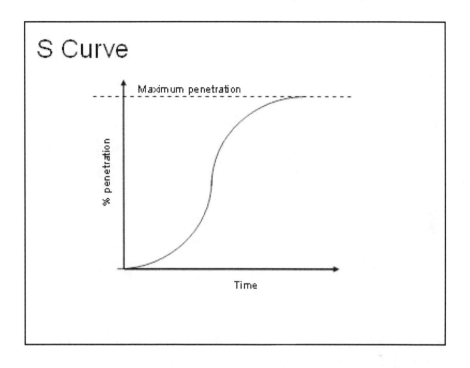

Physicist and engineer Adrian Bejan offers "constructal theory" to explain this pattern. Bejan uses a large river basin as a way of explaining what he refers to as a "flow system." The basin grows fast and stretches far with smaller branches growing out from the main channels. The "design" of the flow system develops over time by evolving flow access—reducing and distributing friction or other forms of resistance. (We'll return to this idea later.) When it comes to the natural dynamics of rich and poor, good things spread from the roots and trunk to the branches, but it's a complex and delicate process.

GET RICH SERVING THE POOR

Harvard Business School professor Clayton Christensen has shown that what he calls "disruptive innovations" either create

35

new markets or reshape existing ones by offering relatively simple, convenient, and/or inexpensive products to a group of customers whom industry leaders have ignored. Some companies have little interest in innovating this way. Profit margins can be lower and sometimes a disruptive innovation doesn't address the needs of a more sophisticated customer base. That's just fine for competitors, though. Companies that realize the value in pursuing disruptive innovation can end up dominating their industries.

Companies like Nokia gobbled up market share in the early 2000s, offering reliable, low-cost, no-frills mobile phones. At the time, the rate of market penetration for these devices could not have been more staggering, and Nokia soon began clobbering companies such as Motorola and Ericsson, which produced geeky high-end phones. Soon, companies began introducing simpler smart phones, and although they were expensive at first, they became disruptive simply because they were so intuitive. The prices for these, too, soon came down. You can now talk, play games, send texts and emails, take pictures, keep appointments, make reservations at a restaurant, buy coffee or airline tickets, and much more, all with your phone. And yet I hesitate to use these contemporary examples, which will all likely be dated by the time these words hit your _____ (insert device du jour).

The mobile device, like the disk drives that allowed Christensen to explain his famous insight, is a perfect exemplar of disruptive innovation. Christensen writes:

> When I began my search for an answer to the puzzle of why the best firms can fail, a friend offered some sage advice. "Those who study genetics avoid studying humans," he noted. "Because new generations come along only every thirty years or so, it takes a long time to under-

stand the cause and effect of any changes. Instead, they study fruit flies, because they are conceived, born, mature, and die all within a single day. If you want to understand why something happens in business, study the disk drive industry. Those companies are the closest things to fruit flies that the business world will ever see.

Perhaps. These days a Droid phone is as good as *drosophila*. And tomorrow, the poor man across town will probably have a phone that's just as good as yours is today.

When it comes to disruptive innovation, there's a simple idea at work: "Companies innovate faster than people's lives change," according to Christensen. Most companies therefore end up offering products that are too fancy, too pricy, and have too steep a learning curve for many customers. When companies stick to these high-end products, they often open the door to competitors who can offer something simpler and cheaper. These are the kinds of products that poorer people want, need, and are willing to buy despite limited resources. And if you're a savvy businessperson, that's what you'll give them. You'll make their lives better and get rich doing it.

THE WAL-MART EFFECT

You might love it. You might hate it. Or you might think it gauche. But Wal-Mart is a disruptive innovator that has probably done more to reduce poverty than any other organization in the world. Educational entrepreneur and FLOW president Michael Strong argues that Wal-Mart is the most effective poverty alleviation organization on the planet:

> Between 1990 and 2002 more than 174 million people escaped poverty in China, about 1.2 million per month. With an estimated $23 billion in

Chinese exports in 2005 (out of a total of $713 billion in manufacturing exports), Wal-Mart might well be single-handedly responsible for bringing about 38,000 people out of poverty in China each month, about 460,000 per year.

…Even without considering the $263 billion in consumer savings that Wal-Mart provides for low-income Americans, or the millions lifted out of poverty by Wal-Mart in other developing nations, it is unlikely that there is any single organization on the planet that alleviates poverty so effectively for so many people.[6]

What Wal-Mart has done to lift millions of rural Chinese peasants out of poverty is truly staggering. But what has Wal-Mart done for the American poor? In a TV ad Wal-Mart ran near the start of the Great Recession, we learned, "Wal-Mart saves the average family about $3,100 a year, no matter where they shop."

How can Wal-Mart save people money if they don't shop there? Other stores have to cut their prices to compete with it. Chris Hollings of the consulting firm IHS Global Insights led a team of researchers to glean the information Wal-Mart used in that 2008 ad, isolating an economic "Wal-Mart effect" by tracking the mega-retailer's growth over time using government data.

Some criticized Wal-Mart for the ad, claiming the $3,100 number is accurate, but misleading. Charles Fishman, Fast Company reporter and author of The Wal-Mart Effect, for example, points out that the median U.S. household income is less than $51,000 (as of 2008). "A family earning $51,000 a year saves about $640 a year compared to what they would otherwise have had to spend."[7]

Even if in the Hollings study the family income baseline might have been inflated relative to the average Wal-Mart shopper, for a lower-income family $640 is still a decent chunk of money—one the family wouldn't have had in Wal-Mart's absence.

"Six-hundred-forty dollars for a typical family still adds up to a TV, a big-screen TV that you wouldn't otherwise get to buy," says Fishman, "or two weeks at camp for a kid who wouldn't otherwise get to go to camp. And so that's not trivial." I suppose it wasn't trivial for Mama Borders, either. Neighbors and family would "carry" her to Wal-Mart and to the hair-dressers once a week.

People criticize Wal-Mart for all sorts of reasons, some better than others. Some worry it disrupts communities. Others say the company uses strong-arm tactics with municipalities when putting in a store. You've likely heard tales of woe about mom-and-pop stores. These criticisms notwithstanding, we have to give serious consideration to Michael Strong's claim that Wal-Mart is the most effective poverty-fighting organization on Earth.

DISRUPTING QUASI-MONOPOLIES

There are two areas in which the benefits of competition and disruptive innovation haven't been able to improve people's lives as well or as inexpensively as we might hope. As it turns out, these are the areas in which government interferes most: health-care and education.

Healthcare – The problem with the U.S. healthcare system is affordability. And that problem is a symptom: The more expensive health insurance gets, the less likely people are to buy a policy. But the underlying disease is complicated. It boils down to five main pathologies, all of which involve interference by government:

1. The U.S. tax code has the effect of incentivizing people to buy health insurance through their employers. This limits competition and choice, and raises premiums for everyone—especially the underemployed and self-employed. With this system, people lose their health insurance when they lose their jobs.

2. People cannot buy health insurance across state lines, which limits competition and choice by creating in-state insurance cartels. People with no nationwide menu of insurance options won't see lower prices and better values because companies that enjoy the liberty of an oligopoly don't need to compete as hard for your dollars.

3. A mixture of public and quasi-private third-party payer insurance schemes encourages people to over-consume healthcare—that is, to buy unnecessary healthcare products and services. The government shifts the costs of over-consumption onto everyone in the form of increased premiums and higher taxes.

4. Many states have excessive coverage mandates—the items you're forced to buy in a policy, such as chiropractic or counseling services, or hormone replacement therapy. In states like Massachusetts, New York, and New Jersey, these drive up average premiums by as much as 20 percent. Though state governments mandate these items in the name of the public good, they often result from lobbying by special interests.

5. Due to the problems of both over-consumption and coming demographic trends, healthcare entitlements such as Medicaid and Medicare are simply unsustainable.

In early 2009, President Barack Obama signed The Patient Protection and Affordable Care Act—or Obamacare—into law. That legislation addressed none of the five pathologies above.

To subject the U.S. healthcare system to market discipline would require a fairly simple set of changes:

- First, Congress would either have to eliminate the subsidy for employer-based coverage, or offer an equal subsidy for those who buy insurance on the individual market.
- Second, Congress would have to enable all citizens to buy health insurance from whomever they choose, in any of the 50 states.
- Third, Congress could expand the contribution limits on health savings accounts (HSA).[iv]
- Fourth, states could make an effort to eliminate coverage mandates, or at least pass "mandate-lite" legislation.
- Fifth, Congress could abolish Medicare and replace Medicaid with a state-level health savings account subsidized annually for the poor and working poor. Savings accumulated in the health savings account (plus compound interest) would cover most Americans into their old age—obviating the need for the costly, wasteful, and morally dubious old-age entitlement.

---

iv   An HSA is similar to a 401K in that it is a tax-deferred, interest-bearing account. Monies left unused in the HSA can be saved for retirement or long-term care plans in one's senior years. HSA contributions are not only tax deferred, but HSA dollars spent on qualifying healthcare items are tax protected.

Even two or three of these five suggestions would have a transformative effect on the cost and quality of care in the United States. Care providers in both goods (e.g. drugs, medical devices) and services (e.g. visits, treatments) would have new incentives to cut costs and improve quality. That alone could represent a revolution in healthcare. A new age of medical innovation would emerge. A new S-curve and eventually increased life expectancy would likely result, especially for the poor. Because injecting market discipline means injecting new opportunities for disruptive innovations, the less-well-off would benefit from rapid uptake of higher-quality, lower-frills care. Unfortunately, the political environment is extremely hostile to these kinds of reforms. Entrenched interests will fight mercilessly to see that they don't challenge their government-created bonanzas.

U.S. health insurance premiums are now going up and up, due almost entirely to policy problems I enumerated in the five pathologies above. It's also true that affordability limits access by the poor to a great degree. Despite all the problems, however, there are still states in which relatively free health insurance markets make plans more affordable. But the fact is, sometimes people just make high-risk choices—such as going uninsured.

To put this into perspective, consider that in Austin, Texas (where I write this), a pack of cigarettes costs about $4.50 (if you buy them by the carton). A pack-a-day smoker will therefore pay about $135 per month. Texas, which has fair-to-middling insurance premiums compared with other states, also has a health insurance plan (Aetna) for a man my age (37 years old) for $135 per month with a $3,500 deductible. Aetna also offers an HSA plan with a $5,000 deductible for $95.83 plus the HSA contribution—say, $50 each month—totaling about $150 per month. (Available HSA funds will pay the deductible.)[v]

Both of these plans pass what I call the "cigarette test." That is, if a smoker quits and can buy insurance for less than the cost of a pack-a-day habit, he can afford it. He can quit smoking and also buy cheaper health insurance. As it happens, about 34 percent of people considered "poor" are smokers, according to Stanton Peele, writing in The Huffington Post.[9] That means that despite the soaring costs of care in most states, at least 34 percent of people who are poor enough to qualify for Medicaid could afford to buy private health insurance.

I realize it's not easy to quit smoking. I am also not suggesting that the government force people to quit and buy health insurance (though many officials are trying their best on both counts). What I'm suggesting is that life is about trade-offs, and if at least 34 percent of the American poor could afford health insurance, they are less poor than we think. In another example of good intentions producing perverse consequences, Medicaid pays people to stay poor (so that they can keep their benefits), offers no disincentives for the same population to smoke, and forces everyone else to pay for the bad habit.

Education – According to Tyler Cowen, the year before Mama Borders was born (1900) "only 6.4 percent of Americans of the appropriate age group graduated from high school. By 1960, 60 percent of Americans were graduating from high school, almost 10

v   These quotes were derived online at eHealthInsurance.com for area code 78749 and assumed the enrollee had not been smoking for at least one year. Consider also that the full effects of the Affordable Care Act have not yet been realized as of this writing.

times the rate of only 60 years earlier. This rate peaked at about 80 percent in the late 1960s and since then has fallen by about 6 percentage points. In other words, earlier in the 20th century, a lot of potential geniuses didn't get much education, but rather were literally 'kept down on the farm.'" I suspect something similar could be said about Mama Borders, who was tremendously bright, not to mention her son Bryan (my late grandfather) or my grandmother Bebe, his wife.

The mostly public U.S. education system—funded by capitalism's bounty—is arguably responsible for the tremendous increase in the number of high school-educated Americans. But something has gone wrong. The system is a John Dewey dinosaur built on a Soviet factory model. Kids' brains are viewed as buckets of the same size and shape. The role of the educator is to pour equal amounts of knowledge in, then introduce a battery of standardized tests to ensure the buckets are filling adequately. The systems spit out these buckets rather like an assembly line. If curriculum designers have anything to say about it, they'll all be educated in terms of a committee's unitary concept of good education.

Although U.S. public schools have doubled spending per pupil since I was born in 1973, learning outcomes have remained flat (according to those self-same standardized tests meant to leave no child behind). The public education system has become bogged down with waste and inefficiency. More resources won't help. The poor experience the worst of this system, whether in inner-city schools where the principals act as wardens, or rural ones where football stadiums are valued more highly than chemistry labs. The fact is, even intelligent people with the best of intentions frequently disagree about what a good education is. But, however parents define a good education, central authorities have proven unable to mete it out. If the government allowed the market to shape the education system, it would hasten the rise of educational entrepreneurs. That means treating parents like customers.

We have to give parents choices. We have to stop treating students as if they were outputs from a factory rather than individuals, each with unique interests, aptitudes, and potential. We have to give parents and students skin in the game, even if that means subsidizing the poorest students with vouchers or tax credits, which they could use to make better choices. Ideally, a fully private education system—robustly supported by philanthropy—would be possible. For now, expanding choice and diversity in teaching approaches at the margins will do wonders to rouse Americans from their zombie-like commitment to the status quo.

There are early signs of an educational revolution despite Dewey's behemoth. In North Carolina, educational entrepreneurs like Robert Luddy are building high-quality, low-cost private (and charter) schools that are getting fantastic results, especially when measured against the status quo. In Milwaukee, parents have been using educational vouchers to pull their kids out of failing and dangerous public schools. In Texas, educational innovators like my wife, Ariel Miller, and Jeff Sandefer employ Socratic teaching, collaborative projects, and online learning—all while keeping costs down. Their efforts represent a wholesale abandonment of John Dewey's factory model and the bloated behemoth that enshrines it. These educational entrepreneurs are disruptive innovators.

SOMETHING TO DO

The American poor now have a tremendous array of entertainment choices, amusements, and reading materials available to them at low cost. "Today ordinary people have time to enjoy those amenities of life that only the rich could afford in abundance a century ago," writes economic historian Robert Fogel. To this, Dierdre McCloskey adds: "…a lot of it spent on rap music rather than Mozart, alas; and on silly toys rather than economics courses, unfortunately. But also on book clubs and birdwatching." In other words, while someone of more sophisticated tastes might not approve of poor folks' amusements, they are abundant. Consider that by 1994, a full 92.5 percent of all Americans had a color television set, whereas in 1934 hardly anyone would have had the time to watch it, much less afford it, even if it had existed.[10]

Just three weeks ago, I saw a laptop for $200 at a big-box store. I couldn't believe my eyes. With that purchase, plus a broadband connection for $16.99 a month, someone of very little means can find virtually anything to do. Gaming consoles are going way down in price, too. People are finding hours of entertainment on smartphone apps that are available for free.

Some researchers have even hypothesized that video games, which have drawn in so many young men ages 16 to 30, share some responsibility not only for the precipitous drop in crime rates nationwide[11], but for steady increase in cognitive abilities[12]. Of course, there are other factors involved. But if this is true, how can something that seems like such an obvious waste of time result in so many ancillary social benefits? It might be difficult for members of the educated elite to accept, but capitalism's goodies are doing more for society than is apparent at first blush—for you, for me, and especially for America's poor.

The poor person in America is the richest poor person in history. They have unprecedented access to the comforts of the 21st century. That doesn't mean people aren't suffering: At this moment, someone out there is living with psychosis and sleeping under a bridge; a young woman with two children is having trouble affording childcare this month and has to work a second shift at a restaurant to make ends meet; a middle-aged man will discover he has a chronic medical condition that will cost him a lot to treat, and could force him to trade in his new truck for an old one. Each of these people has a story. Some are tales of poor circumstances, and others of poor choices. It's tempting to think that with all the material abundance we have today, we should move heaven and earth to see that no one ever has to experience poverty again.

But consider for a moment what brought so many people like Garland and Mama Borders out of poverty in the first place. Today's unprecedented abundance came about for a reason, and history is littered with accounts of civilizations whose "prosperity and success led to the emergence of predators and parasites in various forms and guises who eventually killed the geese that laid the golden eggs," says economic historian Joel Mokyr.[13]

Postscript: They Grew America

As with many other developing countries, America was once an agrarian nation. That is, people just like Garland and Mama Borders grew it. Thomas Jefferson once wrote that, "Cultivators of the earth are the most valuable citizens. They are the most vigorous, the most independent, the most virtuous, and they are tied to their country, and wedded to its liberty and interests, by the most lasting bonds." If Jefferson is right, our most valuable citizens now constitute less than 2 percent of the U.S. workforce, compared with 41 percent the year Mama Borders was born.[14] That's good news. It means our parents and grandparents sowed a great inheritance for us, and we have reaped it.

And yet we're impatient. The late Virginia School economist Warren Nutter writes gloomily about the paradox of our prosperity.

> Progress did not, by and large, aggravate inequities, but it made us more aware and less tolerant of them. Sharpening contrasts in circumstances aroused our humane sentiments, sentiments that could be better afforded by virtue of augmenting affluence. Progress shook loose the age-old endurance that man had customarily displayed for his lot and bred in its place an attitude of insatiable discontent with the pace at which remaining problems were being met. And so we find ourselves in a society in which progress and discontent are engaged in an almost desperate race with each other.[15]

May we learn to be more patient. May we channel our discontent into innovation.

In this age of abundance, we may never be able to return to the farm life Thomas Jefferson so admired. But we must venerate the institutions that got us this far, and leave them intact for posterity. For if we don't, we may find ourselves returning to conditions my Mama Borders was happy to leave long ago.

2

How Rare is the Entrepreneur

With winch and ropes and hooks
We stacked the bales up clean
To splintery redwood rafters
High in the dark, flecks of alfalfa
Whirling through shingle-cracks of light,
Itch of haydust in the
Sweaty shirt and shoes.
At lunchtime under Black oak
Out in the hot corral,
–The old mare nosing lunchpails,
Grasshoppers crackling in the weeds–
"I'm sixty-eight" he said,
"I first bucked hay when I was seventeen.
I thought, that day I started,
I sure would hate to do this all my life.
And dammit, that's just what
I've gone and done."

– Gary Snyder

The Sacramento River winds through California farm country. A road conforms, snakelike, alongside. To the left of our car passes a freshly-built levy—mostly hiding fields beyond. To the right are intermittent structures between river and road—fences, driveways, and houses. The houses seem inconsistent. Because rich people usually cluster in gated communities, I expect every structure along this stretch to reek of ostentation. I am, after all, on my way to meet a multi-millionaire. But this mixed settlement along the river doesn't strike me as a place a wealthy person would live. Many of the houses are large, but a few are run down. Still others seem normal to me—middle class.

Even the grand home at which we eventually arrive isn't imposing. It's lovely, and must be worth millions, but it's tucked away in a kind of don't-mind-me refinement. The house looks to have been designed to the specifications of someone who needs solace. It was not meant to signal status. Guarded by large old trees, the house's façade is composed mostly of wood in warm tones. The California autumn has not yet muted the colors in its garden, which invites you to walk around the house in every direction. Its front columns are simple, sylvan with hints of gothic. The place comes across as a homestead built for a quiet, reflective patriarch.

I'm there to visit Chris Rufer, who is probably the richest person I know. In fact, even if we completely factored out debt—that is, if wealth was measured only in assets—I'd be many orders of magnitude less wealthy than he. I guess he's been a millionaire at least 100 times over, but that would only be a guess. I'm not there to interview him for *Forbes* and stick him onto a chart somewhere under Larry Ellison. I'm there to find out what makes him tick and how he made his fortune.

I only know a handful of super-wealthy people. It's not just that I lack the resources to run in their circles. It's also that wealthy people are rare, and wealthy people like Rufer are even rarer—like diamonds or Van Gogh paintings. And there are good reasons for that rarity. Chris Rufer possesses qualities that most of us lack; intangible, but real.

Dialogue

Before we settled into our interview, I gave Rufer a book in which I had published a chapter. The gift was probably as much for me as for him. I wanted to show him that the interview would be worth his time. For someone like Rufer, the opportunity cost[i] of sitting down with a writer is probably greater than I make in a year. I had to show some plumage, and offer a token to thank him appropriately.

Rufer is tall, maybe 6-foot-3. Feathery eyebrows offer clues about his age. When he smiles, he still seems serious. His gaze is keen and his eyes seem to exist for two purposes: to solve puzzles and to size you up. I was there to interview him but immediately he engaged me in a kind of Socratic dialogue. His expression suggested I frustrated him a little. He's used to people giving him yes-or-no answers (I tend to play Devil's Advocate; it's a curse).

"Can you think of any circumstances under which someone harming you would make you better off?" he asks me in a stately library in the bosom of his beautiful home. Bruce Benson's brilliant but obscure *The Enterprise of Law* is among the tomes.

"Well…" my mind grinds away at philosophical conundrums about police protection and national security, which Rufer and I discuss briefly. But as I get further into the conversation with him, I force myself to be a little more binary with my answers. Doing things Rufer's way will give me a better idea how he thinks. I soon learn that this is the way he shares his worldview. In other

---

i   *Opportunity cost* is the cost of any activity measured in terms of the value of the best foregone alternative.

words, answering his questions simply and directly leaves you with the sense that you've traveled with him through a set of premises. You have shared his perspective, at least for a moment. It turns out his worldview is remarkably scalable, as we'll see. While Rufer is self-effacing about his raw intelligence, he is something of a philosopher by nature. He solves business problems and makes his cases by asking crisp, step-wise questions. This may be one key to his success.

Soon enough, Rufer ceded control of the interview back to me.

BUILDING AN EMPIRE WITH A TOMATO TRUCK

I can't think of anything less sexy than tomato paste—except perhaps the trucks that drive the tomatoes to the processing plant. And yet tomatoes and trucks made Rufer his fortune. It could have been anything, anywhere. If he'd grown up in North Carolina, he might be a furniture mogul. If he'd grown up in Idaho, he might have been a potato magnate. Rufer grew up in California's Central Valley, so his company, Morning Star, is the logical outgrowth of dropping someone with his gifts into what he terms "cow country."

Chris Rufer was an introverted kid with natural smarts. He felt lucky to have gone to UCLA, having earned only a 3.01 grade-point average in high school. He knew he was going to start a business after college and, in fact, he effectively started his business before graduating. He rented a truck one summer when classes were out and the tomatoes were being harvested. He'd had to find two jobs—one at a gas station and one at a factory—just to put together the capital to rent the equipment. As it happened, Chris knew trucks because his dad had owned and operated one.

Behind the wheel of his first truck, Rufer worked through the summer, hauling tomatoes as fast as he could. At one point he thought about quitting.

"If I quit now," he said to his dad, "I'll end up losing a couple thousand dollars."

"Hang in there, it'll work out," his dad had said.

So he worked through that first summer to make only $719 in profit, which he spent on food and rent. He made less money than some of the more seasoned drivers that year, but unlike his competitors, Rufer had an uncanny sensitivity to what was going on around him. As he waited in inefficient lines at the fields, the cannery and the grading station, Rufer picked up more and more information about the ecosystem of tomatoes and processing. He found problems to solve.

Time being money, the young driver had calculated how much he was losing doing things the same old way, and started thinking about how a tomato business might run more efficiently.

"You really should take the tomatoes and skip the scale, skip the grading station, go right to the factory and scale them and just unload them in the flume or sorting tables at the factory," Rufer said. "I knew I'd be making good money if I didn't have to wait all this time. I could get 20 loads instead of eight."

Sitting there in the queue gave Rufer time to use his smarts. He applied what he'd learned at UCLA under the tutelage of such great economists as Armen Alchien, who was a trailblazer on prices and the theory of firms. Rufer calculated, iterated, and solved problems. He walked around and talked to the farmers, watched the field hands sort the tomatoes and observed the patterns within the system. As he thought, he began redesigning the whole process in his head.

"I figured: sort them in the flume by skimming off the greens and letting the good ones pass. You'd save a lot of money and your trucks would move a lot faster," he said.

Rufer had no control over the factory, so he kept thinking about how to game the system. The guys at the grading station got wise to it when Rufer began skirting what he considered poor practices.

"You'd get there and there would be 15 or 20 trucks waiting to get onto the scale," he said. "Studying the system a little, I figured out how the paperwork system worked. I started skipping the scale line and going to the grading station line. By then the line would be down and I'd get through the whole process faster than the other trucks."

Rufer had been cheating a byzantine system, but cheating nevertheless. It turned out that the inefficiency stemmed from California's regulations on grading and deliveries—dumb laws that had been on the books for years. And the poor design of the harvesting practices and processing plant created bottlenecks. Instead of continuing to cheat the system, Rufer eventually fought to have things changed on both the business and regulatory sides.

The Kernel

As I listened to Rufer's story about his truck-driving days, I grew a little impatient. I wanted to get to the heart of his entrepreneurial rise—the kernel from which a master narrative, or *a-ha!* moment, would spring. At one point, I interrupted his truck story.

"Okay, so you made a little money doing this truck thing during the summer. But at some point you had to change course. At some point you're not hauling tomatoes anymore. What happened?"

"We were always hauling tomatoes," he said flatly. "We run 240 trucks and 400 truck drivers."

I should have known better than to interrupt. This was the kernel. The essence of Rufer's tale was that he'd built his empire one tomato truck at a time. And early on, he had used his ability to "telescope"—micro to macro and back, present to future and back, solving problems, developing a grand vision, and administering his growing business step by step. He'd started with his scratch pad, calculating fixed and variable costs, and sketching ideas. In the back of his mind, he always saw the big picture. Tomatoes and tomato paste processing had essentially become an outgrowth of the countless mental revisions Chris made while trucking.

By his second harvesting season as a trucker, Rufer had become more confident. He had figured out how to reduce his fuel costs and enlisted the help of others to begin running multiple trucks. He started thinking about what kind of money he could make if he ran a fleet of trucks. Most working stiffs just want to make money and go home, but Rufer wanted to do everything better. Instead of twiddling his thumbs in his truck or talking junk with the other drivers, he crunched numbers, ran marginal analyses, and designed and redesigned systems in his head.

"Man, if I could just change this and this and this, I could get rich," he said, reflecting on his mindset in those days. "But at the time, there were just too many outside factors: what the growers were doing, what the harvesters were doing."

Rufer's tendency to tear things down into their constituent parts and identify weak links came as naturally to him as breathing. And eventually his tomato-hauling business outgrew trucking, enabling him to exert tremendous influence on the steps that used to slow him down.

"The difference is to see the whole—the outside factors impacting your business, instead of just the narrow factors of your business."

Family, Education, and OCD

Before I tell you any more about how Rufer built his tomato-paste empire, I should let you know that he credits his genes, family, and formal education in equal measure. His grandfather had run a filling station and taught him the value of hard work and gaining a basic head for business. He earned an economics degree from UCLA, a degree in agricultural sciences from California Polytechnic (Cal Poly), and returned to UCLA to get his MBA. By the time he'd bagged his final degree, he was already ahead of most of his peers. He had started building his business and getting grime under his nails. Rufer knew the rhythm of the seasons. It was as if what would become Morning Star had been germinating in the central California soil all along.

Bob Chitester, who produced Milton Friedman's landmark *Free To Choose*, had introduced me to Rufer. Chitester joined us for the interview and asked, "Did you have to dig down deep to be successful?"

"Not really," Rufer admitted.

"So it's hardwired," I said.

"Yes," Rufer admitted "It's not unusual for entrepreneurs to have at least a mild case of obsessive compulsive disorder. Whatever it is, I've got it."

Most of us think about Edison's adage about success being 1 percent inspiration and 99 percent perspiration. For some, it's 99 percent compulsion. There is a very real sense in which entrepreneurs are born. I imagine Howard Hughes sitting in his hygienic inner sanctum giving orders to the one or two people he trusted. Rufer didn't strike me as a Hughes; his mild case of OCD is what you'd want if you like to have both success *and* friends. But this pathology, talent—whatever you want to call it—is a critical ingredient of Rufer's success. What most of us think of as persistence and patience might just be a gentler form of obsession.

"I want things in order. My mind wants it to fit," Rufer explained, "and my mind has a drive to figure the puzzle out—to make sense of the information I'm receiving."

"But what about the bigger picture? The longer view?" I asked.

"Isn't it similar for you as a writer?" Rufer asked, lapsing into his Socratic style.

"I suppose it is," I replied.

I thought about this very book. Writing anything—especially something in long form—requires the writer to settle on a big-picture theme or idea that unifies the work. Then you've got to outline. Then you write. And that involves rendering the details, letter by letter, sometimes improvising. None of this includes the re-writes and the editing, which is a more collaborative smoothing process. Mentally, though, you have to be prepared to click down two or so orders of magnitude. Then you have to click back three or four to see if it all works as a whole. All this happens in your head. Writing is the ability to do this with just words and concepts, but in business you're doing it with resources and people.

Then there is enlightened risk-taking—the "vision thing" successful innovators have. When Rufer was on the verge of moving from trucking tomatoes to processing them, the industry group-think was that tomato paste had little value. It's just a byproduct, they thought.

"Making products out of tomato paste was not all that well known," Rufer recalled. "Heinz, Campbell's, and other companies were making tomato paste within their factories," but outside California, no one saw any value in it.

But one entrepreneur's trash is another's treasure, and Rufer had the economics down. He noticed trends such as improving technology and believed he could create a new, valuable market. Investors were still living in an old paradigm. Rufer believed his business model was correct and that people would want what they did not yet know they wanted. Turns out he was right.

"After five or six years of pounding the pavement on Sand Hill Road in Menlo Park, in Davis, in Fresno...I probably logged fifty-thousand miles trying to raise money," Rufer said.

He finally raised money from three growers, but could only negotiate 10 percent of the profits. The major investor told Rufer no one his age ought to make a million dollars in a year. Still, Rufer took his 10 percent and built a plant. The company that eventually became Morning Star had been born, and after a few years, the investor wrote a check to Chris Rufer for one million dollars.

VISIONARIES, ORGANIZERS, AND HYBRIDS

Rufer described what it was like for him to build and run a business. He likened the process to creating a painting. First, you move in close, employing just the right brush strokes and swirls in the layered daubs of pigment. The flush of a woman's cheeks, achieved with the master's bristles, are premixed on the palette. Then move back, far back. Appreciate the gestalt: the faces in the foreground, blurrier objects in the background, zigzagging reflections of trees in water.

"You can't paint the painting back here, though," said Rufer, showing distance with his hand. "You have to move in close to create the details."

Rufer was not suggesting he is a kind of artist, though maybe he is. It's another way of describing that telescoping process in his mind—micro to macro, future to present and back. It's being able to see what will be possible three years out while simultaneously formulating the steps needed to get there. That requires a rare combination of gifts.

Good entrepreneurs are visionaries or organizers. Great entrepreneurs, such as Steve Jobs or Henry Ford, are both. Recall that the once-great General Motors never had a visionary-administrator hybrid at the helm. Most people don't realize that Billy Durant was the visionary and Alfred P. Sloan was the administrator. Historian Burt Folsom writes admiringly of Durant:

> In 1904, after test-driving a Buick over the potholes in Flint and the mud of the countryside, [Billy Durant] took the challenge of building the car industry almost from scratch. Durant the salesman sprang into action. He entered the Buick in a New York auto show—and came home with orders for 1,108 cars: not bad considering that only 37 Buicks had ever been made. In 1908, after just four years making cars, he had the best-selling car in the business. [...]
>
> Durant and his main rival, Henry Ford, both envisioned mass appeal for the car. Ford, however, thought his company should be built around one

standard car: his low-priced, no frills Model T. Durant, from his years in the carriage business, knew that if he were to prevail as the auto leader he needed many different types of vehicles to cater to different incomes and tastes. He scoured the country with the idea of having Buick merge with other companies that could carve out a niche in the auto market. He bought Cadillac for its luxury cars. He formed General Motors in 1908 by consolidating thirteen car companies and ten parts-and-accessories manufacturers.[16]

Durant was a visionary, but by 1911, General Motors was losing money. Ford was selling more cars so a group of Boston stockholders ousted Durant from the GM leadership. In the wake of Durant's ouster, they tried to run GM more conservatively. But Durant's time was not yet over, according to Folsom.

With capital and expertise he mustered from friends, he started making the Chevrolet, a new economy car that quickly captured a large share of the market. Durant then cleverly traded much of his Chevrolet stock for GM stock, and soon held a controlling interest in both companies. In 1916, he triumphantly returned to GM for a final four-year term in the driver's seat.

During his second presidency, Durant bought Fisher Body and Frigidaire to add to his Chevrolet, Oldsmobile, Cadillac, and Buick. Joining the GM team were Charles Kettering, who invented the self-starter, and Alfred Sloan, a brilliant organizer who wanted annual model changes.

It took Durant to set a course and overcome the gravity at lift-off. But it was the organizer Sloan who helped GM grow and remain competitive well into the 20th century. According to the Alfred P. Sloan Foundation:

Mr. Sloan was elected President of General Motors in 1923, succeeding Pierre S. du Pont, who said of him on that occasion: "The greater part of the successful development of the Corporation's operations and the building of a strong manufacturing and sales organization is due to Mr. Sloan. His election to the presidency is a natural and well-merited recognition of his untiring and able efforts and successful achievement." Mr. Sloan had developed by then his system of disciplined, professional management that provided for decentralized operations with coordinated centralized policy control. Applying it to General Motors, he set the corporation on its course of industrial leadership. The next 23 years, with Mr. Sloan as Chief Executive Officer, were years of enormous expansion for General Motors and of a steady increase in its share of the automobile market.[17]

Durant and Sloan are both synonymous with entrepreneurial greatness today—at least among business historians and MBA types. But each brought a different kind of acumen and a different kind of management philosophy.

MAVEN, RELATOR, OR EVANGELIST?

Authors Bijoy Goswami and Malcolm Gladwell share another way of understanding entrepreneurs, which can be sourced to *The Bhagavad Gita*. In *The Tipping Point*, Gladwell discusses the role of three basic behavioral types in spreading messages.[18] But as Goswami points out, these "core types" appear in just about every sphere of life. They are: Mavens, Relators, and Evangelists (MRE). *Mavens* are motivated by knowledge. They want to discover and create knowledge. Think Einstein. *Relators* are motivated by relationships. They're well-connected, seeking to form new relationships and deepen the ones they have. Think Princess Di. *Evangelists* are motivated by action. They energize others to act and take action on their own. Think Gandhi.

The rarest value creators may be hybrids of the above. If the rarest entrepreneurs are both visionaries and organizers, or Mavens and Evangelists, Rufer may be among the few who can be called both. Maybe he's a different creature altogether. The point is not to put him into a Venn Diagram for MBAs, but to understand what makes him rare.

SELF-MANAGEMENT

Harvard management guru Gary Hamel says that "management is the least efficient activity in your organization." To most people, that's counterintuitive: Isn't management there to make an organization *more* efficient? But Hamel was no doubt inspired to make that claim once he'd met Chris Rufer. You see, Rufer believes something very odd for an executive: management is unnecessary.

At Morning Star, there is no hierarchy. Employees have different responsibilities, to be sure, but the self-management philosophy means the company organizes itself in the manner of an organism—that is, from the bottom up. Planning a company in rigid units and silos, as the father of "scientific management" Frederick Taylor famously suggested, is bad juju—at Morning Star, anyway. Companies need not be organized like machines with people as cogs. According to Rufer, companies are living systems composed of living beings, each of whom has a brain, responds to incentives, and can solve problems through collaboration. If you have these things, you don't need a layer of people whose job it is to order others around. Command and control can be counterproductive.

Self-management derives from concepts familiar to those who are suspicious of bureaucracies:

- "Flatter" organizations
- Self-directed work teams
- Employee empowerment
- Reduced bureaucratic processes
- Distributed decision-making

None of the above aspects works in isolation. They are part of a holistic system of management, which Rufer has turned into a guiding philosophy. Morning Star sets it out as follows:

> Self-Management, simply stated, is an organizational model wherein the traditional functions of a manager (planning, coordinating, controlling, staffing and directing) are pushed out to all participants in the organization as opposed to a select few. Each member of the organization is personally responsible for forging his own personal relationships, planning his own work, coordinating his actions with other members, acquiring requisite resources to accomplish his mission, and taking corrective action with respect to other members when needed.[19]

What are the implications of this management philosophy?

Formal hierarchies dissolve. The traditional model awards certain people within an organization the authority to issue orders which others must carry out. Self-management recognizes that those considered "subordinate employees" in other organizations often have more highly localized and specialized knowledge. That is, employees are usually "the ones who have the greatest insight into the management of their day-to-day functions and who are [...] in the best position to take immediate action when circumstances demand a response or a change in course."

Sometimes an individual ought to have more decision-making power, sometimes less. But Rufer believes all of that can be negotiated internally by a team that stands to benefit from local, well-reasoned decision-making. The team decides what colleague makes what decisions in what contexts—sometimes on the fly. And, according to self-management, the profit centers of the organization benefit from getting more out of every team member. "Colleagues" also benefit from the more autonomous arrangement because people are happier when they are trusted and given greater latitude to make good decisions. That doesn't mean they always do; failures happen, but devolved decision-making reduces the likelihood that any failure will be catastrophic.

"Everybody does better if they're freer to pursue their own paths," Rufer said about self-management, whereas in most companies "a manager fits other people into a system and says 'here's how you relate to other folks.' And that's pre-defined."

Rufer believes in holding people accountable, while giving them much more responsibility to take action and seek out others for collaboration. "Trusted people will gain influence," he said. "True leaders will come about." Self-organization follows because self-management embodies the basic ideas of individual freedom, voluntary association, and the rule of law. You are *equal* before the rules and you are rewarded relative to your ability to *be productive* for your team and, by extension, the organization. It's no coincidence that Chris Rufer thinks that's the way society ought to work, too.

The big paradox is that most organizations embrace hierarchy—stiff, bureaucratic and byzantine. That is, most companies concentrate power at the top and waste resources on excessive planning and hiring middle managers who produce little. Managers and executives accustomed to hierarchy resist change. In contrast, adherents to self-management work as if they keep F. A. Hayek books by the bedside. They believe allowing people to organize themselves is a more natural and humane way to work toward a common goal. In such organizations, change is less difficult. "Authorities," as such, become arbiters in resolving conflicts, tone-setters, visionaries, and people whom team-members designate to make immediate project decisions (if necessary). The employees—scratch that, colleagues—subordinate themselves to the mission.

The burning question is: does it work? In the *Harvard Business Review*, Gary Hamel writes:

> Over the past 20 years, Morning Star's volumes, revenues and profits have grown at a double-digit clip, claims Rufer. Industry growth, by contrast, has grown by 1% a year. As a private company, Morning Star doesn't share its financial results, but I was told that the company has funded virtually all its growth from internal sources, which suggests it is robustly profitable.[20]

In my conversations with Rufer, he echoed Hamel's claim. He sought partner-investors early on in order to break into the tomato-processing business, but by the time that arrangement wrapped up, Rufer simply reinvested his profits to grow. This self-sustaining growth and profit cycle has created thousands of jobs and made Rufer a rich man. When I say rich, I mean he has a net worth some would consider a "grotesque maldistribution."

But is it? Or is it a good thing that Rufer is wealthy? That is the question I've committed to answering in this book. That is: Are the Chris Rufers of the world entitled to their wealth? And who is best positioned to answer this question?

PROFIT AND LOSS

If I haven't yet convinced you that entrepreneurs are rare people with rare gifts, perhaps we can put all of this another way: Profit is good. I realize that's not a common campus narrative. Indeed, the kids down in Zuccotti Park, site of the original Occupy Wall Street demonstrations, would have told you profit is evil and growth is bad.

But these narratives miss the mark. Profits arise due to a win-win situation in which the economic pie gets bigger due to investment, production, and exchange. This results from increased efficiency and good investment, leading to bigger slices for consumers *and* producers. Profit-driven economic systems have produced unmatched technological innovation and brought people astonishing benefits.

Profit is not just the reward entrepreneurs get for creating good things for their customers. In a world of scarce resources, profit is an indication that said resources are being used wisely. Profits are not a product of the exploitation of labor, as Marx wrote, but an indicator that things are getting better. Losses mean things are getting worse, because losses indicate resources are being wasted and value is being destroyed. We should see profits and losses not so much as ways of determining how rich an individual is getting, but as a way of monitoring the health of a whole society. For many people, that is a major shift in perspective.

Sadly, most people don't appreciate the profit-and-loss system. According to a study by social psychologists Amit Bhattacharjee, Jason Dana, and Jonathan Baron, distorted populism reigns:

> People apparently have little faith in the power of markets to create and reward value for society. Across actual firms [...], entire industries [...], and hypothetical organizations [...] our participants associated greater levels of profit with social harm and less social value. Further, they saw

greater profits as undeserved and at the expense of others. Though firms themselves were not seen as generally evil or devoid of value, profit was viewed as evil. Increasing firm profitability (or profit motive) greatly detracted from perceived social value. [...] These results are quite in opposition to the view of markets espoused by economists and scholars that supply, demand, and competition will most reward profit-seekers that provide what society wants. Even in one of the most market-oriented societies in human history, people do not believe in the invisible hand.

Zero-sum thinking runs deep, even as we see the benefits of profits and losses all around us.

In his 2007 book *Basic Economics*, the irreplaceable Thomas Sowell writes that profit and loss are equally important in forcing companies to use scarce resources efficiently:

> Industry and commerce are not just a matter of routine management, with profits rolling in more or less automatically. Masses of ever-changing details, within an ever-changing surrounding social and economic environment, mean that the threat of losses hangs over even the biggest and most successful businesses. There is a reason why business executives usually work far longer hours than their employees, and why so many businesses fail within a few years after getting started. Only from the outside does it look easy.

Sowell taught economics at UCLA from July 1974 to June 1980, and made a particularly lasting impression on a young undergraduate named Chris Rufer.

WASTE: ELIMINATE OR EMBRACE?

Like other great businesspeople, Rufer understands that companies have a powerful incentive to reduce waste. To eliminate waste is to create more value—which can be shared with customers, suppliers, and employees in your business ecosystem. If a company can find a cost-effective way to use less fuel or put its waste products to creative uses, it will. (Recall that before Rufer, tomato paste was considered a byproduct of limited use.)

By contrast, government bureaucracies don't worry about profits and losses, and have fewer incentives to reduce waste. On the contrary, governments often have incentives to *increase* waste. Most government offices define success in terms of how big their budgets are, and try desperately to spend every penny so that their coffers are refilled. In *Stealing You Blind*, author and policy analyst Iain Murray laments:

> "We are spending more on [insert name of program]" is a badge of honor for any bureaucrat or politician. Yet it's actually a sign of failure. Spending more to help more is not a sign that the program is working, it is a sign that it is failing to address the ill it is meant to cure, whether that be poverty, obesity, insert your cause here.

Murray goes on, page after agonizing page, describing waste, corruption, and abuse at every level of government. From government officials in collusion with union bosses to municipal poobahs licking their chops at the lifetime pensions they've given themselves—it all comes at taxpayers' expense.

I don't want to leave you with the idea that government can't do good things. But without market discipline, it's difficult to tell whether government is doing anything well or efficiently. The prospect of profit and the avoidance of loss change an organization's behavior. Without this mechanism, the public sector is far less likely to use resources as efficiently as the private sector—without which, after all, the government would get no revenue.

Profiting at Chris Rufer's Expense

There is another dimension to the idea of profit: what a customer gets out of the deal. Absent fraud and buyer's remorse, the customer always profits in an exchange. Economist Murray Rothbard once asked rhetorically: "How can both parties benefit from an exchange?" He answered as follows: "Each one values the two goods or services differently, and these differences set the scene for an exchange. I, for example, am walking along with money in my pocket but no newspaper; the newsdealer, on the other hand, has plenty of newspapers but is anxious to acquire money. And so, finding each other, we strike a deal."[21] It's not rocket science, and this fact of mutual advantage scales up to society as a whole.

Far from Marx's notion of profit as "surplus value," profit is a reward for intelligent risk-taking, for stewarding resources responsibly, for exercising your skills entrepreneurially, and especially for creating value for other people.

Whenever you buy ketchup, soup, or spaghetti sauce, you might have Chris Rufer to thank. Of course, there is a sense in which you thank him with what economist Walter Williams calls "certificates of performance." Yes, it's just ketchup—it's easy to take for granted—but without Rufer, ketchup (or spaghetti sauce, or even my home-made barbecue sauce) would probably be more expensive and of lower quality. Without all of the other entrepreneurs in the world, none of the good things we take for granted would be available, often at low prices. Every time you give these entrepreneurs your money, you send them a signal that they're satisfying a want or need.

In exchanges, both parties benefit, even when one party is huge. Whenever you exchange with a company—even an *eeeevil* corporation—you are benefiting from the cooperative efforts of its employees. That makes economies of scale possible. You're trading with a group of people who are working— sometimes 'round the clock— to bring you something that is worth *more* to you than the money you gave for it. You profit. The company may or may not profit. You go home and eat fantastic pulled pork coated in sauce made from Morning Star's high-quality tomato paste, which costs you mere pennies on each dollar of true cost. Morning Star takes its pennies from the price of the barbecue sauce you buy to cover its costs as it plants, harvests, and transports tomatoes, refuels its trucks, maintains its plants, advertises its products, runs its farms, pays its farmers, produces its goods, and pays its workers (and, of course, as it pays its federal, state, and local taxes).

Morning Star's team members know that if they're not profiting, something's wrong. Either they're wasting resources or wasting time, and they can only suffer losses for so long before the company goes out of business. When they do turn a profit, some of it goes to expanding the business. That means hiring more people, outfitting new equipment, improving business processes, and turning out better and cheaper products. In other words, some profit gets re-invested. After that re-investment, whatever is left over goes to Chris Rufer and any colleagues with whom he has made profit-sharing arrangements.

WHO OWNS YOUR TALENT?

"But wait," says the skeptic. "Didn't the great philosopher John Rawls think that Chris Rufer's talents and skills as an entrepreneur are arbitrary? We can't all be born as wonderful and amazing as you've painted Chris in this. You already wrote above about how Rufer won his remarkable case of OCD in the genetic lottery. What he creates with his talent is valuable, yes. But we only need to leave him enough of his rewards to keep on doing what he's doing. The rest should go to 'social goods.'"

The inimitable economist Michael Munger elaborates on this point on the popular podcast *Econtalk*: "The things that you know, that you do, your character—those are collectively held. They are not privately owned, according to that theory of desert. That's a very discomforting idea, isn't it?"

In the abstract, it means "society" owns your talents. In practice, of course, it means that the state and various special interests own your talents should you choose to exercise them. But even if we agreed that the state owned everything above some percentage needed to keep you doing what you do, not everyone is motivated by the same rewards, or even by money. There is no magic marginal rate that will keep all productive people at work. As the top marginal tax rate increases, we see that people opt for leisure at different rates. And the problems don't end there.

Some people don't care about money much at all. Some prefer leisure time to working—watching TV or playing beer pong. If we really think our individual talents are publicly owned, taxing income amounts to forcing people to work, without pay, for a portion of their time. Indeed, if some own the labor of others, why would we tax the productive but leave the lazy to lie around? What if, for example, a man wants to live a more bohemian lifestyle instead of working? Or camp out at a demonstration? If "society" owns a portion of his talents, isn't society justified in forcing him to work?

Where I come from, they call that slavery. If not, then how is taxation sufficiently different from forced labor? And if we're uncomfortable with slavery, why would we tax those whom we've already admitted create value, but leave those who create no value to enjoy lives of leisure?

Mike Munger again:

> If you start from the premise that all our talents and character are collectively owned because they are morally arbitrary, then the only reason that anyone gets to keep profits is to motivate them to do what we want them to do for the public good.

Still, Munger demonstrates that—embedded in that premise—is the admission that *entrepreneurs create value in society.*

> I just made an argument saying profits are actually a sign that I am doing something for the collective. I am creating value. The mancgere [trader] is doing something that makes people better off. Well, my opponent might concede that, but say: 'Okay, but then we'll only give them enough profits to motivate them to do what we should want them to do. We don't have to give them the full amount.'

But if entrepreneurs really are value creators, as the Rawlsians admit, it's going to be hard to argue that the Chris Rufers of the world aren't "paying their fair share." At minimum, the burden of proof falls on the socialist to show that any resources the state skims from the entrepreneur's profits for the social good are beneficial *in excess* of whatever social good would have emerged from the alternative use. And that, folks, is by itself a difficult burden. As we said, bureaucrats have no measuring stick for whatever value they create, and deep incentives to waste resources and serve special interests. But even if, in the absence of a profit-and-loss system, a Rawlsian were able to prove the value of society's alternative use for Chris Rufer's profits, the problem of forced labor lingers. Rufer, however wealthy he is, is still being used. He is a kind of slave.

STEWARDSHIP

I tactfully bring up to Rufer that some people hate people like him simply for being rich.

"I couldn't possibly consume all the assets I have," Rufer said. "Most people like me are not conspicuous consumers. We're stewards of resources."

The entrepreneur is not one who steps over bodies to amass riches so he can lock them away from the poor. He does not take baths in gold coins minted with the image of his own face. The entrepreneur—and indeed Makers of all kinds—is a steward. A failure of stewardship means his riches evaporate, along with value for customers and suppliers, and any jobs or innovations that might have flowed from his profit-seeking activities.

As we spoke, Rufer offered an allegory that stuck with me. "I don't understand people like Warren Buffett," he said. "I mean, I'm not against charity. It's his money and he can do whatever he wants with it. But for him just to give away half his shares in Berkshire Hathaway is to give away capital…resources that could be used to build something sustainable. It would be like taking the planks off of a sturdy ship at sea to build fires that warm you up for a night or two. It just doesn't make sense."

I thought long and hard about Rufer's allegory. From Warren Buffett's perspective, we can understand that helping distressed, destitute people in Africa might be of paramount concern. But

Buffett's gifts will trade long-term value creation for temporary relief. So Rufer is right.

For most people, this idea is paradoxical at best. For others, reason simply loses out to good intentions. I suspect even after reading this, some people won't let go of the idea that relieving short-term anguish is better than creating sustainable prosperity. They'll see Mother Teresa, who allayed the suffering of tens of thousands, maybe hundreds of thousands of people as having done more for humanity than Norman Borlaug, whose agricultural advancements nourished millions.[ii] If we are serious that all value is personal and subjective, there is no arguing with either Buffett or Rufer. But if we start from a more utilitarian point, we see that the countries that allow people to deploy private capital in the service of creating prosperity are the ones that need less of Warren Buffett's charity. Stewarding resources makes their benefits available to more people. Charity has its limits.

RARITY

I have tried to convey just how rare Chris Rufer is. He not only helped to create a whole new market, one tomato, one truck, and one customer at a time, but he is also revolutionizing management. He will continue to create value beyond the rewards he receives from Morning Star, as CEOs everywhere start to emulate him and apply his management philosophy.

When he made his first $45,000, Rufer could have gone out and bought a BMW. Instead, he invested it in a plant. He could

---

ii   If you've never heard of Norman Borlaug, he's the person who created plant strains that increased agricultural yields by three and four times. He's known as the father of the Green Revolution and is thought to have saved hundreds of millions of people in India from starvation.

have spent the untold hours he devoted to organizing trucks, trailers, and tomatoes reading comic books or cruising at the beach. Whether he indulged the OCD that comes from deep within, or channeled his inner Mammon, Rufer has made millions of people's lives better. In return, they all gave him certificates of performance. Today, Rufer's company has grown to include three tomato processing factories, a cannery, an agricultural services and tomato harvesting company, a greenhouse and transplanting company, and—the cornerstone of the business to this day—the trucking company.

Rufer feels no guilt about his wealth. He knows he has built an empire of value. He understands fully how he keeps his capital working, each and every day, to generate value for people and turn profits doing it. Unlike many moguls who walk around with guilt complexes, Rufer finds no sense in the phrase "giving back."

Rufer never took anything to begin with. Instead, he created, and he shows no signs of stopping.

3
MAKERS AND TAKERS

Don't hate the player, hate the game.

– Ice-T

When the people find they can vote themselves money, that will herald the end of the republic.

– Benjamin Franklin

This is a tale of two food cities. But it's also the story of Makers, Takers, and the rules each lives by.

In America there are basically two kinds of wealthy people: those who get rich through making our lives better and those who get rich by using the political process to transfer wealth from others. You'll find Takers anywhere officials have the power to pick winners and losers in the economy—whether through regulations, subsidies, or favors. Likewise, you'll find Makers anywhere people are free enough to get a good business off the ground. Trouble is the rules don't always favor the Makers.

Nobel Prize winner Douglass North, in his 1993 prize lecture, said:

The organizations that come into existence will reflect the opportunities provided by the institutional matrix. That is, if the institutional framework rewards piracy then piratical organizations will come into existence; and if the institutional framework rewards productive activities then organizations—firms—will come into existence to engage in productive activities.

Great civilizations emerge where Makers can flourish. Once-great civilizations declined once the Takers started to outnumber the Makers.

Greece. Rome. Britain. America may soon follow. In these prosperous centers, the firewall between business and the state had been dismantled. All lost ground because they succumbed to the influence of Takers—also known as special interests. While many believe government power should be wielded for the greater good, most of what is done in the public's name is really just "politics without romance."

But don't take my word for it.

White Tablecloths

From Washington, D.C., you can travel south on I-95 through lightly rolling central Virginia. Cross the state line. There you'll pick up what's left of tobacco road. Take that to Raleigh.

The capital of North Carolina has always been a strange mix of ole-boy networks and populism, much like the rest of the state. Despite its proximity to the high-tech Research Triangle Park, Raleigh itself is more like a mini-Washington, D.C., only the backbiters and bureaucrats talk a little slower.

On downtown's Fayetteville Street you'll find The Mint.[i] It's a white-tablecloth restaurant that could very well have been plucked

---

i   Actually, you won't. Before going to print with this book, I discovered the Mint just went out of business. Michael Sanera writes: "As we predicted when the doors opened in 2008, the city subsidized Mint restaurant has closed its doors after a net loss of $400,000."

from Chicago's Gold Coast or New York's Upper East Side. Despite Raleigh's questionable urbanity, The Mint is one of maybe a handful of "world-class" restaurants in the area. And if it weren't for a kind of cosmopolitan penis envy on the part of Raleigh's big wigs, The Mint would probably never have come into existence.

In 2007, the city of Raleigh gave The Mint $1 million in subsidies in addition to at least a year's worth of free rent in a city-owned building. Town poobahs had decided Raleigh must have country-club eating closer to the legislature and administrative buildings. How, after all, could important people be expected to broker big deals over plates of barbecue and slaw?

Raleigh has always had a chamber-of-commerce mentality. It extends back through nearly 100 years of Dixiecrat tradition. In other words, starting and running a business in North Carolina has always been about pleasing the political class. This is not to pick on Democrats; an animal we might call a "chamber-of-commerce Republican" inhabits the state, too, only it lives mostly in Charlotte. The Democrats have almost always held the reins in the city of Raleigh, not to mention legislative power in the state. In truth, when it comes to the business of picking winners and losers, these two creatures, R and D, are virtually indistinguishable in North Carolina. Neither is pro-entrepreneurship. Both are pro-business. And there is a difference.

Take the business of eating out. As high-end restaurants like The Mint get subsidies, push-carts and food trucks are effectively banned.

JOB CREATION

Suppose you're having a hard time making ends meet. Instead of lining up to get a welfare check at the Department of Social Services, you decide to start a micro-business selling food. What would you encounter if you tried to start a food truck in Raleigh? At the state level, writes the intrepid reporter Sara Burrows:

> A Department of Environment and Natural Resources rule adopted in 1980 dictates, 'Only hot dogs shall be prepared, handled, or served from a pushcart.' Other than hot dogs, only prepackaged food from approved restaurants may be sold. State law allows a greater variety of food to be prepared and sold from food trucks, but trucks are more expensive and more heavily regulated than food carts.

If state regulations weren't enough, city ordinances make things virtually impossible for micro-restauranteurs:

> While some cities allow [food trucks] to park in metered spaces or designate a lot for them downtown, food trucks in Raleigh can operate only on commercially zoned land, with a permit, for up to 20 days. A limited number—two per block—of non-motorized pushcarts are permitted to set up on city sidewalks, but they cannot locate near a restaurant selling similar food, and they must be of a certain dimension, weight, and material.[22]

Burrows once asked Raleigh City Councilwoman Mary-Ann Baldwin why the city restricts the number and location of mobile food units. Baldwin rather brazenly admitted the regulations are necessary to protect established restaurants and keep the streets free of unsightly trucks.

"You want to balance what's good for the entrepreneur with what's good for your restaurant owners," the *Carolina Journal* quotes Baldwin as saying. "You don't want to hurt [restaurant owners] and put them out of business. They've made a huge investment." (I would have expected the usual shtick about health and safety, so Baldwin gets credit for honesty.)

So do food trucks put big restaurants out of business? It's possible, but isn't that the nature of free enterprise? Competition? Creative destruction? Customers win? Something better replaces what goes out of business. That's a decision customers ought to make, not city planners.

Managing partner Rick Jones of the Raleigh Restaurant Group (which owns The Mint) is what we might indelicately call a Taker. In other words, if it were not for the taxpayer's dollars that kept Jones' Potemkin restaurant on the taxpayer's dole, Raleigh's citizens might have let something really interesting take root. Who knows what delicate saplings might have sprung up and blossomed had city planners not subsidized The Mint and forbidden food trucks?

Not all the blame goes to Rick Jones for gaming the system. He didn't make the rules and, if he hadn't cashed in, someone else would have. *Don't hate the player, hate the game.* But it's time we started thinking about changing the rules so that we reward Makers, not Takers. Both Makers and Takers get rich but only one group deserves it. And to think that Rick Jones got wealthy at the expense of some taxpayers who could never afford to eat at The Mint! Well, let's just say there's something wrong with that.

PETTY FASCISM

Councilwoman Mary-Ann Baldwin is what I refer to as a petty fascist. While I normally hesitate to use the 'F-word,' it applies in Raleigh's case.

"Where socialism sought totalitarian control of a society's economic processes through direct state operation of the means of production," writes Sheldon Richman, "fascism sought that control indirectly, through domination of nominally private owners. Where socialism nationalized property explicitly, fascism did so implicitly, by requiring owners to use their property in the 'national interest'— that is, as the autocratic authority conceived it."[23]

Replace "national" with "city" interests and the F-word is perfectly apt. I'd bet Raleigh's petty autocrats benefit from *quid pro quo* arrangements with corporate restaurateurs such as Rick Jones. It's just one of innumerable examples of crony capitalism in America— Takers living at the expense of Makers.

Town planners get into their heads that they are elected to decide what the city's character should be. These wise elites should figure out everything from restaurants to light posts to paint colors—down to the minutest detail. All will be decided according to their superior notions of a good city. And that is, frankly, why cities like Raleigh lack grit and culture. Sure, the area is nice enough. But apart from boxy government buildings, downtown has become increasingly sterile and fabricated—all according to plan.

Culture and commerce cannot be planned from the top down. It emerges from the people, communities, and markets. In the seminal *Life and Death of Great American Cities*, Jane Jacobs once wrote that cities "have the capability of providing something for everybody, only because, and only when, they are created by everybody." Why? Because "[t]here is a quality even meaner than outright ugliness or disorder, and this meaner quality is the dishonest mask of pretended order, achieved by ignoring or suppressing the real order that is struggling to exist and to be served." That is culture, life, and prosperity from the bottom up.

Cities like Raleigh and neighboring Cary are fine if your idea of a great food is Carrabba's or The Mint. But people who like to taste the interesting experiments of humbler entrepreneurs will find little to offer in places that subsidize corporate cronies and keep the little guys from ever getting into the game. Such places have about as much culture as ultra-pasteurized milk. What's worse: Opportunities for people of little means get steamrolled when politicians collude with big business. And yet this happens all the time. The ghosts of stillborn businesses hover around the town halls of America, and yet no one can see or hear them. They are the casualties of a regulatory state that has grown too big and too costly.

ONE CUSTOMER AT A TIME

Fourteen-hundred miles away, things are a little different—at least when it comes to eating out.

"Damn, that's a good taco." That's what Mike Rypka kept hearing over and over again. He knew if he kept hearing it, he was doing something right.

My first experience with one of Rypka's tacos changed my entire taco concept. And I'm no novice. I have tasted tacos far and wide: from the *taquerias* nestled in Northside Chicago neighborhoods to the street food of the Yucatan. All were tacos that had, in some sense, set the bar for such fare. Until I tried Torchy's.

I ordered a "Dirty Sanchez." Scatological reference notwithstanding, imagine someone with lots of tattoos handing you your food from the window of an Airstream. It comes in a plastic basket with little cups of hot sauce on the side: scrambled eggs sharing a double-wrapped, soft-corn-tortilla bed with tempura pobla-no peppers, cheese, escabeche (pickled) carrot-spears, avocados, and spicy ranch dressing. Carrots? Yes. The pickled carrot spears animate the taco with hints of crispy and tangy. The avocado is central, sensual. The sauce unites everything in creamy coolness. Those firm, steaming eggs make you forget that the Dirty Sanchez has no meat.

It takes chutzpah for a guy from Virginia to come to Austin, Texas, and start a taco truck. "You can't throw a stick without hit-ting a Mexican restaurant in this town," Rypka said, recalling his start. "Were we crazy?"

I don't want to understate Rypka's experience. He had studied at Johnson and Wales in Miami. He had cooked for 3,000 heads a day at the World Bank, served dinner to President Clinton, and run kitchens as an executive chef at very high-end restaurants in Chicago, L.A., and Houston. He had done all of this after start-ing when he was only 15 at—of all places—a Popeye's Chicken in Springfield, Virginia. Rypka says that's where he fell in love with food. "Weird," I thought, but I didn't argue. The man was a culi-nary genius.

A resume like Rypka's might make most of us cocky and yet that's not what I sensed in him as we chatted over coffee. This was a guy with a passion for his craft and a belief that ordinary people can have delicious food at a decent price. "If I could do good quality, high-end food for the masses, that's what I wanted," and by "mass-es" he meant a few Sixth Street partiers looking for hangover cures or a couple of working stiffs on their lunch breaks. Little did he know what masses would come to mean.

HUMBLE BEGINNINGS

Rypka said he never set out to do anything but get into a situation where he could cook his own food, make his own rules, and not have to report to anyone except his customers. "I didn't have rich relatives or anything," Rypka said, "so we had to start small." Turns out Rypka had a buddy with a rehabbed food truck—more or less a caterer's R.V. "He couldn't sell the thing to save his life. Back then, nobody wanted a food truck. These days you can hardly find one anywhere."

I asked Rypka what he did to get started. He grinned a little as he reflected.

"I maxed out my credit cards. I took a loan out against my house," he said. "And I didn't get a paycheck for almost a year because I was putting everything back into the business."

Rypka convinced a downtown property owner to lease space in his lot—this at a time before hipsters made food trucks cool and The Food Network made them mainstream. Surprisingly, the Austin officials didn't harass him, though the city can be draconian in other respects. In 2005, most people thought of a trailer as a place where rednecks live and/or recreate, or maybe how Mexican immigrants sell food in the *barrio* (certainly not a trained chef).

And this, by the way, is another aspect of Rypka's brilliance as an entrepreneur: branding. He knew he had to signal something special. He did not settle for painting something sloppy on the side of his truck. Instead he set to work "with a girl at Kinko's" to design a logo that would capture Austin's vibe and allow him to stand out in a city that hosts quite a few strong local brands. Working at night, Rypka settled on the essence of what would become the Torchy's logo:

a cartoon devil baby with a pitchfork. The fiery font is distinctive: "Torchy's" above and "Tacos" below, with the imp-child in between. A left-to-right scroll through the center reads "Damn Good." So the whole impression is of Torchy's 'damn good' Tacos as a gestalt, which calls to mind a playful tattoo. Perfect for Austin.

The live music capital is a city full of cosmopolitans, Johnny Cash fans, professionals, cultural creatives, the occasional cowboy, hipsters, and a lot of people with tattoos. It's a city of beautiful contradictions. The contrasts work together like pickled carrots, fluffy eggs, avocado, poblano, and ranch. In Austin, Rypka had struck a chord.

Bear in mind Mike Rypka was serving good food at the genesis of the Austin food truck craze, of which he—along with food-truck phenoms Hey Cupcake and Flip Happy Crepes—formed the nucleus of the city's mobile food culture, a culture that has swept much of the United States in recent years.

300

Today, Torchy's Tacos employs more than 300 people. These are people who can now pay their bills and have opportunities to advance within a good company. Despite recession, Rypka and his team are in the process of opening a tenth store as of this writing. And I dare say Rypka is probably in the "one percent" now. From a used taco truck, to ten stores and growing: How did they do it? "One customer at time," Rypka said. He put together a great team and he gives them tons of credit. But he started from almost nothing. No business plan, no begging for capital. A loan here and there, but otherwise, they leaned on neither corporate investors nor colluded with politicians.

Simply put: Austin didn't ban food trucks. Rypka thrived in a business environment that allowed him to start small and experiment.

There are other types of food in Austin, too. From hole-in-the-wall ethnic, to Tex-Mex chains like Chuy's, to Texas brisket, to experimental sushi like that served at award-winning Uchi. Did any of these great places need their investments protected from Austin's food trucks? Has Austin's vibe been anything but enriched by the food truck culture? Let's just say that the city would have a revolt if it tried to ban them at this stage.

Vibrant cities like Austin have wonderful food ecosystems *because* of micro-entrepreneurs. Food trucks congregate along South Congress Avenue in areas that remind one of strange attractors. People flock to the area *because* they know the food trucks are there. Sometimes they patronize them, other times they want to sit indoors. It doesn't seem to affect the surrounding restaurants that thrive in the area, such as Perla's (seafood), Snack Bar (hipster American) and Zen (Japanese fusion).

So this leads us to a question: What would Austin, Texas, look like if the city had not allowed the original Torchy's taco truck? And what would Rypka be doing today? Still working for a corporate outfit like Sodexo? What about his 300 employees?

The moral of these two stories is that the opportunities that arise from entrepreneurship can easily be legislated or regulated away in the name of all sorts of things. But we should really ask ourselves: Are the aesthetic preferences of town elites worth never letting good things come into existence? Should tablecloth restaurants be allowed to siphon off of hardworking people while people like Steve Pruner of Durham, North Carolina, are getting arrested for selling hot dogs from a cart without licenses? And even if hot dog vendors and food trucks had the ability to put every big corporate restaurant in town out of business—which is doubtful—wouldn't that be a reflection of the people's will? (People vote best with their dollars.)

Politics Without Romance

Nobel Prize winner James Buchanan put the central problem of American politics with scholarly concision:

> If the government is empowered to grant monopoly rights or tariff protection to one group, at the expense of the general public or of designated losers, it follows that potential beneficiaries will compete for the prize. And since only one group can be rewarded, the resources invested by other groups—which could have been used to produce valued goods and services—are wasted. Given this basic insight, much of modern politics can be understood as rent-seeking activity. Pork-barrel politics is only the most obvious example. Much of the growth of the bureaucratic or regulatory sector of government can best be explained in terms of the competition between political agents for constituency support through the use of promises of discriminatory transfers of wealth." [24]

What Buchanan described in 122 words is a great power nexus. Politicians give advantages to special interests in exchange for power. Completing the nexus, do-gooders provide moralistic cover for most of it (health and safety, public good, saving the planet, and so on). Citizen-consumers, like you and I, lose. Power and wealth are concentrated on the political class and the corporate class. The costs of that power and wealth are dispersed over everybody else in the form of higher taxes, higher prices, and limited choices.

As I write this, America is still in a recession. We have been for a while. True recovery will not come via dropping largesse from on high like manna from taxpayers. Nor will it come from crony capitalism of the sort that you'll find in Washington, D.C., Raleigh, (or yes, even Austin). It will come from genuine entrepreneurship led by people who start as small as Mike Rypka and who perhaps end up as big as the late Steve Jobs. These are people who satisfy our unmet needs. They serve us and they make our lives better. In that sense, they make us richer, all of which is the essence of growth. Making better rules for entrepreneurship—micro and macro—is the way America can be great again.

How to Tell a Taker from a Maker

So who are the Takers and who are the Makers?

There are five basic types of Takers in the world: the Deadweight CEO, the Opportunistic Politician, the Activist-Lobbyist, the Bloated Bureaucrat, and the Public Parasite.

The Deadweight CEO is in many respects a product of the system. He is good at finding opportunities for his company to profit, but he is indifferent about whether those profits come from making or taking. If a subsidy goes to his bottom line, he'll take it. If he can invest in lobbyists to ensure his competition gets hobbled by an obscure regulation, he'll pay for lobbying. If he can collude with government in any way that benefits his company, he'll do it. Famous Deadweight CEOs include Jeffrey Emmelt of GE, who gets taxpayer money for everything from non-cost-effective solar panels to wind turbines. GE would have no such "business" if it weren't for government largesse—the costs of which are distributed onto you and me. Of course, the Deadweight CEO can be a restaurant owner or cab driver with a medallion (license). They run zombie businesses large and small whose corporate cultures are often marked by a lack of innovation and dynamism.

The Opportunistic Politician has the power to ensure that the Deadweight CEO gets his anti-competitive regulation or subsidy. But the politician wants something in return: a political war chest that will allow him to stay in office for a long time. The Opportunistic Politician is rarely interested in principles. The system rewards his abandoning those principles to engage in log-rolling and getting into bed with corporations that are looking for special favors and market advantages. Of course, the politician rarely bears any political cost for this sort of backroom dealing because voters are largely ignorant of what's going on. And, in fact, politicians tell us about all of the purported benefits of what they do, but none of the costs. Few of us have time to check to see whether our congressman votes to subsidize turbine makers, mohair producers, or any of a million other Takers bidding for favors that will secure his incumbency.

The Activist-Lobbyist could be separated into activists and lobbyists, but for our purposes they can be melded together. Both are representatives—useful intermediaries—between Deadweight CEOs and Opportunistic Politicians. "How could this be?" you may be thinking. Consider that climate-change activists want reductions in man-made CO_2. Well, guess what? So do major energy companies, such as Duke Energy, with large nuclear and natural gas portfolios. If Congress were to pass a carbon tax, Duke Energy would have to pay the tax, but it would have to pay a heck of a lot less than its competitors with heavy interests in coal (which releases more

CO_2). Lobbyists for Duke Energy converge on Congress to ask for a carbon tax. It seems counter-intuitive: big corporate lobbyists licking their chops, begging to be regulated. Then, of course, the activists for global warming converge on Congress to ask for the tax, too. (Economist Bruce Yandle calls these "Bootleggers and Baptists" coalitions.[25]) Guess who will pay for the new tax? You and me. And so it goes for food safety legislation, agricultural subsidies, emergency bank bailouts, and high-speed rail projects. Activist-lobbyists make all the noise, we pay all the costs.

The Bloated Bureaucrat is a person who sees him or herself as an indispensable public servant. Whether it's the board of education paper shuffler in your hometown or a green planner at the U.S. Department of Energy, these bureaucrats produce very little but take in a lot. They often have enviable salaries, Cadillac health insurance, and lifelong pensions. In some states they're even unionized! (Fox, meet hen house.) They're paid more compared to the average private-sector employee and each thinks the entire edifice of civilization would crumble without his or her department, of which they are a critical cog. Bureaucracies rarely shrink and almost always grow—even if they outlive the use for which they were created. The trouble with a Bloated Bureaucrat is that it is difficult to tell whether he or she, while being capable and well-intentioned, is creating value in society. Because these bureaucrats operate outside the discipline and feedback mechanisms of the marketplace, we have to place considerable faith in their contributions to society, relative to their cost.

The Public Parasite could be you. It could be me. And it certainly is our neighbors. The Public Parasite demands healthcare benefits at 65 despite having a million-dollar house in Boca Raton; will probably live twenty years beyond retirement; and will consume much, much more than he was ever forced to contribute to the system. The Public Parasite wants new roads in his district every year (whether said roads are needed or not) and will tell a little white lie about his income to ensure his kids all get free lunch at school. He wants Social Security and subsidized ballet, and will stand in line at the checkout paying with food stamps while playing games on his brand new smartphone. He is willing to give The Opportunistic Politician his vote to ensure he gets all of it.

THE TEMPTATION TO TAKE

Jonathan Rauch, in his excellent and woefully underappreciated book *Government's End,* asks you to imagine you're the president of Acme Big Flange Company. You have $1 million to invest in the growth of your company. What should you do? You have a couple of options. The first option is to buy a high-speed flange-milling machine or maybe a better inventory-control system. Over ten years, this will give you a 10–15 percent annual return—that is, $100,000 to $150,000. Not bad. But there is a second course:

> For $1 million you could hire one of the best lobbyists in Washington. This fellow is a former staff member of the House Valve and Flange Subcommittee: He knows the legislators, he knows the issues, and he is persuasive and ingenious. With his help, you could invest some of your $1 million in campaign contributions to members of the Valve and Flange Subcommittee. Though you can't count on buying anyone's vote, your money would by you access, which your competitor might not enjoy. Your lobbyist and your PAC might win you a tax break, a subsidy,

or, best of all (because it's least visible to the public), a law or regulation hobbling mini-flange mills. Any such tax break, subsidy, or regulation could easily be worth, say, $10 million a year. [26]

So here's the question: Are you better off investing in a milling machine or a lobbyist?

Before you answer conclusively, let me add a new dimension to Rauch's thought experiment. Suppose you know your competition is already investing in a lobbyist. What do you have to do with your $1 million at this point? Suppose also that the prize is $50,000 for every dollar invested. Now it's a lobbying arms race. What Rauch calls the "parasite economy" is booming now because you and your competitors are in a deadly game of, well, gaming the system—which all of you are now forced to play. It's winner take all. If there are three companies bidding for the prize, that's three times the waste because, of course, none of these bids go to productive things. Society loses, especially taxpayers and consumers who have no idea what's going on. All it takes is for one player in one industry to hire a lobbyist.

"I think it may be the thing feeds on itself," says economist Gordon Tullock, whose pioneering work exposed the Taker nexus. "Every time you have a successful lobbying effort, that advertises the value of lobbying." [27]

CHARACTERISTICS OF MAKERS

We've seen that, increasingly, our system of government rewards Takers. Makers still exist, but they are becoming increasingly rare as the "institutional framework rewards piracy." But let's not get ahead of ourselves. Who are the makers?

There are also five basic types of Makers: the Creative Entrepreneur, the Earnest Executive, the Insightful Investor, the Savvy Speculator, and the Hard-Working Employee.

The Creative Entrepreneur is a visionary. He not only has big ideas, but he can also see them through so as to put people and resources together to get a company off the ground. He may or may not be good at administration, but he has the good sense to partner with someone who does. At root, the Creative Entrepreneur has a special ability to see how to create value for people—to serve them at least as well or as inexpensively as his competitors. By definition, he is able to make folks' lives better using fewer resources than those he serves are willing—*willing*—to let go of. The essence of the Creative Entrepreneur is, as the venerable Israel Kirzner put it, an "alertness" to undiscovered opportunities, maybe even as yet created markets. Think Steve Jobs. Think Mike Rypka. Think Henry Ford.

The Earnest Executive is a leader and administrator. Her ability to make good decisions as an organization grows is critical to success. She is the one who can make things happen, manage growth, make tough decisions, organize the company into profit centers, find the fat, trim the fat, pick the right people, reward the right people, empower the right people, and determine the most promising areas for new growth. She has to understand her competition and keep them in check and she has a relentless commitment to value for the customer. Sometimes you find the rare person who is both a Creative Entrepreneur and an Earnest Executive in one. (Again, think Steve Jobs.) But usually you have to get these two teamed up or have one pass the torch to the other, as in the case of Billy Durant and Alfred P. Sloan. The former founded General Motors; he was a visionary. The latter, according to Peter Drucker, was "the first to work out how to systematically organize a big company. When Sloan became president of GM in 1923 he put in place planning and strategy, measurements, and most importantly, the principles of decentralization."[28]

Or think of unheralded CEOs such as BB&T Bank's former CEO John Allison, who refused to give out adjustable rate mortgages and other dodgy government-backed loans that ended up causing the financial meltdown of 2008. Allison's company came out smelling like a rose when his bigger competitors were in very serious trouble. (Of course, everyone knows his competitors got bailed out.) Allison's integrity and commitment to true value in mortgage products made his company stronger. The Earnest Executive normally runs healthy companies that are innovative and purpose-driven.

The Insightful Investor has the resources—i.e. the capital—and he knows where to put it. Whether he sees a promising idea sketched on a napkin in a coffee shop near Sand Hill Road, or he's using capital to fertilize an existing company that promises healthy growth, the Insightful Investor cannot simply follow the trends. He has to gain the insight to find investment opportunities in which he will not see his resources evaporate. Think of Peter Thiel, who got in at the ground floor after Facebook's Mark Zuckerberg stumbled into his office in 2004 (Thiel also co-founded PayPal). Recall those guys on Sand Hill Road who had to hold their noses when a couple of smelly computer builders named Wozniak and Jobs fell into their midst back in 1977. We love these two, but without those Insightful Investors willing to sniff beyond the underarms, there would have been no Apple.

The Savvy Speculator is a kind of investor but it's important to draw a distinction here, because the Savvy Speculator has a different kind of bent. Where the investor sees opportunities in people and companies, the Savvy Speculator is a minute-to-minute big-picture arbitrageur. Think of it like this: Tornadoes hit an important logistics hub in an area that specializes in grains. The Savvy Speculator takes this information and, through good timing and knowledge of shifting circumstances, understands that this grain hub will be disabled for a while. He might try to move assets based on the idea that the price of grain could temporarily spike due to the disabled hub. He also might see an opportunity for foreign grains due to the tornadoes. Is there an opportunity to buy in substitute commodities—such as corn—that were not affected by the tornadoes? The Savvy Speculator also might understand that within three to six months, the grain hub will be restored to full capacity and seize the opportunity to buy low now and sell high. Much like an ant following a pheromone trail, his interests are narrow.

In the big picture, however, speculators' function in society is to get resources where they need to go given the circumstances of the marketplace. These are circumstances of either scarcity or abundance. Speculators can bet right, or bet wrong, but the fact that they bet at all is essential to a well-functioning economy. To the extent the Savvy Speculator is able to make reasonably good judgments about these large-scale events—as well as the behavior of other speculators—he profits not only from being smarter, but from being patient, persistent, and resilient. Indeed, most traders make money from about 20 percent of their trades. Say what you want about people on Wall Street or the Chicago Merc, but they work tirelessly—often obsessively—to ensure that at the end of a bad trading day their fortunes have not evaporated. Untold are the myriad stories of traders who were not insightful and left the investment game humbled, with only lint in their pockets.

The Hard-Working Employee is familiar to us, and yet this person is often as unique and varied as the organizations and roles he occupies. From upper management and accountants to creatives, shipping clerks, and janitorial staff, each Hard-Working Employee creates value by specializing in some activity the organization—and eventually its customers—needs.

Makers such as those described above create a virtuous ecosystem. As we suggest, these maker categories can overlap. The action happens when Makers do what they do best and interact with each other for mutual benefit and mutual gain. Sometimes, of course, Makers compete with other Makers. But this competition gives us beneficial effects, as well, because when Makers compete they're almost always trying to give us the best product at the lowest price. They know if they don't, another Maker will.

To Make or To Take? That is the Question

Now that we've explored these major categories of Makers and Takers, imagine letting them loose into the wild. Also, suppose for the sake of discussion that half are Makers and half are Takers. Will one side eventually overwhelm the other? It depends on the rules. I admit this gets things a little backwards. As we've suggested, a Maker or a Taker is just as often a *product* of the rules. But to get to our key intuition, let's suppose we dropped an equal number of Maker-inclined and Taker-inclined folks into a rule matrix. What would happen? It's simple: If the rules favor Makers, we'll eventually get more Makers. If the rules favor Takers, we'll get more Takers. In other words, though we may never completely transform everyone predisposed to being either/or, the rules of the game have a lot to do with what a body becomes. Why? Because rules are systems of incentives. Like a Brit inclined to drive on the left, once across the pond he will very quickly find incentives to drive on the right side.

Increasingly, however, the rules favor Takers in America. That is because the rule of law is being corrupted. When I say "the rule of law" I don't mean simply that we have laws cranked out from a sausage grinder by lobbyist-funded lawmakers. I mean that laws, in order to favor Makers, must apply equally to everyone or, similarly, equally to every company. If the rules can be changed to favor interest groups, Takers will find a bonanza. Incentives matter, after all. So, in America, each and every day we get closer and closer to a Takers paradise.

That's bad news: From the point of view of any individual in this great nexus of Makers and Takers, it increasingly pays to be a Taker. If we zoom out, when people go from being Makers to being Takers, society becomes poorer in three critical ways. First, transferring resources from other's pockets to yours takes resources. There is an army of intermediaries who need to be paid— Activist-Lobbyists and Opportunistic Politicians among them. Remember, these people produce nothing of value. They're merely parasitic go-betweens. Second, and more worryingly, all of the resources that *could have gone* to productive things now go to the taking system. Third, among all these Takers there are very, very smart, courageous, talented, and well-intentioned people, but their smarts, courage, talent, and drive are going into the parasite economy. What do you find in the banana republics of the world or among the ruins of once-great civilizations? Parasite economies. They are filled not with evil people, but with people who find what little they can among the twisted maze of laws fashioned for the benefit of the few.

TAKER'S AUCTION

Before closing, let me offer a final thought experiment designed to unpack how much waste goes into the parasite economy.

I have $1 for which I have decided to hold an "all-pay" auction. Imagine you're with a group of other people in my "lobby." Everyone in the lobby starts bidding for the money and, everyone who bids, pays—hence, "all pay." I start the bidding at 25 cents. Someone chimes in with a bid. They'd be a fool not to take a dollar for a quarter. When I move the bidding to 50 cents, I have another taker. We're getting hot now! When I ratchet the bidding up to 75 cents, you bid this time. After all, that's still a quarter's worth of profit to you.

Okay, now something weird happens. I offer a $1 bid for the $1. Guess who takes it: the guy who bid 50 cents and now stands to lose it—remember, each bid must be paid. Now you're thinking, "Wait a minute, if I bid $1.25, I'll still lose less than 75 cents, so maybe I'd better bid $1.25 now." You wouldn't be wrong, except the person who bid a dollar for the dollar is now thinking she'd better bid $1.50, reasoning in exactly the same way you are. Finally, the bidding closes at $1.75. You lose 75 cents for playing. A lot of other people lose money, too.

According to economist David Zetland, channeling the 1983 movie War Games, "The only strategy is not to play the game." (I'm indebted to Zetland for this thought experiment, by the way.) The trouble is, if you're not playing the lobbying game, your competitors might force you to. After all, they are trying to change the rules of the institutional matrix to *their advantage*. If you don't play, you could lose even more. But the overall result is ungodly deadweight loss to society.

WHO CHOOSES? WHO BENEFITS? WHO PAYS?

Once we learn to distinguish the two types, we can identify them and bring sunlight. But how do we figure out who's a Maker and a Taker? And how do we disrupt the Taker's nexus so as to make the environment more hospitable for Makers? This, of course, is the trillion-dollar question.

First, you as an individual can become better at figuring out whether Takers are at work. Say you're near the water cooler or at a dinner party and the discussion turns to politics. Sometimes you don't know exactly how to make the argument, so wouldn't it be simpler if your conversation partner could help make your argument for you? A simple, useful exercise for unpacking the problems of political economy is to ask the following questions: Who benefits? Who chooses? Who pays? What's fair play?

Take any issue—any subsidy or regulation, for example—and ask those four questions. The rationale that flows can get you very far indeed. It's the citizen's equivalent of Deep Throat's "follow the money."

But if we're worried about the process Jonathan Rauch calls

"demosclerosis,"[ii] how can we begin to disrupt this seemingly un-stoppable Takers nexus that has corrupted so many societies? The following is a tentative list of suggestions in no particular order.

1. *Change the Metarules* – Ideally, we could change the rules so that the separation of business and state was as separate as that of church and state. More likely, we'll have to change the way laws are made (the rules of lawmaking) to preclude the passage of legislation that runs counter to the rule of law—i.e. the "metarules." Most metarules are constitutional in nature. So, in the United States, you'd have to change the Constitution to restrict the whole game of legislating winners and losers, or at least change the incentives of legislators through term limits.

2. *Change the Rules* – Changing the rules is not as powerful, but it's something. For example, in the United States you cannot ban lobbying because it would be both an abridgement of free speech and the right to petition government for the "redress of grievances." But perhaps it would be possible to institute a requirement that all lobbying activity be transparent and accountable. For example, what if Congress were to pass a law requiring all petitions to government be recorded and made available online? Of course, very few politicians have an incentive to bring sunlight to their activities. But one can dream.

3. *Call out the Takers* – If more people were to become good at following the money, it would be simpler for journalists,

---

ii   Jonathan Rauch defines "demosclerosis" as "government's progressive loss of the ability to adapt" as a side-effect of the postwar style of politics that emphasizes interest-group activism and redistributive programs.

citizens, and bloggers to call out the Takers, make examples of them. With enough civic consciousness about cronyism and the parasite economy, perhaps you could get to a point where 1 and 2 (above) become more likely. At least we might be able to derail some of the more egregious examples of favor seeking.

4. *Create Opportunities for Exit* – What if it were easier and cheaper to play by different rules? What if, for example, it were possible to live and do business off the coast of societies whose laws have become illiberal or predatory (say, by seasteading)? What if it were possible to create a free economic zone within a country whose laws have become too byzantine (as they have done in China and are doing currently in Honduras)? Creating opportunities for exit—or competition among sets of rules—is a pragmatic way of dealing with rules that favor Takers.

I admit the four suggestions above seem rather pie-in-the-sky, but we shouldn't lose hope. Once we are able to bring the difference between Makers and Takers fully into the public consciousness, there may be a way to make the world a better place by unleashing the creativity and enterprise of those committed to making our lives better. That means more and richer rich people. But that's okay: The future of our nation—indeed, of our world—depends on them.

4
NEVER MIND THE GAP

One also encounters a depraved taste for equality in the human heart that brings the weak to want to draw the strong to their level and that reduces men to preferring equality in servitude to inequality in freedom.

— Alexis de Tocqueville

A and B put their heads together to decide what C shall be made to do for D. The radical vice of all these schemes…is that C is not allowed a voice in the matter, and his position, character, and interests, as well as the ultimate effects on society through C's interests, are entirely overlooked. I call C the Forgotten Man.

— William Graham Sumner

Bill Gates and Warren Buffett are sitting at a diner drinking malted milkshakes. This is not the first line of a joke. Someone snapped a picture of this scene in Omaha, Nebraska, back in 2010. The image appeared with a *Forbes* [29] article about a plan the two were hatching. Two of the world's richest men were discussing an idea that came to be known as the $600 Billion Philanthropy Challenge.

"Gates and Buffett started what can be called the biggest fundraising drive in history," Carol Loomis wrote of the moguls.

They'd welcome donors of any kind. But their direct target is billion-aires, whom the two men wish to see greatly raise the amounts they give to charities, of any and all kinds. That wish was not mathematical-ly framed at the time of the New York meeting. But as two other U.S. dinners were held (though not leaked), Buffett and Gates and his wife, Melinda, set the goal: They are driving to get the super-rich, starting with the *Forbes* list of the 400 wealthiest Americans, to pledge—literally *pledge*—at least 50% of their net worth to charity during their lifetimes or at death.

The pledge is an ambitious and noble undertaking. It means persuading others to give a lot of their money to good causes. And interestingly, it had come on the heels of Buffet's 2006 commit-ment[30] of more than $1 billion a year to the Bill and Melinda Gates Foundation, the world's largest charity. But what does it mean?

REVEALED PREFERENCE

Economists have a concept they refer to as "revealed prefer-ence." This is a fancy way of saying you can get a good idea about what people want by observing what they do. People's actual choic-es reveal their preferences. It doesn't always work. People are com-plicated creatures and can be motivated by multiple, often conflict-ing desires. You might not want to visit your in-laws, but you want to keep your spouse happy. In this case, you have demonstrated a preference, not so much for spending time with in-laws, but for maintaining domestic tranquility. Still, most of the time, we can figure out someone's preferences through her actions. If somebody spends an hour at the movies rather than at the park, we can make an educated guess that she preferred the movies to the park. It could be that a park hijacker told her to "go to the movies—or else!" But chances are she ranked the movie higher than the park among the available alternatives of things to do that day. Then she acted.

Similarly, if Warren Buffett gave large sums to the Bill and Melinda Gates Foundation rather than giving those same sums to the Thiel Foundation, we can make a pretty good guess that Buffett prefers giving to the Gates Foundation. Again, revealed preference—which is rooted in people's real choices—can tell us a lot about what people prefer.

Only about a year after Gates and Buffett decided to convince other billionaires to give half of their net worth away to charity, Buffett said: "My friends and I have been coddled long enough by a billionaire-friendly Congress. It's time for our government to get serious about shared sacrifice." Specifically, Buffett wanted the federal government to tax the rich at a higher rate—even if that means double taxation.

All of this prompts the question: Is Warren Buffett serious about shared sacrifice? It depends on what you mean by the term. If shared sacrifice means helping the world become a better place, Buffett is, indeed, serious about both entrepreneurship and sacrifice. As we point out, the Oracle of Omaha is giving boatloads to charity each year. But I'm not so sure he's serious about billionaires paying more in taxes. Buffett's is an example of Machiavelli's cynical twist of an old line from Cicero: *Videri Quam Esse*—"to seem rather than to be." How do we know? Revealed preference.

In a now-famous op-ed in *The New York Times*, Warren Buffett admits "Last year my federal tax bill—the income tax I paid, as well as payroll taxes paid by me and on my behalf—was $6,938,744. That sounds like a lot of money. But what I paid was only 17.4 percent of my taxable income—and that's actually a lower percentage than was paid by any of the other 20 people in our office."[31]

After his *Times* piece came out, a lot of people wanted to know why Buffett didn't just pay more in taxes. Nothing prevents one from writing a check to the U.S. Treasury for any amount he likes. And yet it appears he did not. If he did, it was not an amount that would have caused the percentage he paid in taxes to equal that percentage paid by any of the other twenty people in his office.

So what can we conclude about people such as Warren Buffett? We can, at least, say he's inconsistent. I suspect others in the tax-me-more coalition are too. He wants to give but what his actions reveal is that, deep down, Buffett really wants a fine organization like the Gates Foundation to be the steward of his philanthropy. Through his actions toward the $600 billion pledge, Buffett also demonstrates he wants others to be charitable. So far, so good.

Finally, we can reasonably surmise that Buffett's actions speak louder than his words on the subject of taxes, too. For if he truly believed that the cluster of causes championed (and debts incurred) by the federal government were causes requiring shared sacrifice, he would have tried to convince his friends to give half their net worth to the Internal Revenue Service and not to charity. He did not. And if he thought the federal government was a worthy cause, he would himself have diverted all those billions per annum away from the Bill and Melinda Gates Foundation to the IRS. He did not.

So why didn't he?

When it comes to taxes, maybe Warren Buffett prefers to seem rather than to be. Maybe the ghosts of grade-school justice are whispering to Buffett: *If they don't have to, you shouldn't have to either.*

Writing an op-ed for *The New York Times* is a relatively low-cost way to signal rectitude. Similarly, dangling a chad in the voting booth is relatively low-cost for any given voter to signal the same. Both actions let you get all puffed up on righteous indignation for less than it costs to write a check to the IRS, much less buy a meal for a homeless person.

Buffett could respond that, far from being sanctimonious, he just wants to be sure that rich people share the same tax burden as the middle-class people such as those in his office. If that means raising taxes on the rich, then that's fair. But if proportionality were the issue, he could easily have used his *Times* column to suggest *lowering* tax rates for the brackets occupied by those other twenty people in his office. Perhaps they should pay no more than 17.4 percent—what Buffett ended up paying. That's still more than the very top earners pay in countries such as Hong Kong and Switzerland. (He did not make that suggestion.)

We have gone a long way toward exposing Warren Buffett's contradictions, but they are really beside a much larger point because when it comes to his *actions*, Buffett has some good things to say. What his actions tell us is that resources do more good in the hands of individuals and organizations than in the government's hands, and philanthropies do a better job of seeing to people's genuine needs than the federal government. On those two points, it would be hard to disagree.

AN AUTHORITY ON SUPERWEALTH

Whatever Warren Buffett truly thinks about the idea of fewer resources going to the government for redistribution, I want to take the position that it's a good idea. But who am I? Let's just say I am someone as qualified to talk about the little guy as Warren Buffett is qualified to talk about his rich friends.

The occupiers have settled in to the public consciousness now, for better or worse. Somewhere in their chants is an inchoate worry about the growing gap between rich and poor. Many of the marchers themselves are children of the rich. They've had no hand in making the silver spoons with which they eat or the iPhones with which they organize. And yet they demonstrate against corporations.

But let's focus on their purported concerns: Should we worry about the gap between rich and poor?

The Congressional Budget Office finds that between 1979 and 2007, income grew by:

- 275 percent for the top 1 percent of households,
- 65 percent for the next 19 percent,
- Just under 40 percent for the next 60 percent, and
- 18 percent for the bottom 20 percent.

This seems like a pretty damning picture. Even if we were to argue that some of this data doesn't account sufficiently for non-income goodies at the bottom (such as entitlements), this picture makes a lot of people worry.

Before I make my case, I should tell you a little about myself. I once had dreams of being rich but I have decided to trade the prospect of great monetary rewards for the happy life of a writer.

Today, my financial situation is so plain you could feed it to a toddler. Our primary car is a 2008 Scion Xb. Our second family car is a 1995 Mazda Protégé with flaking paint. The Scion isn't quite paid for. Like many people, my wife and I were upside down in a home and we had to do some creative borrowing to sell it. Now we rent. We have never set foot on a yacht. Our net worth qualifies us to give no wealth management advice whatsoever—unless that advice takes the form of what not to do. I doubt we can tell the difference between caviar and roe.

Yet, compared to two-thirds of the world, we live like royalty.

That's just one of the reasons I want to defend superwealth. More specifically, we should stop worrying about the so-called "gap" between rich and poor. I want to make that case from my perch here in a humbler region of the socio-economic spectrum. I believe we should also learn how to celebrate the wealth creators and the philanthropists like Warren Buffett both for what they create and for their willingness to give. Still, you might be wondering, "Why would anyone in his right mind want to defend wealth disparity?" It sounds like I'm defending poverty but nothing could be further from the truth.

A Thought Experiment[i]

Let me be clear: This is no dispatch from Galt's Gulch. It is a genuine attempt to bring a little common sense to what has become a cascade of concerns about the gap.

To get through some of the less useful rhetoric, the key is to find out first where someone is coming from in his gut. What really motivates him? What are his basic assumptions? These questions might violate Milton Friedman's admonition against questioning people's motives. But to my mind, you can tell a lot about a person by seeing what lights his fire.

---

i   Portions of this section appear in articles published by The Freeman and in The Daily Caller.

And on the subject of the rich-poor gap, I suggest engaging people in a simple thought experiment:

If you were king (or queen) for a day and you could choose between only two states of affairs (A or B), which would you choose?

A—Permanently institute a policy that significantly reduces the gap between rich and poor.

B—Permanently institute a policy that makes everyone better off, including the poor.

Try it out. Take your time. Before jumping to any conclusions, think about these choices carefully. It's not a logic test. As I said, the thought experiment is designed to unpack our intuitions on the subject of rich and poor. I realize the article's title ruins the punch line a bit. But there is no "right answer." No tablets will be handed down.

Still, I hope to persuade you that, given the two options, one makes a lot more sense than the other. Indeed, if we could all agree to choice B, we could make a major step together toward a common goal. After all, almost nobody wants to see the conditions of the poor worsen and almost everybody wants to see the conditions of the poor improved. Among those committed to answer B, differences of opinion may lie in *how* we get to the common goal of improving the lot of poor people. In other words, reasonable people can disagree about the means but if we could all agree we would like everyone to be better off—*especially the poor*—we would be way ahead of the game.

THE ATAVISTS

Alas, matters are not so simple. Before singing any fireside *Kumbayas,* we have to admit there are a lot of people out there who would choose A (possibly you, Dear Reader). Consider a smattering of examples of folks I'd put in Group A, which we'll call "The Atavists" for reasons I'll explain in a moment:

- Famous atheist Sam Harris says, "Yes, we must cut spending and reduce inefficiencies in government—and yes, many things are best accomplished in the private sector. But this does not mean that we can ignore the astonishing gaps in wealth that have opened between the poor and the rich, and between the rich and the ultra-rich. Some of your neighbors have no more than $2,000 in total assets (in fact, 40 percent of Americans fall into this category)[ii] ; some have around $2 million; and some have $2 billion (and a few have much more). Each of these gaps represents a thousand-fold increase in wealth." Harris calls resistance to wealth redistribution "quasi-religious."

- *The New Yorker's* James Surowiecki believes "there's a yawning chasm between the professional and the plutocratic classes, and the tax system should reflect that. A better tax system would have more brackets, so that the super-rich pay higher rates. (The most obvious bracket to add would be a higher rate at a million dollars a year, but there's no reason to stop there.) This would make the system fairer, since it would reflect the real stratification among high-income earners." Surowiecki adds: "A few extra brackets at the top could also bring in tens of billions of dollars in additional

ii   Surely Sam Harris means net worth, not total assets. It's a forgivable mistake but a mistake nevertheless. Note that, as of this writing, I'm one of Harris's neighbors with "no more than $2,000" in net worth due to debt, but I have more in total assets. If 40 percent of Americans had no more than $2,000 in total assets, this would be at odds with home ownership data, which stands at over 65 percent despite the collapse of the housing market.

revenue." (Read: A drop in the proverbial bucket.)

- Nobel-prize winning economist Joseph Stiglitz shares a similar view in *Vanity Fair*: "Some people look at income inequality and shrug their shoulders. So what if this person gains and that person loses? What matters, they argue, is not how the pie is divided but the size of the pie. That argument is fundamentally wrong."

What thread ties these perspectives together?

Atavists have a couple of things in common. First, they share a Pavlovian response—*tax the rich*—any time there is a perceived social ill. This elixir is offered before any other treatments for what may be deeper, underlying diseases, of which at least *some* inequality may be a symptom. The second is epicyclical thinking, which we'll return to in a moment.

Let us entertain a rather seditious question: Before deploying one more IRS agent, why not first fix any policies that *cause* wealth disparity? Whether we identify with Group A or Group B, there should be few if any circumstances under which we tolerate wealth transfers from poor to rich. And if we open our eyes, we can see examples of such discriminatory transfers everywhere.

1. *Corporate Welfare*—Bank bailouts, agribusiness subsidies, pork, you name it. Politicians are doling out corporate welfare at every level of government (think Solyndra). One way to reduce inequality is to stop transferring wealth from taxpayers to Takers.

2. *Regressive Regulation*—Excessive regulation makes goods and services more expensive for everyone and raises the costs of starting a small business. The big businesses love it

because they can afford the regulations and they know that the regulations will *keep out smaller competitors*. Such policies deny poor people opportunities. Regulations are regressive. Let's roll them back.

3. *Loophole Labyrinth*—Our complicated tax code is designed so that it is easier for wealthier people to purchase the talents of CPAs who find loopholes. For the poor and middle class, tax lawyers may not be worth a nickel. Let's flatten taxes and close loopholes. How about a 15 percent flat income tax and a 15 percent flat corporate tax? Let's stop enriching IRS bureaucrats and H&R Block executives and start enriching all the people who serve customers better.

4. *The People's Pyramids*—Local boondoggles such as light rail and sports arenas mean higher sales taxes. That burden falls disproportionately on the poor who pay for local sales tax increases whether or not they patronize the stadiums, visit the convention centers or ride the light-rail lines. States should forbid developers and sports owners from bilking municipal taxpayers. (Bureaucrats argue these boondoggles improve the local economy and ultimately benefit the poor. But they're wrong.)

5. *Medicare Monstrosity*—Why should struggling young people have to fund the healthcare expenses of rich seniors in Boca Raton? Medicare requires just such transfers. We can start by means-testing Medicare or abolishing it altogether. Elderly people who cannot afford basic healthcare can get Medicaid—or better, a vouchered version of Medicaid.

6. *Cadillac Care*—Duke University law professors Clark Hav-

ighurst and Barack Richman write that: "[T]he U.S. health care system operates more like a robber baron than like *Robin Hood*, burdening ordinary payers of health insurance premiums disproportionately for the benefit of industry interests and higher-income consumer-taxpayers." So, people with good jobs get tax-protected insurance while the working poor have to fend for themselves on the individual market. That's crazy. We need to unlink employment and health insurance.

7. *Bloated Bureaucrats*—Iain Murray in his excellent book *Stealing You Blind* writes: "'We are spending more on [insert name of program]' is a badge of honor for any bureaucrat or politician. Yet it's actually a sign of failure. Spending more to help more is not a sign that the program is working, it is a sign that it is failing to address the ill it is meant to cure, whether that be poverty, obesity, insert your cause here." We've got to starve ineffective bureaucracies by applying cost-benefit analyses and tying them to budgets and/or by implementing a Taxpayer Bill of Rights.

8. *'Incentives' Arms Races*—"Economic incentives" are designed to attract existing companies from this state or that, but they are just another form of corporate welfare. Politicians think they should lure companies from other states with your tax dollars, but this process is self-destructive—particularly as some of these companies are insolvent. We should demand states abandon the incentives arms race, for it is the worst form of "trickle-down" economics.

9. *Minimum Wages*—The minimum wage is an idea born out of good intentions but the unintended consequences can be

devastating. Every time Congress raises the minimum wage, it raises the cost of hiring new employees. That removes the bottom rungs of the economic ladder for many—especially black teenagers. We should abolish the minimum wage or at least cut it in half.

10. *Big Labor*—Unions, both public and private, are labor cartels that artificially raise labor costs. The perverse effect is that workers who aren't unionized have higher barriers to entry. Unions use government power to enrich themselves and use forced union dues to fund political campaigns. They transfer resources from taxpayers and deny opportunities to folks who would otherwise work at market wages. We need to remove state crutches from private unions and abolish public-sector unions outright.

I could go on. "Progressive" policies that have the unfortunate side-effect of enriching the wealthy at the expense of the poor are just necessary evils most Atavists are willing to overlook for their abstract idea of the greater good. Besides, says the Atavist, it's easy to mitigate the unintended effect of those policies: just raise taxes and redistribute!

But why not stop all this epicyclical thinking? Why not make the rules apply more equitably instead of tilting the tax code more? Why shouldn't the first thought be to reduce the burdens of the state on the poor? And why not let value creators such as Steve Jobs and Warren Buffett get rich honestly so they continue to offer goods, services, and opportunities people want?

To the Atavist, it usually doesn't matter whether you're a Maker or a Taker. You can be a Jeffrey Emmelt who enriches himself by lobbying for government subsidies and military contracts, or a John Mackey who offers wholesome foods to health-conscious consumers. If you're super-rich it's all the same. It's the wealth that's taboo. Why? How you got rich is not a primary consideration if it's one at all. What roils the Atavist is the very existence of the rich. Individuals, with their unique contributions, get reduced to plot-points on an income distribution graph.

Venture capitalist Kip Hagopian picks up on this problem when he concludes: "The flaw in virtually all of the intellectual arguments on the issue of the progressive income tax (both pro and con), is a lack of appreciation for how income is determined. Because of this, the crucial implications of the distinction between income derived from aptitude and income derived from work effort have been left out of the debate." Indeed, for there to have been any wealth to redistribute, there had to be an initial distribution. That's an unsexy way of saying that rich people had to create the wealth to begin with.

Let's not forget that taxation and redistribution have other perverse effects. If you pay people to subsist they'll forego opportunities to become upwardly mobile. And if you punish people for being productive, you'll get less productive behavior. Because these problems are so central to the operations of a healthy economy, Atavists usually deny or ignore such problems.

Witness former Obama economics advisor Jared Bernstein in the *Christian Science Monitor* opting for the former tack:

> But the thing I and others don't mention enough is that in theory, there's no reason to expect people to respond to higher tax rates by working less. That is, they could just as easily decide to work harder to make up the loss in their after-tax income.[32]

While there is something a little unsavory about treating anyone like a pack mule just because you think you can, the idea that someone might work harder if taxed more is more likely to be true among people in lower tax brackets. These folks have more outstanding financial obligations and might be forced by circumstances to make up the extra income. In the face of taxes that punish more effort, the independently wealthy are far more likely to opt for a life of leisure.

Stone Age Ethics

I've written elsewhere that those who are unnerved by the gap between rich and poor are not so much ethically enlightened as they are in the grip of an inborn hoarding taboo. Most of us share this taboo to some degree because we're all human, but for some of us it burns in the DNA and becomes expressed as indignation. That's why I've been calling Group A "The Atavists."

Stone Age instincts lie at the core of this egalitarian worldview. Without discussing that too much here, I join evolutionary psychologists Leda Cosmides and John Tooby in thinking this Stone Age emotional response evolved over millions of years. But these feelings are not always appropriate in a modern context. Our human ancestors rooted around in the bushes for life's necessities. Not everyone was successful finding food each day. It was a good idea to share your grubs, berries, or guinea fowl today, for tomorrow you might not be so lucky.

So in small groups of hunter-gatherers, a howl for redistribution at the sight of want makes good evolutionary sense. In an age when hoarding could mean weakening the group and surpluses could more easily be shared than traded, the evolved disposition became "share and share alike." But such a rule makes far less sense in the context of a modern, large-scale society—especially where politics replaces propensities to act as an individual. I'll save the rest of this discussion for another time. Suffice it to say, people's feelings about the gap originate largely in our human past. And we'll do well to keep them where they belong.

THE PERSPECTIVES GAP

Before moving to the fundamental issues that divide groups A and B, let's call Group B "The Better-Offs." This group wants to improve the conditions of the poor, even if that means the rich could get richer. The idea is that if everyone can be better off, that's okay—despite unequal outcomes. According to The Better-Offs, things are getting better all the time because it's possible for savvy investors and clever entrepreneurs to get super-rich. And that fact should be celebrated, according to The Better-Offs.

The stage is now set. Between The Atavists and The Better-Offs, there are five major gaps in perspective.

1. *Harming the Rich or Helping the Poor*—To care about the conditions of poor people is not the same as worrying about how much money rich people have. Our thought experiment above is meant to tease out this difference. Maybe a more straightforward way of putting the point is: Would you improve the conditions of the poorest people modestly if it meant making the top one percent richer? A "no" answer suggests one cares more about what the rich have than what the poor lack. I suppose "no" could mean one believes that the only way significantly to improve the condition of the poor is for

the government forcibly to take more resources from the rich. But that is less likely. An Atavist's primary concern is equality of outcome. A Better-Off's primary concern is mitigating poverty.

Timothy Noah's multi-part series in Slate is a good example of Atavism on display.[33] The series includes passages such as the following:

> All my life I've heard Latin America described as a failed society (or collection of failed societies) because of its grotesque maldistribution of wealth. Peasants in rags beg for food outside the high walls of opulent villas, and so on. But according to the Central Intelligence Agency (whose patriotism I hesitate to question), income distribution in the United States is more unequal than in Guyana, Nicaragua, and Venezuela, and roughly on par with Uruguay, Argentina, and Ecuador. Income inequality is actually declining in Latin America even as it continues to increase in the United States. Economically speaking, the richest nation on earth is starting to resemble a banana republic.

Gasp! A banana republic? We're turning into Uruguay?

Let's skim over such uninformative hyperbole as "grotesque maldistribution" because if any sense can be brought to such language it would come in the "how" questions of wealth distribution not the "what" questions. (Namely, did the rich get rich through honest entrepreneurship or by bribing government officials to keep out competitors? There is a difference.)

A little common sense trumps Noah's misuse of the Gini Index.[iii] In other words, if you define a "banana republic" in terms of the gap, then the United States, Hong Kong, and Singapore are all banana republics. We know that people from Singapore are not clam-

---

iii   The Gini Index is an economic measure of income inequality based on Lorenz Curve. A society that scores 0.0 on the Gini scale has perfect equality in income distribution. Higher the number over 0 higher the inequality, and the score of 1.0 (or 100) indicates total inequality where only one person corners all the income. It is also used as a measure of other distributional inequalities such as market share. The index is named after its inventor, the Italian statistician Corrado Gini (1884-1965).

oring to get into Myanmar (any more than Americans are clamoring to get into Venezuela). But by Noah's logic, North Korea, Venezuela, and Myanmar are veritable utopias. I don't think Noah would want to commit to that *reductio*, but he does. Measuring wealth gaps in a given country doesn't tell us anything about poverty or opportunity. It only tells us a statistical spread between the richest and poorest. Despite very little income inequality in North Korea, common sense tells us living in the bottom quartile in Hong Kong is still a better deal—at least if you're a member of The Better-Offs.

2. *Win-Lose or Win-Win*—Despite protests from of a couple of Nobel laureates who should probably know better, the market is not a zero-sum arrangement. All this discussion of the "gap" and the "Great Divergence" obscures the fact that, whenever people engage in voluntary exchange, all parties benefit.

Recall Joe Stiglitz above: "Some people look at income inequality and shrug their shoulders. So what if this person gains and that person loses? What matters, they argue, is not how the pie is divided but the size of the pie." This straw man doesn't look like anybody I know. The whole point of a free economy is that exchange is by definition mutually beneficial. A market is inherently positive sum. Outside the market—that is, when one person gains and another person loses—only one of four things could have happened: coercion, theft, fraud, or some variation of the first three sanctioned by the state. Wealth transfers—whether from poor to rich or from rich to poor—are inherently zero-sum. That means someone has to lose in order for someone else to gain. The Better-Offs want a "win-win" society, so it's not just a question of the size of the pie, but how the pie gets baked. The presence of more rich people (absent crony capitalism) is an indicator that things are getting better for everyone.

3. *Static Statistics or Upward Mobility*—Sam Harris laments that 40 percent of Americans have a net worth of less than $2,000 (at least, we assume he meant net worth, because "total assets" is plainly false). One problem with this factoid is that about a quarter of the population is under 18 years old, which leaves about 15 percent of adults with low net worth, if Harris is to be believed. I don't know many kids with a net worth over $2,000, but I'm comfortable with the fact that my 5-year-old has little more to his name than a box of Legos and a couple of Wii games. Otherwise, the remaining individuals in this low-net-worth group may have wildly different circumstances. There could be people among them with high incomes but boatloads of debt, college kids with little besides Ramen noodles and a laptop, or people who lost their behinds house-flipping houses in 2008. And, of course, there are some really destitute people out there. But the point is, there is a lot more to any statistical snapshot than meets the eye. We can't simply appeal to statistics as if they were scripture.

Economist Steven Horwitz has explored the data on wealth distribution more deeply. He says it's true that the poor's share of total income today is less than that of the rich when compared with, say, thirty years ago. But that doesn't matter, Horowitz says. The income pie is much larger than in the past, so the poor's income is still *greater* than in the past. Absent the government doing counterproductive things like stimulus packages, the pie almost always gets bigger over time. So the income of the poor is better today than in the past despite an increased share of total income for the wealthy.

Statistical snapshots can also be misleading because, when it comes to incomes, people are mobile. When we track groups over time, we can see that much of the rich/poor mythology is based on statistical artifacts like the one that snookered Sam Harris. New low-net-worth people—e.g., young people and immigrants—are constantly coming online to replace those who have started climbing the prosperity ladder. This tracks with the "American Dream" narrative that has brought people to these shores for more than a century. People usually start off by eking out a living by working hard (that is, if the government doesn't pay them to work less). With experience, they become wealthier. That doesn't mean there aren't people who get stuck in the lowest income bracket throughout their lives. It means there are far fewer of them than people like Sam Harris care to admit.

4. *Income or Absolute Wealth, Well-being*— A minute of work today buys you a whole lot more than a minute of work did twenty, fifty or one hundred years ago. Poor people enjoy cellphones, refrigerators, TVs, inexpensive food, and a far higher standard of living because their purchasing power is so much greater than in the past.

In 1920, a working stiff had to work thirty-seven hours at the prevailing wage to buy a gallon of milk. In 1997, our working stiff only had to work seven minutes. To buy a pair of Levi's, you had to work ten hours, thirty-six minutes. In 1997, three hours and twenty-four minutes. And, of course, in 1997 it would take nine minutes to buy a unit of computing power (MIPS); no computing product was even available in 1920. Zooming out from justifiable pessimism about the short- to medium-term, things are looking better all the time. This data also shows that a mostly win-win economy works over time. Competition among firms that want to serve customers better yields continuous improvement across tax brackets. And much of the really big gains are difficult to quantify—especially when it comes to the poor.

In fact, the most expensive things people have to worry about come from areas in which government meddles the most, such as healthcare and higher education. By historical standards, our poorest quintile today is much better off than any time in human history. That's because the cost of living, broadly speaking, is going down while living standards are going up. In the short-term, who knows what miseries central banks and legislatures will bring us. Printing money will likely cause the United States to lose purchasing power. National debts might bring whole nations to their knees. But in the long run, we still have reason to be optimistic.

Philosopher and economist Deirdre McCloskey, channeling Adam Smith from more than 200 years ago, put it rather simply:

> [A] rich man cannot, after all, eat much more than his chauffeur can, speaking of sheer volume and nutrients. Nor can he wear right now more than one pair of Italian designer trousers, speaking of mere leg-covering ability. Nor can he live in more than one enormous room at a time, speaking of gross roofage and wallage.

Add this to Steve Horwitz's calculation of the labor hours it takes to buy a half-gallon of milk today compared to one hundred years ago. Things start looking pretty good for the American poor. There are also millions of new things available today—beyond shoes and roofage—that were not available to anyone only fifty years ago. So it's not only cheaper to buy a chicken with your labor, but it's now possible to trade less effort for a mobile computing device, or have people bring you a chicken dinner and then clean up after you. And that means it's easier to be poor than at any other time in history.

5. *Compulsion or Compassion*—Among Better-Offs, some might have a slightly different take on all this. There's something unsettlingly Benthamite about the idea of any given person being better off. Perhaps we should think of a positive-sum society as being a happy byproduct of good institutions that protect freedom and property, as opposed to a policy goal per se.

With the original thought experiment, of course, we are only trying to reveal deeper underlying commitments of Atavists and Better-Offs. Atavists, for example, are more often than not comfortable with compulsory compassion; that is, if you've got it and someone else needs it, the state is justified taking it from you by force. The Better-Offs see things a little differently: They usually think of compassion as no policy at all, but a personal value. Compassionate acts flow freely from people who hold those values. They cannot be legislated by Congress and enforced by IRS agents. And indeed, attempts to centralize compassion usually succeed only in removing that very same value from one's breast, as more and more people leave their charity at the voting booth. (We'll return to this point later.) At the same time, many Better-Offs think there is something untoward about viewing the wealthy as an ATM, particularly as most (though perhaps not all) are committed to values that are directly at odds with the ends of income equality.

So, now that we've identified these gaps of perspective, what do they tell us?

Give Better-Offs a Chance

When we pull back the moral mantel, concern about the gap between rich and poor reveals a kind of aesthetic fetish. For all the talk of social justice, it is difficult to ground an Atavist's concerns in anything that looks like justice. And the further away from indignation about the rich an Atavist moves, the closer he gets, by inches, to joining the Better-Offs.

The punch line here is that all this fretting about the gap is a great big blinking distraction. I'm sure I offended some of the more egalitarian readers by referring to them as Atavists, which I guess smacks of saying they are acting like cavemen. That is not really my intention. Rather, I want people to dig down deep and confront their commitments. Ask yourself honestly if you might be confusing an aversion to wealth accumulation with concern for the poor. If you are not, you may very well be a Better-Off like Dierdre McCloskey, who says: "We will not have the heaven-on-earth of perfect equality, ever, and I lament this fact. But equality over the long term…has been increased by capitalism, and in absolute terms the poor even in the 1980s and after got better and better off."

Still, those who see America in zero-sum terms will continue to think that disdain for the rich and concern for the poor are somehow linked by socio-economic reality. They'll argue that a free economy makes people rich at the expense of the poor, or that there is really no way to help the poor without soaking the rich. But for those who understand that the world can be positive sum, we can agree with Milton Friedman, who said: "The society that puts equality before freedom will end up with neither. The society that puts freedom before equality will end up with a great measure of both."

We do not want to pigeonhole Atavists and Better-Offs into any crude left-right dichotomy. After all, there are plenty of Better-Offs whose primary commitment is to the well-being of any given person, but who still see taxation and redistribution as the only realistic means to that end. Still, if there were more Better-Offs in the world, we could move the locus of our national conversation to a place that's far less polarizing. We might have only to settle the question of whether various redistribution schemes are more effective than, say, a world in which more Bill Gateses and Warren Buffetts are free to create wealth and give it away—a world in which entrepreneurship and superphilanthropy are unleashed.

5

How Wealth Works: Rich People's Money

Blaming speculators as a response to financial crisis goes back at least to the Greeks. It's almost always the wrong response.

– Lawrence Summers

I made a lot of money for my clients.

– Bernie Madoff

I waited. For two months I heard little from John except that it was coming.

I was patient. I knew he'd just taken the top job at his firm. To take time out to respond to my questions would cost him money. You see, I'd been corresponding with John to better understand what he does, what "Wall Street" does. I knew in broad strokes. Traders and speculators of all types do something essential: they *deploy capital*. To most people that's pretty meaningless, but if you know that capital is resources used to produce other goods and services, the picture starts to get a little clearer.

Capital is the yeast that lets the economy rise. Or maybe capital is the heat that bakes the economic pie. Notwithstanding these imperfect metaphors, I want to communicate to readers that most of these masters of the universe aren't just playing fast and loose within a rigged game (although that can be true). As former Clinton Treasury Secretary Larry Summers once said, people have been blaming speculators for millennia—well before Senator Bernie Sanders (D-Vt.) found it politically useful. Yet investors, including speculators, are part of the value-creation process. I needed to unpack that fact a little more, which is why I turned to John (who asked that I not use his full name).

"I am in the investment management business," John finally wrote. "My company manages funds on behalf of people and institutions. We charge a fee for this service. My firm makes money only when we perform well for our clients and they perceive the cost for our service to be of value. If we consistently perform and outperform our competitors, we retain our clients and we grow our business by attracting new clients."

Sounds like a sound bite from a commercial on CNBC, but John's self-description is the essence of people who manage money successfully. And managing money successfully means doing it sustainably.

ANONYMITY, BUSES, AND A DIGRESSION

John is among the one percent. Maybe he doesn't want to be identified because he doesn't want Occupiers camping out in the parking lot of his offices with clever signs. Maybe he simply doesn't crave any kind of fame—assuming this book could make him famous. Whatever his reasons, John wants to remain anonymous. And because he's the main character in this chapter, we will honor his wishes.

The times I've spent with John have not been smoking cigars in leather wingback chairs or sipping *Châteauneuf-du-Pape* in a private jet. No, the two occasions we've spent significant time together we were passengers in a hired bus—a yellow Thomas school bus complete with pleather seats and diesel odor. We had a great time. We chatted about this and that—sometimes deep things, sometimes not—but there was never a shortage of conversation on that bumpy ride. I would never have guessed John had studied at Harvard, much less that he was rich, had someone not told me. John's mien betrays a guy who would be comfortable almost anywhere.

CAPITAL IDEAS

With that digression, we have to ask: Why is it that people like John are essential to the functioning of a market economy? What would the world be like without people like him? Honestly, I think some people imagine folks in John's stratum bathing in gilt tubs full of $100 bills. But John clears up that misconception:

> Once discretionary purchases are exhausted, people who have generated capital that they cannot deploy more fully in their principal businesses will seek other attractive options for it. One thing they do not do is simply sit on it. Wherever there is capital, there is a counterparty that is the steward of it—even if it is just cash held in a bank (most people don't use mattresses). So the bank will invest it in other enterprises. In this way, capital is never idle; it is always seeking its optimum utility, and *is available for others to make use of.* (Emphasis mine.)

Many readers might have found that paragraph difficult. If so, it might be worth reading again. You see, that idea is really the crux of the matter. If I could sum it up, it would be like this: In a market system, *rich people's money is constantly working for the benefit of you and me.*

Financial intermediaries perform a valuable service in the economy by helping direct capital flows toward productive uses. They do this by analyzing investment risks for people who aren't so good at it. I'm better at writing. John is better at analysis, and he's held accountable for results. Sometimes they get it wrong. Barring the Bernie Madoffs of the world, wealthy investors are, by definition, the ones who succeed and help their customers succeed. As New York asset manager "Mad Dog" Mattes put it to me, "If people fail to achieve the goals established in their business plans, they are fired or drop out. It keeps mediocre achievers out of the business and lets better professionals assist the investing public."

There are many who fail—poor souls about whom we never hear. We only hear about the successful ones when they're being demonized or the criminal ones when they're being prosecuted. But we want the successful ones to do what they do.

"The intermediation of capital is no different than the intermediation of other resources like energy or food," John said. "Very few people would want to refine crude oil in order to fill their car with gas, or grow their own wheat to make bread. The same is true of making capital available for investment. This has become more of a professional, specialist business performed on behalf of those entities that have money to put to work."

So these money middlemen serve a function—they specialize.

As economies grow more complex, tasks within a system have to be separated. In an organism, cells are specialized for functions, such as constructing bone, while others transport oxygen to where it needs to go in the body. In market economies, workers specialize for functions such as building bridges or transporting gasoline. In both cases, specialization is essential for the system to work. Without specialization it becomes more and more difficult for individuals to thrive. The system contains all of the specialized components, which are interdependent.

People like John are a vital part of that evolving system. He describes it better than I could have:

> [This business] has grown more in scale and complexity in recent decades, no doubt as a consequence of the complexity and growth of the developed world and global markets as a whole, particularly as additional asset classes become more accessible and investible. Although one money manager, commercial bank, or investment bank wouldn't change the functioning of the economy, the banking and investment universe provides the overall mechanism for borrowers and lenders and investors and issuers to come together more efficiently.

Getting capital and trade flows to and from the developing world has done more for global human progress in the last 30 years than any foreign aid program ever has done or will do. I realize some people don't like terms like "efficient"; they seem so lifeless. But efficiency is to the economy what health is to the body. When things aren't working right you get sickness and malaise. If people succeed by making bodies and economies better, it's no wonder good doctors and smart investors are wealthy.

COMPETITION

The proliferation of firms managing global assets has meant open competition, which is a good thing. Competing firms means better pricing, better performance, and increased transparency. As with any other industry, if the number of competitors is reduced— or firms are overregulated—the industry gets distorted.

Imagine if there were only a single grocery store from which to buy food. It would be expensive, under stocked, and it would offer poor service. Or what if there were only one make of car? The car would be unreliable and come with few options. These examples aren't farfetched. Just ask someone who shopped for food or owned a Trabant in the former East Germany.

The same is true of financial intermediaries, even for something as simple as banking. John explains:

> The more restricted they were, the less they were able to function efficiently. Until 1978, for example, all bank deposit rates were fixed by the government. It didn't matter where you deposited your money, you'd get the same rate. So the experience of your average bank depositor was not very good. It was also expensive—expressed in fees or low interest rates on savings. All this came with few services, save the occasional free toaster you got for opening an account.

It wasn't only bad for depositors, John continues.

> It was a poor vehicle for borrowers, too. When market interest rates rose, banks were severely dis-intermediated and lost deposits as those funds sought more attractive returns. The availability of lending ground to a halt and the economy suffered. It wasn't until banks were allowed to compete by offering deposit rates that reflected the marketplace, and later, their ability to lend successfully and operate efficiently, that they became the engines of economic growth they are today.

The same is true in money management. There was a time when there was no such thing as a mutual fund. Individuals without investment experience who wanted to own stocks and bonds had no choice but to invest in the markets on their own–subject to a regulator-sanctioned, fixed-commission system. Today, "although the ability of money managers as a whole to consistently deliver out-performance is debatable," John said, "no one can argue that there aren't thousands of fine firms offering a plethora of investment choices with transparent costs, styles and investment return histories openly available to investors. The investor experience is far superior to that of someone in 1920s and 1930s!" And for those investors who do want to manage their own money, the competition for their business has also never been keener.

REGULATION

Financial regulation is complicated and there are vigorous debates about what sorts of regulations are good for preserving the system as a whole while not hampering growth. We haven't the space to launch into those debates, but there is a whole class of regulations that is no good to anyone (except perhaps large, incumbent financial institutions that can afford them as barriers to entry).

A good rule of thumb for determining whether a given regulation is detrimental is to ask whether it limits competition or distorts prices. In terms of limiting competition, the costs and complexity of the regulation can hobble or exclude market entrants. This has two effects: It can mean competitors never get to offer customers better products at lower prices; or it can mean business gets driven to more hospitable climes, that is, into competing jurisdictions where the restrictions aren't so costly or restrictive.

Stepping back, we have to ask if regulations (or subsidies) distort the markets. Options trader Thomas Sparks put it this way:

> The price signal tells businesses whether to direct more or fewer resources to producing a given product. They consider the price of the product and measure that against what it costs them to provide it. Distorting the price signals gums up this process. So, for example, if the government subsidizes housing via tax deductions, artificially low interest rates and more, then they lower the effective price. This drives up demand to irrational levels.

Government policy can create market illusions that make people do things they might not do if they had an accurate price signal (more on prices later). Now, I'm under no illusions: "Socially optimal" regulations are made by people with only good intentions and a perfect understanding of the market process. Yeah right. But seriously, if regulators were used to the rules of thumb I sketched above, very few regulations would ever be written. Markets—profits and losses—discipline and hasten adjustments within the system better than any regulators ever could.

STEWARDSHIP

Earlier we exploded the idea that rich people have mattresses full of cash, but let's take a closer look at the idea of stewardship. How are the wealthy and their financial intermediaries stewards of capital? What does that stewardship entail? To this, John said:

> I'm not sure that wealthy people are stewards of capital any more than anyone else is, only by degree. Everyone responds to incentives and people—rich or poor—make good and bad choices based on their reading of those incentives. Rich people make mistakes with their money, too, but there does seem to be some evidence that wealth that was accumulated by the creator and owner of an enterprise behaves differently than wealth that was inherited, for instance. I think all wealthy people believe that they have a responsibility to nurture capital the best way they can.

Talk about sustainable development. When do you ever hear about capitalists nurturing anything? Remember what Gordon Gekko said in *Wall Street*? "It's not a question of enough, pal. It's a zero-sum game: somebody wins, somebody loses. Money itself isn't lost or made, it's simply transferred from one perception to another." If John is right, Gordon Gekko is full of shit. And yet, that's largely what people think about our financial stewards.

Recall that in our earlier chapter "How Rare is the Entrepreneur," Chris Rufer wondered if Warren Buffett giving away his shares in Berkshire Hathaway to the Gates Foundation was sort of like pulling the planks from a ship at sea to keep warm for the night. The point is, of course, debatable. Is it a better use of resources to invest them in sustainable ventures or to give them away to worthy recipients? Which is more beneficial to society? Is it better to create a new company that might conceivably employ many people, or donate money to a charity that funds something that is much needed but will never grow to be self-sustaining? We need not answer this question definitively.

In thinking about what's best for society, we shouldn't forget that people might just have rights we ought not violate in the name of the "greater good." But one thing is clear: If we're being honest about the difference between the private sector stewards of capital and the political allocation so often carried out by the public sector, there is simply no contest. As veteran trader Sparks put it: "The beauty of a capitalist system is that capital ends up in the hands of the guys with the judgment to make these calls. I despise Warren Buffett, but he has a gift for judging business prospects against risk, so capital has found him. Government 'investors' in the Solyndras try to imitate him because Warren makes it look easy." But government is hopelessly wasteful by comparison. In the private sector, people are rewarded for nurturing capital. In the public sector, people are rewarded for transferring capital to favored groups. It's just that simple.

Speculators

Historically, speculators have been treated like the Jews: People don't understand them much, but blame them for everything. But speculators should also be celebrated—not so much for their motives, which are no better or worse than yours or mine, but for the good they do.

Economist Donald Boudreaux says speculation "makes resources more abundant when there is great scarcity by encouraging people to use those resources more sparingly when there is relative abundance." He offers a simple illustration:

> Suppose a village on the west side of a mountain range has an unusually good wheat harvest, but a village on the east side loses most of its crop to drought. Everyone agrees that wheat should be shipped from where it's relatively abundant to where it's in short supply. Commerce and market prices ensure that such shipments occur.

> Wheat prices in the drought-stricken east village will be high, while prices in the village with the good harvest will be low. So merchants will buy wheat on the cheap in the west—causing its price there to rise—and ship it to the east village, where it will be sold at a profit. [34]

Of course these merchants are motivated by profit. So what? They perform the beneficial task of distributing supplies more sensibly with their invisible hands. Thanks to the merchants' response to the difference in prices between the two villages, people who need wheat less urgently are encouraged by higher prices to use less of it so people who need wheat more urgently get what they need. Isn't this the best outcome?

Speculators do the same thing, says Boudreaux: "The only difference is that, with speculation, people who need resources more urgently are separated from people who need them less urgently, not by a physical barrier but by time."

Speculators who think oil will be in shorter supply next week can profit by buying oil today and selling it in a week. Thus, oil gets transported across time from today (when it's more abundant) to next week (when it will be less abundant). Without speculation oil supplies get used today, which makes their conservation until next week (i.e. when the scarcity situation is more desperate) impossible. So speculation enables conservation! And, yes, speculation can drive up the price today but the higher prices encourage conservation. Due to that conservation, oil will be less scarce next week. Today's higher prices not only give us incentives to conserve more, but they also prompt oil producers to intensify their efforts to supply more. (Oil stocks that are unprofitable to extract at lower prices can be profitable to extract at higher prices.)

Of course, speculators can be wrong about next week but these speculators have the best incentives to get things right—far more than, say, Senator Bernie Sanders. Speculation errors are kept to a minimum because when traders are wrong they wind up buying high and selling low, the quickest way to the poor house for a commodities trader. They want to avoid losses and to do so they have to be ultra-sensitive to opportunities to transport those resources across time—from a point of greater abundance to one of greater scarcity. It's a good system, so why are speculators vilified? Our friend John puts matters bluntly: "It's just too compelling a narrative to ignore for long, since there must always be someone or something to blame for one's favorite company's share price being driven down or the price of food or gasoline going up."

John's observation is sound. Behind every sanctimonious smear there's a special interest coalition waiting in the wings. But people who actually conduct business rely on speculators to smooth out what might otherwise be more volatile. Indeed, people running companies who depend on commodities for the operation of their businesses don't want huge prices spikes and troughs. They crave certainty and stability. Options traders and other speculators help smooth things out so businesses can plan better, John says.

> Those who trade in markets in which they have no natural economic interest provide a valuable source of liquidity and risk mitigation for the producers and processors who seek forward price certainty in exchange for a modest "insurance" premium. Attempts to reduce or restrict this activity almost always results in higher end costs to the consumer.

Ultimately, supply and demand fundamentals, the financial performance of companies, and the value of the currency itself have the most significant impact on prices.

"A speculator is a trader who will take risk to realize profit in situations a normal investor will avoid," adds Mad Dog Mattes. "They bring liquidity into the various markets, necessary to maintain their health and dynamism."

And yet speculators are almost always scapegoats.

PRICES AS SIGNALS

I hope you'll forgive my detour. I promised we would return to the importance of prices. If you're skeptical of a market economy's ability to yield accurate prices, options trader Thomas Sparks reminds us of his encounter with a well-known former Soviet who appeared in Chicago some years after the collapse. Sparks says: "When Gorbachev came to the Chicago Board of Trade he said that the USSR would've collapsed decades earlier without the West's prices to use internally. When they sent oil from the Urals to Cuba in exchange for sugar, they knew what ratio to use."

In another Sparks story, a Chicago Board of Trade (CBOT) director mentioned that futures products were good for their customers to use for hedging. The director said, "Ninety-eight percent of our customers never place a trade." Sparks asked, "What do they use us for?" "The price signal," said the director. "They look to see where corn and soy beans are trading and decide whether to plant more of one or the other."

It has taken humanity most of its history to appreciate the importance of price signals. Despite how far we've come intellectually, we're still learning those lessons. The great Friedrich Hayek is probably the most important figure to articulate the importance of the price signal. Economic historian Roger Garrison reflects on Hayek's contribution:

> It is a short step from Hayek's appreciation of the phenomenon of spontaneous order to his understanding of the price system as a communication network. The key contribution of the price system to social well-being consists, Hayek demonstrated, is the system's capacity to transmit information from one part of the market to another. In the event of a natural disaster which has curtailed the availability of a specific raw material, for example, the fact of a reduced supply will be effectively communicated to potential users through the medium of a higher price— which also provides the incentive for the socially desirable economizing of the particular raw material (Hayek, 1945, p. 85-86). The need for such a communication network arises out of the fact that the information to be communicated is dispersed throughout the society. [35]

Okay, okay, let's slow that down a bit. Information—that is, knowledge—is dispersed throughout society. That means it's not centralized. But if knowledge is dispersed, why are so many decisions about so many important things made in Washington, D.C.? This was a fundamental question for Hayek, who believed that centralized intervention in the economy was largely a fool's errand.

There are very strong political incentives to distort prices, or at least to enact policies that have the effect of creating price distortions. Politics, after all, is a zero-sum game played in the short term. Sparks says:

> Everything the politicians do is about "hiding the banana," i.e. hiding the true cost of something—whether it's housing, public education, medical costs, costs of programs or the government itself. People view "price" in a negative way, as in the *price you pay*. Politicians get this and try to hide it—pushing economic reality under some rug or other in Washington. But people need to view price as the most important, sacred datum that we have and try to make it as pure—realistic—as possible. Otherwise, we're driving blind.[36]

As Sparks suggests, the political incentive is to obscure economic reality through cost shifting, bubble blowing, or other means. But that is rather like changing the lines on a thermometer. Markets work best—are more stable and more sustainable—when prices reflect economic reality.

THE VALUE OF A DOLLAR AND THE PRICE OF CREDIT

If prices are easily distorted by government policies, why are we so eager to centralize? There are all sorts of possible answers to this question but almost all come down to a human urge to master the world around us. This will to mastery can be born out of good intentions, greed, hubris, or a deadly mix of all. Whatever the intentions, the consequences of centralization can be devastating.

Many people believe that prices are grossly distorted when governors at the Federal Reserve Bank start pulling levers from their private control room. Fed policies are often a mysterious quasi-political game. While some of those policies may be carried out with some purported social good in mind, monetary policy often benefits the elites first. For example, increasing the supply of money may cause investors to go wild for a time—making money in the short term. But if the long-term effect is inflation, the poor have the most to lose in terms of purchasing power. No wonder people are pissed off. The problem is, they're just not sure why, or whom to blame. This is what makes bad monetary policy so insidious. It's like a regressive tax requiring no legislation to levy.

Whatever their stated purposes or intentions, artificially low interest rates, "quantitative easing" and other Fed measures can change our dollar's purchasing power, create boom-bust cycles, or cause investors to take excessive risks. Fed policy can delink prices from the fundamentals. Sparks again:

> To fly your 747 you need certain data inputs (price signals): air speed, altitude, engine thrust, pitch, etc. Your cockpit gauges tell you all this. The government gives you false price signals: "Hey! You're up at 30,000 feet you stud!" when you might really be at 3,000 feet. Or, "You're zipping along at 350 mph and lookin' fine!" when in reality you are only going 150 mph and ready to stall.

Odds are these planes are going to crash sometimes. The question I won't attempt to answer here is: If the government sends bad signals, who is responsible for cleaning up after the crashes?

WALL STREET: BEYOND GOOD AND EVIL

As we try to move forward in an age of hostility toward Wall Street, we have to take care. Wall Street never acts in a vacuum nor does it act within an ideal market system. Market actors—consumers, traders, investors, and ordinary consumers—act imperfectly within what is given and what is given is very often deformed by political realities created by a powerful few.

Wall Street is a metonym that, if we look more closely, has millions of faces. Often Wall Street is you and me. Have you checked your 401(k) statement lately? What Wall Street does can be good or evil. As my friend the writer Jackson Kuhl puts it: "Wealth has no inherent moral value—what is steel compared to the hand that wields it?" One of the morals of this book is that Wall Street, like wealth, is in some sense beyond good and evil. "For every Wall Street profiteer deriding his own clients as Muppets," says Kuhl, "there's a Santa Claus handing out hundreds at a homeless shelter." Or perhaps serving clients well, as my friend John does.

I'm reminded of old cartoon prints from the 1920s and 1930s depicting animus toward Wall Street. Like the *ouroboros*, the history of national wealth is captured by that symbol of a serpent eating its own tail. It's a cycle both vicious and virtuous—one of eternal recurrence, creation, and destruction.

"How ironic that everything old is new again," writes Hamilton, pseudonymous co-founder of the Hamilton Society of Wall Street, "especially when it comes to the public perception of fairness on Wall Street." The Hamilton Society is an organization of traders that formed in the wake of the Occupy Wall Street movement. "Hamilton" is its founder. He knows a thing or two about the past.

> This debate has raged off and on for well over one hundred years, if not longer. [...] As history comes flashing back, suddenly, we are transported once again, to the 1930s when Charlie Merrill, E.A. Pierce and Paul Shields, and a few heroic crusaders took on the vested interests of fraud, lack of transparency and favoritism for "insiders" and championed the interests of the middle class customers. They started a revolution that restored confidence in the securities markets after they had been almost fatally injured after the 1929 Crash.[37]

Hamilton credits Charles Merrill with introducing the middle class to the discipline of investing. Merrill wanted "to promote sensible guidance in building greater wealth through a systematic investment program."[38] Hamilton says one could argue that the visionary approach of Charles Merrill, "grounded in fairness, trust and integrity," allowed America to realize her great wealth.

Looking in the Mirror Since 1978

Charles Merrill might have hastened the inclusion of the middle class into the investment business but it wasn't until 1978 that tax-deferred investment vehicles like 401(k) plans were introduced into the tax code. With that, unprecedented prosperity was unleashed for more people than ever before. Steven Moore calls it the "greatest story never told." Well, we're going to tell it, and Moore's picture is worth a thousand words. (See next page for chart.)

Of course, it's not just the democratization of investment that enabled this kind of growth. Significant policy changes that began with the Reagan administration enabled this new wealth

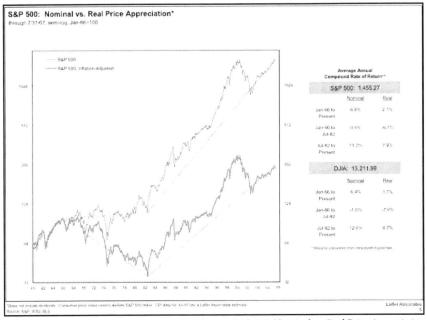

Source: S&P 500: Nominal vs. Real Price Appreciation

to be created. But it was undoubtedly a Carter-era tax loophole exploited by one Ted Benna in 1981 that helped people make pre-tax contributions to these popular investment vehicles. Despite hits taken to growth in the years since 2008, it is difficult to dispute what inclusive investment policies have done for the average investor in the last thirty-odd years. No doubt some of the above picture is of an investment bubble but much of it is not. That's why if people want to find Wall Street today, many simply need to look in the mirror.

THE MEANING OF WALL STREET

People use the term Wall Street without much reflection or distinction. So I asked John what he thinks about the term and about how other people perceive it. His answers were revealing.

> Wall Street has come to mean commercial banks, investment banks, investment managers, etc., basically any place that a person might wear a tie to work and where people get paid an amount of money that the public views as excessive through labor that they don't view as either difficult or socially "necessary." That lately it's an easy target is not surprising: Some of what it does looks mysterious and therefore suspect to outsiders.

Of course, it doesn't help that today Wall Street is also associated with bailouts, which has created more of the kinds of moral hazards that lead to the mortgage meltdown. And the Bernie Madoffs of the world, exceedingly venal and rare creatures, become Wall Street poster children. Our John isn't happy about this state of affairs:

> The more visible participants are not always particularly sympathetic characters. Examples of malfeasance are publicized in finance more than in any other industry (medical malpractice, for instance, occurs daily but seldom makes it to the front page of *The New York Times*). Routine compensation mechanics are incorrectly termed "bonuses."

> And we are all being told that the economic collapse was Wall Street's fault. People have lost money and need someone to blame. Governments, along with a compliant media, always serve up the money changers and deflect some of the blame that correctly should accrue to them. They're usually pretty successful at convincing the average person of this. It has happened throughout history, most recently in the 1930s. The rhetoric today is exactly the same.

When I read John's reflections, I wondered why Wall Street seems always to be doomed to lose the blame game. I think the answer is largely because people need to feel that the state is not the source of any economic problems, but bestrides a white horse and races to our rescue when things go tits up.

BEING FRANK

By now, a waist-high stack of books has been written about the financial crisis of 2008–2009. Some are better than others but careful scrutiny of the evidence reveals a crime scene with government fingerprints all over it. John agrees:

> While the failure of large financial firms during the crash didn't help the stock and bond markets any, and counterparty relationships were highly stressed globally, those failures and the actions of other firms *did not cause the economic crisis*. The antecedents to the crisis with the most significant impact came in the form of unintended consequences of well-intentioned government policies and the subsequent pile-on of government actions meant to stem the crisis. Walking someone through this point-by-point explanation, which I have done, takes about two hours.

It would take us even longer here, but we can offer a glimpse. In what became a perfect storm of factors that included tax policy and artificially low interest rates, one man's behavior stands out. Financial policy analyst Peter Wallison paints a fascinating (and damning) picture of that man in *The Atlantic*. And if Wallison is correct, no one bears more responsibility for the mortgage mess than Congressman Barney Frank.

> Congressman Frank, of course, blamed the financial crisis on the failure to adequately regulate the banks. In this, he is following the traditional Washington, D.C. practice of blaming others for his own mistakes. For most of his career, Barney Frank was the principal advocate in Congress for using the government's authority to force lower underwriting stan-

dards in the business of housing finance. Although he claims to have tried to reverse course as early as 2003, that was the year he made the oft-quoted remark, "I want to roll the dice a little bit more in this situation toward subsidized housing." Rather than reversing course, he was pressing on when others were beginning to have doubts.[39]

The rest, of course, is history. Wallison's numbers don't lie:

> It is certainly possible to find prime mortgages among borrowers below the median income, but when half or more of the mortgages the GSEs bought had to be made to people below that income level, it was inevitable that underwriting standards had to decline. And they did. By 2000, Fannie was offering no-down-payment loans. By 2002, Fannie and Freddie had bought well over $1 trillion of subprime and other low-quality loans. Fannie and Freddie were by far the largest part of this effort, but the FHA, Federal Home Loan Banks, Veterans Administration and other agencies—all under congressional and HUD pressure—followed suit. This continued through the 1990s and 2000s until the housing bubble—created by all this government-backed spending—collapsed in 2007. As a result, in 2008, before the mortgage meltdown that triggered the crisis, there were 27 million subprime and other low-quality mortgages in the U.S. financial system. That was half of all mortgages. Of these, over 70% (19.2 million) were on the books of government agencies like Fannie and Freddie, so there is no doubt that the government created the demand for these weak loans; less than 30% (7.8 million) were held or distributed by the banks, which profited from the opportunity created by the government. When these mortgages failed in unprecedented numbers in 2008, driving down housing prices throughout the U.S., they weakened all financial institutions and caused the financial crisis.

By 2008, a handful of banking execs were working behind closed doors to clean up Frank's mess. These men were human, fallible, and prepared to go to Washington with a begging bowl if necessary. Should they have been so hubristic[i] before the crisis? No. Could they have behaved in a more principled way, like John Allison of BB&T Bank, who refused to allow his bank to give out subprime loans? Apparently. It's hard to say whether acquiescence to government policies (and at times recklessly profiteering from them) makes financial institutions deserving of taxpayer bailouts. But one thing is clear: the system can't go on like this forever.

BAILOUTS AND CAPITALISM

It's tempting to place all the blame on overleveraged banks and to hurl insults at them, but the buck has to stop with the rule makers. We can no more blame the banks than we can blame the coming insolvency of Medicare and Social Security on retirees, or the coming student loan debt. Yes, it takes two to tango, but between those with the money and those with the guns, those with the guns have to own the ultimate responsibility for failure. They make the rules.

In other words, some institution has to *sell power*, and that institution doesn't live on Wall Street. It lives in Washington, making unholy rendezvouses with Wall Street execs in K Street brothels.

Even as we picked on Bernie Sanders for his woeful understanding of market processes, he joined Congressman Ron Paul (R-Tex.) in a rare moment of bipartisan disgust with the machinations of Big Finance in collusion with the government.

---

i John remarks on executive hubris: "There is an asymmetrical control over the destiny of the firm that resides in the executive suite. A very few people making critical decisions can have immediate and magnified effects on these companies, since they are by nature leveraged businesses. And they don't always make great decisions; in fact, they sometimes make incredibly poor ones. In my opinion, fewer than 10 senior executives were responsible for the collapse of Bear Stearns or Lehman Brothers or AIG or Merrill Lynch, certainly not the tens of thousands of people working at those formerly fine firms."

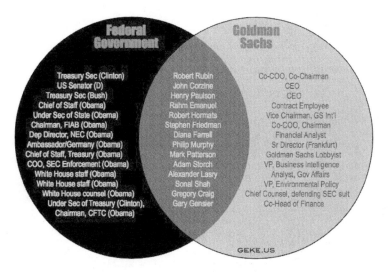

Here's a sliver of Sanders's press release:

The first top-to-bottom audit of the Federal Reserve uncovered eye-popping new details about how the U.S. provided a whopping $16 trillion in secret loans to bail out American and foreign banks and businesses during the worst economic crisis since the Great Depression. An amendment by Sen. Bernie Sanders to the Wall Street reform law passed one year ago this week directed the Government Accountability Office to conduct the study. "As a result of this audit, we now know that the Federal Reserve provided more than $16 trillion in total financial assistance to some of the largest financial institutions and corporations in the United States and throughout the world," said Sanders. "This is a clear case of socialism for the rich and rugged, you're-on-your-own individualism for everyone else."[40]

The Federal Reserve is supposed to be a bank of last resort. It was designed to restore market liquidity in times of crisis. But it has grown into a behemoth whose tentacles stretch globally. It helps prop up failed welfare states like Greece. It enriches bankers whose

149

financial institutions have abandoned the discipline created by the threat of losses.

The Fed's activities often amount to monetary band aids. It can blow up asset bubbles that cause market actors to put off painful, necessary adjustments. It can create both hysteria and temporary amnesia among day traders and it can discourage saving at times when more people should be saving. But I digress. The nexus that comprises the Federal Reserve—complicit private banks and the global system of central banking—may be the status quo but it is not exactly "Wall Street." It certainly is not a free market. And it is definitely not John.

6

How Wealth Works II: The Physics of Wealth

For I agree with you that there is a natural aristocracy among men. The grounds of this are virtue and talents.

– Thomas Jefferson

Life is a series of natural and spontaneous changes. Don't resist them— that only creates sorrow. Let reality be reality. Let things flow naturally forward in whatever way they like.

– Lao Tzu

In 1989, the same year the Romanian people forcibly removed dictator Nikolai Ceaușescu from power, Adrian Bejan became a distinguished professor at Duke University in North Carolina. He had not yet articulated what would become the defining theory of his career but—in some sense—he already knew it in his bones.

Bejan remembers his childhood in Romania as a time in which shortages were common. Under communism, things didn't flow very well. Where the state could not supply something people demanded, black markets formed. Information was restricted too, so people smuggled in books, magazines, and records. The Internet was still the stuff of science fiction.

In in the middle of the Cold War, when meat began to disappear from Romanian store shelves, Bejan's father, a veterinarian, started hatching chickens. He had a light box that illuminated the inside of the egg so he could make sure the embryo was developing properly.

"As a teenager, I stared in awe and wonder at the growth that unrolled before my eyes each day, as the vasculature grew and spread tightly on the inside surface of the shell," Bejan said. "I also noticed that the design I was seeing was the same as that of the river basins on the colored maps I was drawing in school. Where the chicken embryo was evolving on the inside of the sphere, the Danube basin had evolved on the outside of the spherical earth."

These memories formed the Proustian bases of what became constructal theory, an idea so powerful that, once you understand it, you see it everywhere.

Constructal theory sounds highfalutin, but the idea is this: Systems survive when things flow better—all kinds of systems, from natural systems to human systems—and when things flow better, we start to notice patterns in nature that are products of good flow.

"The élan that constructal theory has generated in science is [...] contagious," Bejan said, "and the theory itself so common-sense, concise, and useful that it deserves to be discussed more broadly with colleagues from totally unsuspecting fields."

The young Bejan landed at MIT—scholarship in hand—in 1969. He was a math whiz, but his English was only passable. He also arrived in the United States at one of the most decadent times in American history. The contrasts with his homeland were profound. He left the austerity of the Eastern Bloc to discover a dizzying array of products and services. This abundance must have affected him, too.

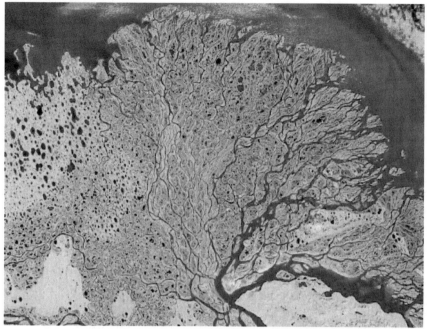

Source: Lena River Delta, image courtesy of NASA

Between arriving in 1969 and expressing the constructal law in 1996, professor Bejan improved his English, completed a Ph.D. in mechanical engineering, and landed a professorship at Duke. It took scores more publications and another decade before he found himself in Nancy, France, in the audience for a talk by the eminent physical chemist Ilya Prigogine.

Uncomfortably, Bejan found himself disagreeing with the Nobel laureate. For those "in the know," Ilya Prigogine walks on water. He is the godfather of complex systems theory, and the giant on whose shoulders many of today's greatest thinkers and scientists stand.

Echoing the scientific community's conventional wisdom, this famous man asserted that the tree-shaped structures that abound in nature—including river basins and deltas, the air passages in our lungs, and lightning bolts—were *aléatoires* (the result of throwing the dice). That is, there is nothing underlying their similar design. It's just a cosmic coincidence.

When he made that statement, something clicked. The penny dropped. I knew that Prigogine, and everyone else, was wrong. They weren't blind; the similarities among these treelike structures are clear to the naked eye. What they couldn't see was the scientific principle that governs the design of these diverse phenomena. In a flash, I realized that the world was not formed by random accidents, chance, and fate but that behind the dizzying diversity is a seamless stream of predictable patterns.

In that moment, the constructal law was born. On the plane back to Durham, Adrian Bejan wrote:

For a finite-size (flow) system to persist in time (to live), its configuration must evolve such that it provides easier and easier access to its currents.

This principle—the core of Adrian Bejan's work—explains a great deal about the movement of capital throughout an economy.

Fractals, Rules, and Complexity

My roommate in college used to write Mandelbrot fractals on his old PC. One day in 1994, he took LSD and watched a fractal for hours. I've done a lot of things in my life, but never LSD. Still, I watched with him. I didn't need acid to be moved by the fractal images. Its tendrils, fronds, and spirals inspired me and set me on a journey of sorts. Fractals are just equations, of course, and fractal images just representations of those equations. There is no magic to it. But when you visualize the geometry, it seems as if you've somehow gained access to God's code.

For those who have never heard of a fractal, just look around you. From the repeating forks of veins in leaves to the spiraling chambers of the ancient nautilus, we take fractals for granted. Recursion is everywhere. Simple geometric shapes repeat themselves without end, giving rise to complex configurations. You can find these shapes everywhere in nature. Using a computer, you can create mountainous landscapes, artificial plants, or hallucinatory river systems that mimic the real thing. You can zoom into these images almost infinitely. Follow one fractal river delta and another opens up. Zoom in on a rivulet and discover a whole new environment with its own river basin—all in Technicolor.

After that I started seeing fractals everywhere. Before my roommate, I didn't even know who Benoit Mandelbrot was. But these beautiful forms had opened my mind to a whole new realm of possibilities. Armed with a new interest in fractals, I began to explore chaotic systems and complexity theory.

The roots lie in complex mathematical equations involving imaginary numbers, but the rules are easy to understand.

First, two concepts: *emergence* and *complexity*. Emergence is the way new patterns arise out of an abundance of relatively simple interactions among lower-order elements in a system. Complexity is the extent to which any of these higher-order patterns are greater than the sum of the elements (and can be studied at that higher level). Examples of complex systems include bee hives, an animal's nervous system, an organism, an economy, and a climate.

I took five basic lessons with me from my contact with these fields:

1. *System Rules*—When it comes to any emergent system, the rules matter. Without rules, there can be no system, much less emergence. Change the rules and the system changes with it.

2. *Simple Rules*—You need relatively simple rules to get complex systems. The more complicated the rules, the less likely you are to get emergence. Simple rules are better because the elements or "agents" in a system are usually too dumb (or it's too costly) to follow complicated rules.

3. *Bottom Up*—Emergent systems need neither a designer nor a central authority. These complex orders require only that the elements of the system—whether we're talking about bees, slime molds, or people—behave according to specific rules. The system emerges from the rule-oriented behavior of the elements.

4. *Ordered Chaos*—Self-organizing systems are robust. They are not perfect but because they are greater than the sums of their parts "the wonderful possibility to be held as a working hypothesis, bold but fragile, is that on many fronts, life evolves toward a regime that is poised between order and chaos," writes theoretical biologist Stuart Kauffman. When we find those systems in the sweet spot between rigid order and chaos, we find profound diversity and we find good rules.

5. *Butterfly Effect*—Small changes in initial conditions can mean big, unpredictable changes elsewhere in a system. This came to be known as the butterfly effect. "I realized," said Edward Lorenz, the meteorologist who discovered ordered chaos in his work, "that any physical system that behaved non-periodically would be unpredictable."

With these basic lessons in tow, I sallied forth.

But a question lingered in my mind. Why the similarities "on many fronts?" I knew there was a reason and I knew it had to do

Ants and Emergence

Some people think the queen issues commands to drones and workers among ants. Innovation writer Steven Johnson very ably describes the process of rule-based emergence among ants:

> [T]he great bulk of ant information-processing relies on the chemical compounds of pheromones, also known as semiochemicals for the way they create a functional sign system among the ants. Ants secrete a finite number of chemicals from their rectal and sternal glands— and occasionally regurgitate recently digested food—as a means of communicating with other ants. Those chemical signals [rules] turn out to be the key to understanding swarm logic.

The system seems to have its own "hive brain." Colonies aren't command and control hierarchies. They are organized by rules from the bottom, up.

with self-organization and rules, but that half-formed answer lacked something. I felt a whole answer lay in what you might call an *élan vital*—an animating force. Most after Darwin have scoffed at the idea of such a force, much less an animator that sets it in motion.

But *why* is it that a nautilus shell expresses a Fibonacci sequence or "golden ratio?" What does this have to do with the fractals in the leaves of trees? How is it that socio-economic phenomena display fractal-like patterns under certain conditions? Why do complex social orders arise from simple rules?

Despite picking on the very idea of *élan vital*, evolutionary humanist Julian Huxley had a similar nagging suspicion when he wrote:

> When I was just last in New York, I went for a walk, leaving Fifth Avenue and the Business section behind me, into the crowded streets near the Bowery. And while I was there, I had a sudden feeling of relief and confidence. There was [philosopher] Bergson's *élan vital*—there was assimilation causing life to exert as much pressure, though embodied here in the shape of men, as it

has ever done in the earliest year of evolution: there was the driving force of progress.

Huxley was getting close. The idea of "pressure" as the "driving force of progress" is not the stuff of literary whimsy or mere metaphor. It is constructal thinking.

FLOW SYSTEMS

Everything that moves is a flow system. Whether animate or inanimate, says Adrian Bejan, all flow systems generate their structures based on the currents they encounter in the wider environment. So evolution applies beyond the realm of biology:

> Flow systems have two basic features (properties). There is the current that is flowing (for example, fluid heat, mass or information) and the design through which it flows. A lightning bolt, for example, is a flow system for discharging electricity from a cloud. In a flash it creates a brilliant branched structure because this is a very efficient way to move a current (electricity) from a volume (the cloud) to a point (the church steeple). A river basin's evolution produces a similar architecture because it, too, is moving water from an area (the plain) to a point (the river mouth). We also find a treelike structure in the air passes in lungs (a flow system for oxygen), in the capillaries (a flow system for blood), and the dendrites of neurons in our brains (a flow system for electrical signals and images). This treelike pattern emerges throughout nature because it is an effective design.

Look for the treelike structures. That's where you'll find the flow Lao-Tsu cautions us not to resist.

I had come across an article about Bejan and his work online. Some egghead from Duke had reportedly explained everything in the world with a single principle: swimming fish, running mammals, and branching trees. I didn't pay it much attention at the time. I was still synthesizing the insights of complexity—the study of emergence and the relationships among parts, wholes, and the rules they live by. Little did I realize, there were more intimate connections between emergent complexity and what Bejan was saying.

I would have passed over it had I not run into a journalist named J. Peder Zane at an event. Zane had been working with professor Bejan on a book (in which the passage above appears). We got to talking and eventually had lunch together to share interests. Before I knew it, I was back at my house Googling constructal law. I soon began to turn this new lens onto my own field.

Channels and Rules

In September 2010, I called professor Bejan for the first time. Because my background lies primarily in political and economic theory, I wanted to see how far he'd extended constructal theory to these subjects. I asked him about the relationship between the constructal law and legal rules (institutions). After all, if the constructal law is a law of nature that extends to animate and inanimate systems alike, might it not also extend to human social arrangements?

Wearily he told me of his recent trip to Edinburgh. Bejan had been on foot, on his way to give a talk on an academic paper, but in a flash of insight he got his own lesson that day. As he began to explain, he shed some of his weariness.

"I kept bumping into people," he said, with just the softest Romanian accent. "Why was this happening? Then it occurred to me: people in the UK drive on the left."

The natural inclination of Scots is to mimic the rules of the road in the relative anarchy of the pedestrian thoroughfare. Bejan had been breaking an informal rule. In order to find flow, he had to adapt to the channels local to Edinburghers.

"Channels are analogous to rules," Bejan said.

I wondered if Bejan had read the work of new institutional economist Douglass North, who speaks of the tendency of certain institutions (rules) to "lower transaction costs." This, after all, is econ-speak for "flow." In his Nobel Prize lecture, North said:

> Institutions are the humanly devised constraints that structure human interaction. They are made up of formal constraints [rules, laws, constitutions], informal constraints [norms of behavior, conventions, and self-imposed codes of conduct], and their enforcement characteristics.

But how much do institutions—formal and informal—matter to the success of societies?

> Together they define the incentive structure of societies and specifically economies. … Only under the conditions of costless bargaining will the actors reach the solution that maximizes aggregate income regardless of the institutional arrangements. When it is costly to transact, then institutions matter. And it is costly to transact.

It's costly to transact, indeed. You have to be able to trust that people will come through on their end of a bargain. You have to be able to find those you want to transact with. You have to be able to count on a wider business environment that doesn't include too many third-party intermediaries, such as regulators, tax men, or strongmen collecting bribes. The rules of the game are critical to economic prosperity over time. Likewise, channels within systems form over time to improve flow.

Phenomena Explained or Predicted by the Constructal Law

1.	The shape and distribution of trees in forests	6.	The physics of swimming animals
2.	The form and function of river basins	7.	The size, shape, and race of Olympic runners
3.	The form and function of circulatory systems	8.	The size, shape, and race of Olympic swimmers
4.	The physics of flight in animals	9.	University rankings
5.	The physics of running animals	10.	College basketball rankings

Vascularization

Just like the fractals I used to see everywhere, I began to see the constructal principle working everywhere. Bejan calls it "vascularization." The big difference is fractals only describe; the constructal law explains. Bejan writes:

> The constructal law does much more than explain the designs we see in nature. It articulates a law we can use to understand why designs emerge and predict how they will evolve in the future.

To get our heads around vascularization, think about trees in terms of their form and function. In the air, why do they branch so? To ensure the inflow of carbon dioxide. In the soil, why do the roots fork the way they do? To optimize the inflow of nutrients and water to the tree. Outflows of waste (oxygen) by trees ensure we get fresh air, which we need in our human cardiovascular systems. The tree's two sets of vascular systems have co-evolved and the plant and human systems resemble tree branches.

In order to accommodate currents in the world, vascularization abounds. Tree-like configurations in everything, from river basins to the transportation networks that deliver your milk, are instances of Bejan's principle at work. For any such system to persist in time, it must continuously provide better *flow*.

Few Large and Many Small

Finally, we arrive at the question of wealth: How do the tree-like/vascular designs we see everywhere in nature extend to economies, corporations, companies, CEOs, employees, investors, and consumers?

"Constructal theory," says Bejan, "is the view that the generation of design in nature is a phenomenon of all physics." All physics includes "everything, animate or inanimate, geophysical and societal." That's a powerful, sweeping claim but Bejan is confident. His law has been so fruitful in its ability to explain so much. Can it explain the rich-poor gap?

Bejan's French collaborator Sylvie Lorente argues that constructal designs exhibit the property "few large and many small." That is, flow systems normally organize like vascular systems in which big currents are connected to ever-smaller streams. If the law stands up across multiple areas, the distributions of resources will exhibit a similar pattern, whether in college rankings, well-paid jobs, or wealth. In the case of income, the constructal law explains why we have a few people with large net worth and many people with small net worth. Wealth is distributed naturally this way, like a scaling law. But the distribution is no cosmic accident—no *aléatoires*. The evolved distribution is functional. Function gives rise to form and form is about *flow*.

Constructal logic explains the strong relationship between energy use and GDP. Advanced nations are wealthy because they can move stuff more efficiently than developing countries. Energy consumption is, simply said, a measure of moving stuff where it needs to go. Is it any wonder, then, that some of the biggest companies in the world have to do with energy and flow? ExxonMobil (energy), Wal-Mart (logistics and retail) and Google (information). The extent to which an entrepreneur, say, can make and move valued products, services, or information is the extent to which he'll be rewarded. Think J.P. Morgan and Henry Ford; in the information space, before Steve Jobs and Bob Metcalfe there were Gutenberg, Morse and Bell.

"Wealth is physics," Bejan says, "because wealth is in some sense flow and movement. And that is measurable. Wealth is not abstract." Because wealth is connected to the physical world, Bejan thinks it underpins the evolved design of flowing economies.

THE PHYSICS OF WEALTH

Branching off from the mother theory, what might an economic corollary to the constructal law look like? Here's my shot at a formulation:

> For an economic system to persist in time (to prosper), its configuration must evolve such that it provides easier and easier access to resources and capital.

Adrian Bejan is no egalitarian. Remember that the young Romanian engineer had already been in the United States for more than 20 years when Nikolai Ceaușescu got what was coming to him on Christmas Day in 1989. Despite the economic malaise of the '70s, Bejan must have noticed the contrasts between his home country and the United States. When it came to the two systems, one flowed and the other one didn't. "The constructal law captures the broad tendency of social organizations to construct evolving flow systems that enable people and their goods to move more easily, more cheaply. This is not a human desire. It is physics."

Bejan now sees plenty of room for what he somewhat inaptly refers to as "hierarchy." This is a term Bejan uses publicly when his preferred term, vascularization, is likely to go over people's heads. Hierarchy to Bejan is not at all like the command-and-control systems envisioned by any *conducător*. It is rather a law of organization and seldom does it make room for "equity" in any egalitarian sense.

Equality of wealth may very well be an affront to laws of organization. As Bejan quips: "Basketball is not communism." Just ask LeBron James. We're not just talking about the money James makes. We're talking about playing time and how frequently James gets the ball. Put another way, winning basketball teams must optimize the flow of balls into baskets. For such optimization, not all men are created equal. There is only equality before the rules of the game.

Our new constructal law of economics dovetails nicely with a host of other ideas in bourgeois economics. The spontaneous order that Hayek pointed to—unplanned orders of tremendous complexity—may turn out often to be "vascular" in Bejan's sense. We can imagine someone buying pork chops at the supermarket. The price tag sends a tiny information signal to the buyer. Let's say the buyer is willing to pay that price. The store manager gets a little revenue in exchange for the pork chops. The manager sends a signal (among other tiny signals) to the corporate office and to its distributors who, in turn, send signals to suppliers/packers. They send signals to pig farmers, who send signals to traders at the Chicago Mercantile Exchange (CME Group).

These price signals flow like a river from a thousand tributaries and a million springs. In other words, price systems are vascular and the system through which these signals flow are not a product of any one person's design. Rather, the system is an emergent phenomenon of lots of people who are cooperating for mutual advantage. At most, the system is governed by an ultra-simple rule: Prices must be free and people must be free. "Freedom," Bejan says, "is good for design."

> Rigid governments lacking the ability to change are just one manifestation of the inevitable forms of resistance that obstruct flow. Instead of struggling under dictators or totalitarian governments, flow configurations evolve in one direction in time: to reduce the effect of friction and other brakes that inhibit their flow. Resistance is inevitable and unavoidable. It is why the world will never be a perfect place and why the most flow systems can accomplish is to keep getting better, that is, to be less and less imperfect. Thus the constructal law suggests the idea of progress, conveys the promise of hope: *Given freedom, flow systems will generate better and better configurations to flow more easily.* [Emphasis mine]

Remember that the next time you hear the term "free market fundamentalism." Given freedom, systems will flow better and better. But what about mixed economies? Some might argue that top-down state interventions or wealth redistribution comports very well with constructal thinking, but not so fast.

As a mechanical engineer, Bejan is interested in applying vascular designs to improve cooling systems and cars but he doesn't think constructal systems can be centrally designed, tweaked, or managed at the macroeconomic level. His reverence for the evolved nature of such systems is apparent when he writes:

> Natural self-organization is even more widespread. It strikes closest to home in the form of connections, links and networks that constitute the societies that we know. These patterns are everywhere we look: transportation routes; urban growth and economics and business structures distributed in clear patterns all over the globe. Simpler, but equally fascinat-

ing structures, are exhibited by spatially distributed populations of other living systems, from domesticated and wild animals, to bacterial colonies.

Don't forget Steven Johnson's ants.

Constructal economics goes a long way toward explaining why some people are stewards of many resources, while others control few. It might also explain some of the "long-tail" phenomena identified by tech and business writer Chris Anderson. In *The Long Tail*, Anderson taught us that a larger share of population lies within the "tail" of a probability distribution—more than we will find in a "normal" distribution. Now the long tail describes the retailing strategy of selling a large number of unique items with relatively small quantities sold of each—usually *in addition to* selling fewer popular items in large quantities. Or, as Bejan and Lorente would say, "few large, many small."

COMPANIES AS CANOPIES

In a mahogany rainforest, the canopy sucks up most of the available resources in sun and air. Mahogany roots suck up the water and mineral nutrients of the earth. Trees are nature's "pumping stations," taking the water from the ground into the air but keeping a lot of that water in their fibers. We get how vital these trees are to the rainforest ecosystem. Rainforests cover only about 7 percent of the Earth, yet they are home to half the world's animal species. Despite gross resource inequalities between the trees and other rainforest flora and fauna—whether in sunlight, water, or nutrients—we tend to think of mahogany trees as great stewards of the rainforest. Every other species depends on them, and they upon the other species. In a single tree, there is also gross inequality in the distribution of resources. The trunk of the tree controls many more resources than a single stem or fluttering leaf. And yet, intuitively, we understand that this is the way the tree flows.

Economic ecosystems work the same way. Imagine that a single company is a tree. The board of directors is like the major roots, while smaller investors are the minor roots. The board enabled the company to grow when it was but a sapling. The executive team—especially the CEO—is like the trunk. The executive team "holds up" the rest of the company, ensuring that the rest of the company gets what it needs (capital) to do its work. Middle management is like the limbs, branches, and boughs growing out from the trunk. The salespeople and front-line employees, though they control fewer resources, are responsible for bringing in resources in point-to-area fashion at the periphery; they are like the stems and leaves. Turn most any organizational chart upside down and it looks like a tree. Of course, matters don't end with the front-line employees. Companies, like trees, are open systems. These porous areas at the periphery are the familiar places we think of as points of exchange.

We should pause here for a moment to remember that this is a metaphor and shouldn't be taken too far. Ultimately, the elemental unit of economics is and will always be the individual. Each person in the nexus of interactions faces his or her own set of incentives, choices, rules, and metarules. But it is striking how these elements self-organize in tree-like fashion—even in companies like Chris Rufer's Morning Star.

So, in the rainforest, animals are the trees' customers: They get oxygen, food, and shelter out of the deal. The trees get carbon dioxide and soil nutrients and they hoard it, just as they hoard most of the sunlight and water. But evolution ensures there aren't many more efficient ways for the forest to function or for its resources to be distributed. The same can be said for economic ecosystems. Companies, and the very capable people who run them successfully, are part of a wider ecosystem in which "gaps" in resource distribution are just as vital as they are to such distributions in nature. And, for both companies and trees, when it comes to the efficient use of resources bigger is sometimes better. In business, they call this "economies of scale."

What about outside the corporate organism?

Sedans and SUVs don't grow on trees. To create them, Ford needs raw materials to flow to its factory (a point) from the surrounding area. This involves multiple channels, including the lines of communication between the factory and suppliers—"Send us ten tons of steel and a million tires"—and the various transport routes (roads, train tracks, air transport routes) generated to ferry those materials to its factories, channels that are now strategically placed around the world to allow the company to increase efficiency.

No analogy is perfect but there are two important reasons to draw such parallels.

First, when we look around at flow systems in nature, we don't find equality anywhere. This isn't the result of any Darwinian dog-eat-dog. It's the result of predictable patterns in which resources are distributed according to system flows. The CEO of a large, multi-national corporation might invite the envy or indignation of street protestors who object to something they neither understand nor had a hand in creating. The CEO is a great steward of resources, both in capital and in human beings. His or her financial rewards should track very closely to the scale of his stewardship. If a market system gives rise to the same sort of flow architectures as the rest of nature, we have *functional* reasons to respect it.

Now, one may not like what nature produces and one might live in the illusion that human beings can outdo nature. This is a fairly typical utopian instinct but if the constructal law is really a law of nature, it cannot simply be revised according to the whims of human designers. That is probably why designs that mirror nature to some extent outperform those that don't. Any manufactured brain that outperforms a human brain will simply be borrowing what's already so great about brains—i.e. harnessing self-organizing properties. Likewise, any man-made form of human social organization will never succeed if it focuses on engineering a better society. It will succeed if people can think of better rules.

And Bejan, like Hayek, doesn't think in terms of atomized parts or centrally led collectives. He sees that flow systems based on good rules are something in between—something that is not perfect, but is likely to benefit any given person.

> This insight challenges the Darwinian concept of winners and losers. In time, some species do flourish and others wither away. … The constructal law teaches us to see all flow systems as components of a single organism, the entire globe, which evolves its design to enhance its flow. They are not competing against each other but working together. The idea of winners and losers might make sense if evolution were a zero-sum game with no direction in time. But because flows morph to increase flow access for the whole, the whole becomes the winner.

And so it is for richer and poorer. "The big need the small," Bejan says, "just as surely as the small need the big." Human ways of managing the flow of resources are extensions of human beings and are therefore just as important as in nature. Perhaps then we should experience the same wonder and awe when we look at the New York City skyline as we do when we look at the Blue Ridge.

Second, corporations do not exist in isolation. They are, a la constructal theorist Sophie Lorente, the "few large" members of a wider ecosystem that includes many small, interconnected "stakeholders." I hesitate to use that term, as it has been adulterated by the parasites of special interest politics, but Whole Foods CEO John Mackey articulates the concept well:

> Surrounding [Whole Foods'] central purpose are the various constituencies: customers, team members, suppliers, investors, and the community and environment. All are linked interdependently. Retail business provides a simple model to illustrate that management's role is to hire good people, train them well, and do whatever it takes to have those team members flourish and be happy while they are at work. The team member's job, at least at Whole Foods Market, is to satisfy and delight the customers. If we have happy customers, we will have a successful business and happy investors. Management helps the team members experience happiness, team members help the customers achieve happiness, the customers help the investors achieve happiness, and when some of the profits from the investors are reinvested in business you end up with a virtuous circle. I find myself continually astounded about how few business people understand these linkages.

Whole Foods Market[i] is a wonderful example of a constructal phenomenon—a large interdependent organism whose *raison d'etre* is creating value for customers.

---

i   I asked John Mackey if I could interview him and write a chapter about him for this book. He declined. He has been demonized in the past. He has a responsibility to his organization first, so I understand.

Intelligent Design?

It turns out the systems that flow best are usually not the ones that are designed or controlled, but the ones that have evolved. Bejan's engineering-design students are mimicking nature after all—not the other way around. This is not to say that we shouldn't try intelligently to design artifacts, such as cooling systems or silicon wafers; Bejan himself is a professor of mechanical engineering. Rather, it is to say that the insights of the constructal law should give us humility before those great and complex systems that evolve organically over time due to distributed processes. These structures are not objects of "intelligent design." They are the results of emergence.

In a Similar Vein

Playing with constructal logic allows for both lateral thinking and systems thinking. In other words, when you let a principle of system flow hang out in the background as you think about this or that, you save yourself a lot of time, energy, and trouble. Bejan's principle is an organizing rule of nature.

Even as I write this, I am involved in a form of vascularization. I have taken many of these quotations from Bejan's and Zane's book *Design in Nature*. I have performed both a kind of synthesis and branching that will bring Bejan's ideas not only to those interested in economics, but hopefully to a wider audience. The current of Bejan's ideas is coursing through the veins of an infinitely complex information system out in the world and is destined to arrive in the higher centers of your brain. Where will it branch from here?

7

THE TROUBLE WITH REDISTRIBUTION

The fair and reasonable desire that all men and women, be able to take part equally in the Lottery inspired indignant demonstrations—the memory of which, time has failed to dim.

> – Jorge Luis Borges, from The Lottery in Babylon

People respond to incentives. The rest is commentary.

> – Steven Landsburg

I want to tell you a parable. Like any good parable, this one has a moral. And, like any good parable, this one ought to be retold. When it comes to parables, sometimes it's hard to find the original teller. Luckily, in this case, we know the author. So, in the timeless tradition of parables, I am stealing this one from Kip Hagopian. I'll keep the skeleton of Mr. Hagopian's story and change the flesh a little to keep things interesting.

HAGOPIAN'S PARABLE

Once upon a time, there were three sisters: Tara, Lara, and Sara Gini. They were triplets, so each was 40 years old. Having been raised in the same home, these virtual genetic duplicates had the same basic aptitude. As it happens, each sister grew up, got married, and had two kids. All three were nurses making $25 an hour. They each worked 50 weeks a year.

Although they were all pretty smart and had basically the same level of education, they differed in their work preferences, or what some might call "work ethic." Tara worked only 20 hours a week. She had a completely different work ethic from her sisters Lara and Sara, who each worked 60 hours per week. Neither Tara's nor Lara's husbands worked. In fact, Tara's husband was what you might call a layabout while she was an avid stamp collector. Meanwhile, Sara's husband worked 40 hours per week as a writer making $50,000 per year (the same hourly rate as his wife).

Tara and Lara spent all of their income and relied on Social Security checks to maintain their lifestyles at retirement. By contrast, Sara and her husband saved a lot of their after-tax income over many years, eventually amassing $300,000. They put this money into an investment portfolio that ended up producing $25,000 a year in interest and additional income. So, the financial breakdown of each family looks like this:

	Tara's Family	Lara's Family	Sara's Family
Work Hours per Week	20	60	100
Annual Salary			
Wife:	$25,000	$75,000	$75,000
Husband:			$50,000
Investments:			$25,000
Total Income	**$25,000**	**$75,000**	**$150,000**

Despite their different work and life priorities, the Gini families were close. The Ginis were so close, in fact, that when a new residential development was built in their town, they each bought a home on the same private street. Each house cost the same. Their three houses were the only ones on the street.

One day, the sisters decided to pool their funds to improve the street. They were concerned about crime and safety and they all wanted a more attractive setting for their homes. So the three families decided to install a gate at the entrance to the street; add lighting for additional visibility and security; resurface the street; and landscape the area to improve the drive up to their homes. All the work cost $30,000.

The sisters were quite happy with the outcome and all felt $30,000 was reasonable given the benefits to everyone on the street. When it came time to divide up the bill, however, the problems started.

Sara thought matters would be easy. Because the benefits to each family were the same, each sister should pay one-third—about $10,000. But Tara and Lara objected.

"Why should we pay the same amount?" Tara and Lara asked. "You make much more money than we do."

Sara was puzzled. "Why is that relevant?" she asked. "Our family makes more money than yours does because my husband and I work longer hours and earn extra money on our investments. Why should we be penalized for working and saving?" Sara looked at her sister and said, "I'm no smarter or more talented than you are. If you and your husband worked harder and saved more you'd make as much as my family does."

To this, Tara replied: "I don't work more because I like my leisure time. I don't save because I want to have things today. Why have things when I'm too old to enjoy them?" Tara was indignant. How could Sara—who was "rich"—ask her to pay the same amount when it was harder for her to do so?

Lara thought things over for a moment and then said, "I've got an idea. Our aggregate income is $250,000, and $30,000 is 12 percent of that amount. Why don't we each pay that percentage of our income? Under such a formula, Tara would owe $3,000, I'd owe $9,000, and Sara would owe $18,000. Since I make three times as much as Tara, I would pay three times as much. Sara, who makes twice as much as me and six times as much as Tara, would pay two times as much as me and six times as much as Tara."

"No," Tara said.

"No?" Lara and Sara responded in unison.

"Why not?" asked Sara "What do you propose?"

Tara was ready with an answer: "Paying the same percentage of our income isn't fair. Instead, let's do it this way: Sara, you pay $23,450; Lara, you pay $6,550; and I will pay nothing. This is the only fair division." Lara was surprised at how completely arbitrary this proposal was. She was also surprised at how disproportionate it was. But because her suggested share was significantly less than what she would have had to pay under her own proposal, she didn't object.

Sara was gobsmacked. "You call that fair?! I make only two times as much as Lara, but you want me to pay three-and-a-half times as much as she does? I make six times as much as you but you expect me to pay almost 80 percent of the total cost while you pay zero? Don't forget, each family is getting exactly the same benefits from this street improvement. Where did you get such a nutty idea?" she asked Tara.

"The United States Federal Government," Tara said. She pulled out a gray booklet. "It's all right here in the IRS tax tables. Under the current tax code, here's what each of us paid in income taxes last year:"

	Tara's Family	Lara's Family	Sara's Family	Total
Income	$25,000	$75,000	$150,000	$250,000
Taxes Paid	0	$6,550	$23,450	$30,000
Effective Tax Rate	0%	8.7%	15.6%	12%

"By an amazing coincidence, our total taxes paid were exactly equal to the $30,000 we spent to improve the street. This is the progressive income tax system all U.S. citizens live under. I don't see why the Gini families ought to live any differently. In fact, I believe all future resource pooling should be divided in this fashion."

"I'm in," Lara said.

So, by a democratic vote of two to one, the cost of street improvements was divided in the following way:

	Tara's Family	Lara's Family	Sara's Family	Total
Dollars	$0	$6,550	$23,000	$30,000
Percentage	0%	21.8%	78.2%	100%

And by a vote of two to one, all future improvements were to be divided up exactly the same way.

THE MORAL(S)

There are a number of morals in Hagopian's Parable. I hope you'll allow me in much of this chapter to elaborate on them. The parable helps to simplify and crystallize some of the trouble with taxation and redistribution from a moral point of view, as well as show just how completely arbitrary[i] a progressive taxation system is.

But there's more. What the parable does not unpack is the incentive effects of the progressive taxation system. In other words, it's not just that progressive taxation might be wrong *ex ante*—that is, an affront to the rights and liberties of Sara Gini's family—but it might have perverse effects when we look at it through a more consequentialist lens.

SOME CAVEATS ABOUT CRONIES

Before we get started, a caveat: Unless we state otherwise, we always assume that whatever anyone earns is *earned*. That means we assume one's income comes not from political favor-seeking, but flows from productive effort. This assumption animates this entire work. If it is not already abundantly clear, this author is no fan of crony capitalism. While I understand that the tax code makes no distinction between crony capitalists and value creators (Takers and Makers), I have to assume that anyone making money is a Maker (despite the fact that Takers abound). Indeed, a less progressive

---

i   That is, unless you start with the principle "From each according to his ability and willingness to work, to each according to his unwillingness."

tax code that offers fewer resources to a limited government would change the ratio of Takers to Makers considerably. If there are fewer resources in the hands of politicians and government bureaucrats, there are simply fewer political spoils to be auctioned off.

DISCOURAGING EFFORT AND INVESTMENT

As we saw, Sara Gini and her husband were both hard workers and savers. But how might they behave in some Part 2 of this parable? If they are punished for working harder and saving money for retirement, they have less incentive to work hard and save for retirement. Indeed, they might get tired of living with the unfair pool and say, "To hell with it, then. We'll just act more like Tara and Lara."

As a consequence, they would produce fewer goods and services and accumulate less wealth than they would under a less "progressive" tax. Society would thus become poorer and Sara's family would become poorer, too, both now and into the future. And it is uncontroversial that the proportion of those who pay taxes is skewed: According to the Tax Foundation, the top 1 percent of income earners paid 36.7 percent of all income taxes in 2010. The top 5 percent paid 58.7 percent, and the top 10 percent paid 70.5 percent.[49]

But the problems don't end with the effects on Sara's family, which is part of the productive class. What about those who get the coerced product of Sara and her husband's hard work? Prior to any subsequent changes to Sara's behavior, the transfer payments discourage the recipients from both earning more and investing more in their earning potential. For example, under a progressive tax system, the costs of being lazy are reduced, so idlers like Tara and her layabout husband get incentives to be idle more often. According to economist Robert Higgs, "When they can get current income without earning it, they exert less effort to earn income."[50] And, of course, when people like Tara and Lara expect to get something in the future without earning it—like Social Security and Medicare—they invest less both in their human capital and save less for retirement. No wonder some Americans are less upwardly mobile.

According to Brookings Institute fellow Scott Winship:

> The most direct way to increase upward absolute mobility is with policies that promote strong economic growth, which in turn requires a focus on economic efficiency. But here relative mobility comes back in—because low relative mobility is inefficient. The mass of people stuck at the bottom is likely to represent an incredible costly misallocation of human resources. Of course, one-fifth of the population has to be in the bottom fifth, but that quintile does not have to be filled so disproportionately with the children of disadvantaged parents. Many people in the bottom fifth are likely to have made the same bad choices as their parents before them. Different people will hold them more or less accountable for their shortcomings, and that is a major fault line of American politics.
>
> But many people in the bottom fifth have presumably "worked hard and played by the rules." Reducing economic and other barriers in ways that do not encourage gaming of the system should, then, help some subset of Americans rise out of the bottom, increase their productivity, and thereby promote economic growth that will help everyone else too.[51]

Winship is mostly right here. Upward mobility is indeed improved by policies that encourage growth—and I'd add *not redistribution*. But what policies encourage growth? The answer, of course, is those policies that encourage productive activity and wise investment (Read: not a progressive tax code). On either side of the fault line of American politics, then, lie one's thoughts about the degree to which someone should be "more or less accountable." Because the progressive income tax is designed to keep a large welfare/entitlement state, the result is that many people are less accountable. The so-called "social safety net" has become a sticky web that ensnares people—rich and poor—keeping them in a kind of economic torpor. Those who might be Makers increasingly become Takers.

The consequences of redistribution are, thus, incentives to become dependent. Failure to exercise one's own abilities means those abilities atrophy. People forget how to help themselves. They don't invest in developing marketable skills and, after a generation or so, this dependent class never learns to help themselves. Witness the erosion of self-reliance that Tocqueville once admired. After some years living in the safety net, the process becomes intergenerational. A population soon doesn't know how to teach their children to be self-reliant. Instead, they teach their children how to game the system and a dependent class forms. To make matters worse, an army of supplicants form who have been charged with the responsibility of aiding the dependent class; this army, too, is dependent on transfers.

"Very often legislation intended to help the disadvantaged, in fact, pays people to stay disadvantaged," said Thomas Sowell in a famous 1980 Commonwealth Club address. "It penalizes them to the extent that they attempt to rise from disadvantage." Sowell adds ominously: "Vast empires can be built on these programs. [They] definitely prevent poverty among bureaucrats, statisticians, economists and many others. ..."[52]

We're not just talking about those poor who draw "benefits" from Temporary Relief for Needy Families (TANF). We're talking about the Taras and Laras of the world, people you probably know. We're talking about wealthy baby boomers nearing retirement who, thanks to Social Security and Medicare, will sponge off of younger, poorer people for years to come. We're talking about real people who know that, if they just gain one more pound, they'll be considered "morbidly obese" by the state and thus qualify for lifelong disability payments—which in turn means they'll never work another day. (What's ironic is that, if we caught any of these people working despite their disability designation, we'd quite justifiably consider them frauds.) Of course, these wards of the state require well-paid people to administer them—bureaucrats who, on average, receive more in salary than their private-sector counterparts[53] even though they produce few goods or services that anybody values enough to pay for voluntarily.

To refer to someone as a "bureaucrat" is not meant to denigrate him. In fact, many government employees can and do help people. Many at least ardently believe they do but by-and-large their help is temporary and it creates a rather perverse system in the longer term that does more harm than good.

A work ethic does not live in a vacuum. The will to work can outlive disincentives to produce and invest for a while, but not forever. On the other hand, if every citizen bears more of the direct costs of idleness, a work ethic is more likely to find life in a person—along with other virtues, such as a guarded concern for neighbors who are genuinely in need.

POOR EXAMPLES

Members of the dependent class are poor, yes, but they are poor examples, too. I can hear it now: "Blaming the victim" falls so easily from the lips of those who benefit from this dying system. But if the state pays people enough to be bad examples for their kids, family, and friends, they will be. After all, what do one's kids, family, and friends observe? They see simply that they can receive goods, services, or money from the government without earning these things. The onlookers eventually adopt an attitude that they, too, are "entitled" to such transfers. A culture of dependency on government emerges along with this dependent class and, of course, to keep the checks rolling in, they only have to be willing to pay up with the currency of power: their votes.

Here's where the political fault lines start to fracture the landscape even more. It's no longer just an issue of more or less responsibility for oneself and one's family. Special interest groups start to accrete around these distributions of largess. The American Association of Retired Persons (AARP) may be the largest single interest group in the United States. They stand white-haired, brandishing clubs and bats near the pipeline and are prepared vigorously to defend seniors' goodies on Capitol Hill. But despite all the money in Washington, D.C., resources are finite. The AARP must compete at the trough against other interest groups, from the military-industrial complex, the wind and solar interests, people on Medicaid, the NAACP, Big Agribusiness and many, many more. Political conflict among these groups is inevitable because only so many snouts can line the trough.

"Political maneuvering creates or exacerbates conflicts among groups defined by their eligibility to receive particular kinds of transfers," writes Robert Higgs, "old against young, black against white, rural against urban, female against male, Northern against Southern, homeowner against renter, and so forth without visible limit." As a result, resentment grows.

Young people figure out that their Social Security taxes are going straight into the coffers of retirees who are already better off as a group. They also cotton onto the notion that they'll likely never see any of their own contributions, unlike today's retirees and baby boomers who have seen "an extraordinarily high effective rate of return on their contributions," according to Higgs. (Currently the average married couple gets back everything ever paid in, with interest, in just over four years.)

THE DISSOLUTION OF COMMUNITY

The famous communitarian philosopher Michael Walzer writes:

I argue that "justice demands" a more egalitarian distribution in our society because of what medical care means to us, the value we collectively assign to it, and the decision, already made, to provide it out of communal resources for some but not all the members of the community. ... [54]

The problem with Walzer's idea and the whole "communitarian" idea of equality is that it destroys community. In the real world, people fight over transfers. The more "communal resources" there are (read: state controlled), the more fights we'll see. And while his "some but not all" caveat might ward off the specter of unfunded liabilities for a time, there's no escaping the problem that people compete fiercely in the zero-sum game of political resource allocation.

All of this fighting over transfers destroys real community; people balkanize around their interests rather than coalescing around their communities. As Higgs reminds us, "neighbors lose their sense of belonging to a common cause with collective interests and joint responsibilities," despite all of the communitarian rhetoric. People start to view each other as "patsies or moochers," Higgs adds.

Similarly, political economist Mark Pennington writes:

> It is not, therefore, the principles of association and disassociation that are more likely to "atomise" people, but the coercive nature of a tax-financed welfare state. There is little or no opportunity to develop fraternal feelings between taxpayers and the recipients of welfare state services, most of whom are complete strangers and who have no reason to engage with one another directly.

The opportunities to develop feelings at all are often anything but fraternal.

Imagine waiting in the checkout line with cash behind someone using food stamps. Do you look more closely to see what else they're buying? As soon as you see the steak and beer, do you start to wonder whether they really need the food stamps at all? You work hard for your money, after all, but found yourself having to forego the New York strip. Would you have it if your taxes had been lower? Whatever the merits of your scrutiny, the wider point is not just the questionable fairness of the food-stamp-using neighbor with steaks and beer, it's that the system makes us regard each other in ways that are not healthy for community or sense of mutual aid. As economist Donald Boudreaux writes:

> But when provision of goods (especially ones for which there is no serious case to be made that they are public goods) comes to be the object of collective action, people in the minority will naturally feel put-upon when forced to pay for strangers' goods and services—put-upon not only financially but, in many cases (as in this one) morally as well.[55]

Yes, morally. Remember Piss Christ, the controversial government-funded art that depicted a crucifix in a vial of urine? Or how about more recent moves to force religious institutions to pay for contraception? Never mind the cognitive dissonance we feel when we see someone getting public assistance who clearly doesn't need it. "Entitlements" divide, largesse factionalizes us.

Crowd Out

Once we get a sense that the state is responsible, we lose our charitable instincts. "Someone else is taking care of it," we think justifiably. Then we either stop giving or divert our charitable resources to causes other than the poor. Self-help institutions languish; where churches, lodges, temples, clubs, and other mutual aid associations once flourished, we now have the welfare/entitlement state with its attendant army of paid overseers. Crowding out of the voluntary sector causes many private associations to wither and die; many are long dead. Because government institutes a single welfare policy, there is no room for experimentation so new approaches to empowerment and assistance that might create less dependency never get tried.

Not only do the self-help and mutual-aid institutions wither among the needy, but so do charitable groups supported by the better off. If you're inclined to help the less fortunate, you now have less incentive to contribute or organize yourself for that purpose. When a large centralized system of compulsory compassion leads people to *let government take care of the problem*, we lose something important. The charitable impulse gets reduced to a cheaper act known as voting. You may leave the booth puffed up on your sense of compassion and goodwill, but your efforts amount to little more than shirking your responsibilities to your neighbors.

More and more citizens drop out of their communities. They let the government take over more and more. State growth becomes normalized—something that seems inevitable—and politicians justify their existence essentially by suggesting the state undertake activities previously carried out by the private sector. We aren't surprised and many people fail to question the state's ability to carry out the activity. The state comes to be viewed as the universal fixer of social problems—where ever-increasing budgets are needed to fix more and more problems—that the government itself almost always creates. If the government already feeds the poor, provides preschool education, and pays medical expenses for old people, why shouldn't it provide your health insurance and your college loans, too?

CORE FUNCTIONS

Once upon a time, people thought of government as being responsible for a few core functions. Indeed, the whole point of writing the United States Constitution (including the enumerated powers) was to encode those core functions and leave all other functions to the states and to the people. Today, this thinking is considered quaint—a relic of a different time. The modern administrative state is supposed to solve all problems from the center. A wise elite is meant to administer the solutions—that is, until those solutions become intrusive. By then it's too late to reverse it. The interest groups have accreted around the program, subsidy, or regulation. Intrusion becomes the health of the state.

Only budget realities prevent the wholesale proliferations of every program under the sun. Most programs face little opposition when they are instituted, either because people are ignorant about them, or opponents will be accused of being reactionary. But even big, national programs often seem like a good idea at the time, especially if a party is looking to purchase allegiances of new constituent groups. Witness the Republicans' willingness to institute the Medicare prescription drug benefit in 2003. The party that was supposed to be the party of limited government got into the prescription drug business. In the relatively recent case of Obamacare, there had been vociferous opposition from the public and yet a Democrat-controlled Congress ramrodded the legislation through—abandoning both its own rules and the will of the people. Democrats spent a tremendous amount of political capital and took heavy losses in the 2010 election. But as of this writing, Obamacare is entrenching itself day by day.

THE FORGOTTEN MAN

Redistribution involves more than the one who pays and the one who gets. In between stands the bureaucrat who determines whether someone is eligible, keeps the records, and often intrudes into the personal affairs of those they're charged with assisting.

As William Graham Sumner famously wrote, "A and B put their heads together to decide what C shall be made to do for D." The trouble is that B, the mediating bureaucracy, consumes resources that could have gone to more productive uses, including poverty alleviation. In other words, for the government to transfer a dollar to D, it's never enough to get the dollar from C. A hefty "commission" must be paid to support B. Society is made poorer because that commission isn't going to anything productive. Of course, the bureaucracies themselves, once they exist, become stubborn interest groups. The rank-and-file become masters at justifying the existence of the bureaucracy: Only they possess the expertise and data necessary to address the problem. Paradoxically, they need the problem for their continued existence. Funny how the problems never seem to go away.

PERFECT STORM

Now that great swaths of Americans are dependent on welfare and entitlements, we're facing not one but three separate fiscal crises: Medicaid, Medicare, and Social Security. Together they amount to a perfect storm of unfunded liabilities that, as of this writing, are already starting to make landfall as the baby boom generation retires. Because this generation has been required to pay into this system their whole working lives, they expect to get something out of it. The trouble is they'll take out a lot more than they ever pay in, and the intergenerational transfers will be devastating without some kind of reform.

According to Conn Carroll, writing in *The Washington Examiner*, "That is over $318 billion that just Social Security and Medicare are adding to the deficit in 2011. Throw in the $269 billion we'll spend on Medicaid this year, and the big three entitlement programs added over half a trillion dollars to this year's deficit all by themselves." By 2021, entitlement spending is projected to rise to $3.27 trillion—bringing the national debt to nearly 90 percent of GDP, according to the Congressional Budget Office. Without reform, this represents economic catastrophe the likes of which we've never seen. To put this into perspective, if the GDP is defined roughly as the market value of all goods and services produced within a country in a given period, roughly ten years from the date of this book's publication there will be more government debt than the value of everything produced that year. The Takers will have overwhelmed the Makers.

It's Wrong

Looking at the unintended consequences of the redistributionist state is important, but at some level we just have to look at things from a moral point of view. As George Will remarked in one of his *Washington Post* columns:

> Not only does redistributionist government direct wealth upward; in asserting a right to do so, it siphons power into itself. A puzzling aspect of our politically contentious era is how little contention there is about the ethics of coercive redistribution by progressive taxation and other government "corrections" of social outcomes it considers unethical or unaesthetic.[56]

Progressive taxation and coercive distribution is ethically questionable. In fact, I'd go as far as to say it's wrong. Stealing is wrong. Stealing through the coercive apparatus of the state is also wrong. The difference between individual theft and state-sanctioned theft is a difference only of degree.

In his *Anarchy, State and Utopia*, the great philosopher Robert Nozick reminds us that as long as a holding—whether land or money—is justly acquired and justly transferred, whatever distribution arises is just. Third parties have no right to disrupt or change these just distributions. They can justify doing so based on an aesthetic fetish like equality of outcome, or out of the deepest concerns for the poor. No distributive "principle of justice can be continuously realized without continuous interference with people's lives," writes Nozick. And he's right. Just ask Sara.

So What Do You Suggest?

It's easy to be a critic and Benjamin Franklin was probably right about the inevitability of death and taxes. But if you were to ask me to replace our current system with something a little more reasonable, I'd suggest one of three proposals:

- A flat income tax of about 15 to 17 percent starting at around $30,000 per household. Households earning below $30,000 would pay no tax. Households earning $70,000 would pay 17 percent after the first $30,000.
- A national consumption tax and the repeal of the federal income tax. Various consumption taxes have been proposed but 20 percent sounds reasonable enough. For the sake of compromise, one might build in a feature that allowed means testing for how the tax impacts the poorest.
- A single or "Georgist" tax that would tax property/real estate ownership. This was Milton Friedman's preferred tax, but it's probably more politically infeasible than the two above.

The most politically feasible tax is the flat income tax starting at $30,000. Because it starts at $30K it is still "progressive" in a sense, and it is true that the Taras of the world could continue to take advantage of the investment savvy and productive effort of the Saras. That said, it would be a far better system than the one we have today.

The first reason to favor a flat tax is that, unless you work for H&R Block, doing your taxes is a colossal waste of time and effort. In total, my wife and I probably spend eight to sixteen hours per year just doing taxes. That's eight to sixteen hours we can't use to improve my wife's new private school, to play with our little boy, or to clean up the house. It's no fun, either. And when you calculate the hours Americans spend just complying with the complicated tax code, it adds up to 6.1 billion hours, according to Janet Novack of *Forbes*.[57] If time is money, that's money wasted, and if you pay others to do your taxes, you're still wasting money on unproductive activity even if it's being carried out by others.

Second, as we suggest, the flat tax above isn't really flat. It ensures that people at the lower end of the socio-economic spectrum are protected, but everyone pays something into the system.

Finally, the flat tax isn't easy to cheat. Politicians won't like this fact, but everyone else will. As investment guru Ron Muhlenkamp points out, "When the rules are clear, it's hard for the public to cheat. It is also more difficult for the politicians to write rules making it legal for parts of the public to pay less taxes without cheating." As of 2011, that was 72,536 pages of tax code complexity. In all those pages are opportunities for cronies and tax attorneys to benefit. And, indeed, there are opportunities for rich people to benefit. To make it fair, make it flat. We'd take no more than five minutes filling out a single card or web page, either of which could be submitted in no time. It would wipe out whole platoons of useless functionaries and tax preparers. Thankfully, these people would find meaningful employment elsewhere putting their talents to productive uses.

Some might object that the rich won't pay enough in taxes. We've spent most of the book explaining why that's okay. But Ron Muhlenkamp puts it in much more pragmatic terms in his book *Ron's Road to Wealth*:

> Folks, the truly rich don't need taxable income—they have assets. They can either live off their assets or invest in municipal bonds, which are exempt from income taxes. Income taxes don't tax the rich; income taxes tax those who are trying to get rich.[58]

Muhlenkamp is right. Just ask Warren Buffett.

The other problem is that wealthy people can also afford to pay people to help them get out of paying taxes. To this day, people balk at Arthur Laffer and his famous "Laffer Curve." The Laffer Curve shows the relationship between tax rates and tax revenues. That is, as tax rates come down to reasonable levels, people stop investing so much in trying to avoid them. According to Laffer, there is a sweet spot in taxation that allows governments to get an optimal level of revenues. Muhlenkamp again:

> After Reagan lowered the top tax rate, the tax avoidance schemes no longer made sense. So the doctors went back to being full-time doctors [instead of spending one day per week avoiding taxes]. They made more money and as a result they paid more in taxes than before the Reagan tax cuts. So did a lot of other productive people, which gave us the strong economy of the 1980s.

Now, we might quibble about what that "optimal" tax rate is and we might quibble about whether government should set the optimal rate in order to get maximum revenues (which feeds Leviathan). But we shouldn't quibble about the reality of tax avoidance and the incentives people face when they are confronted with high marginal rates, tax code complexity, and money to spend on cracking tax attorneys.

In short, ironing out the tax code—so it's simple and flat—will get us closer to a state of fairness, efficiency, and overall prosperity.

8
Statistics and Sabotage

Our understanding of the rich and the poor has been skewed by what we choose to measure, and not realizing how different are the classes of goods that the rich and poor consume.

– John V. C. Nye

As soon as an indicator becomes a target for conducting policy, it loses its informational value.

– "Goodhart's Law," as attributed to Charles Goodhart

Numbers: They have the quality of being beyond question. Two plus two equals four; not five, not three. Numbers seem air tight—like the truths of logic. When you start to gather numbers and put them together to make a picture, that's when the trouble starts. When it comes to the social scientists, numbers are supposed to limn some truth about the world. Aggregating numbers can result in one of the three types of lies famously identified by Mark Twain: "lies, damn lies, and statistics."

If you have a data set that seems to prove your point, it's tempting to go around and beat your opposition over the head with it. However, there are a number of problems with this approach. First, people seldom question just *how* data are gathered, through methods fragile unto themselves; second, it's easy to omit some critical aspect, or leave out a key piece of information, that is likely to change the entire picture; and, three, statistics can lead people to infer what cannot be legitimately inferred.

In this chapter, we'll explore a few of the ways statistics on inequality get abused, misused, and repurposed to mislead people. I can't speak authoritatively about any given person's motivations, but when you consider the intelligence and stature of some of the people who offer these examples, their errors strike me as either gross oversights or lies (at least in the sense Twain meant). I'll leave that for you to decide.

WAGE STAGNATION

In certain hands, it's surprising how mutable numbers can become. One good example is the use, misuse, and abuse of statistics about U.S. wages over time, and one of their most visible saboteurs is Harold Meyerson of the *Washington Post*, who has used his column to claim:

> [We] face an economy that's been warped by two developments we've not seen since FDR's time. The first of these is the stagnation of ordinary Americans' incomes, a phenomenon that began back in the 1970s and that American families have offset by having both spouses work and by drawing on the rising value of their homes.[59]

Thirty-plus years of stagnating wages? It would seem that capitalism doesn't work for the little guy.

Former Labor Secretary Robert Reich joins the pity party. In a self-styled YouTube video, Reich claims that "since 1980, the American economy has doubled in size...but adjusting for inflation, most people's wages have barely increased." Barely increased, despite the rich getting richer.

New York Times columnist Paul Krugman has been spreading the wage stagnation virus for at least a decade. Among them, I suspect all this is meant as a collective pile-on of a tax policy that has existed more or less since Ronald Reagan sat in the Oval Office.

Context is Critical

If we look carefully at these data—as well as at some important phenomena they fail to capture—we might arrive at a very different set of conclusions than those above. Luckily, some bigger brains than mine have taken on the challenge: George Mason University economists Russell Roberts and Donald Boudreaux.

First, consider that the data on wages don't include non-monetary income for which poor people qualify, such as food stamps and Medicaid. Nor do they include non-monetary forms of compensation such as contributions by employers to workers' health-insurance plans. Russell Roberts, consulting U.S. Census data, says:

> Unfortunately for Meyerson's unrelenting pessimism, median family income (median, not mean) corrected for inflation, was up 23% between 1973 (a good year in the early 1970s that the gloom and doomers like to call the good old days).

> Is that increase due to both spouses working? For families where both spouses work (so holding constant the number of workers in the family), the increase is 36%.

> These income numbers do not include employer contributions to healthcare or retirement unless they get converted into income. They correct for inflation using a flawed index that probably overstates inflation by 1% a year for the last ten years. They include composition effects

of an increase in immigration that reduces the measured median by adding in newcomers who have fewer skills.

Like me, Meyerson is not an economist. So perhaps we should give him the benefit of the doubt. Then again, if you wield a pen for one of the world's most influential news organizations, you'd better check with someone capable of interpreting the data.

REICH UND ARM

I gather there is no layman's excuse for economist and former Labor Secretary Robert Reich parroting Meyerson's claim almost verbatim. Even if we agreed that "wages have barely increased," we would have a hard time arguing that *total compensation* has barely increased since 1980. Thanks to government policies—some better than others—we get more and more of our compensation in non-wage forms like pre-tax healthcare benefits and employer contributions to 401(k) plans. No reasonable person claims that we shouldn't count these payments as compensation and yet Reich leaves them out.

What's worse, Reich tortures the data by ignoring the economic effects of immigration. That's when a fresh supply of low-skilled labor enters the U.S. job market, finding opportunities made available by economic growth. In other words, you can't suggest the economy has been on hard times (except for the rich) since 1980 while ignoring the enormous benefits that have gone to immigrants. "In the past three decades," writes St. Louis Federal Reserve economist Rubén Hernández-Murillo, "the percentage of foreign-born people in the United States has risen rapidly. In 1970, foreign-born people represented 5 percent of the population, compared with about 12 percent in 2003. The percentage of foreign-born workers of total U.S. employment is even higher—about 14.8 percent as of last year [2005]. ... Overall, the flexibility of U.S. labor markets has allowed the economy to absorb the increased flow of immigrants."

Don Boudreaux's response to Reich's stagnation thesis is now well known among econ geeks. But you and I should appreciate it, too. Boudreaux asks us to consider the effects of immigration and claims that Reich "confuses statistical categories with real people." To unpack this charge, he offers an analogy with a family:

> Let's say that you annually keep track of the height of your three kids. This year, their average height is 4' 2." Next year, you have a fourth child and you calculate the height again. The addition of that infant will lower your kids' average height, even though your first three kids have grown in height during the year. Clearly, you wouldn't conclude from the lower average height that your kids are shrinking in size. That would be absurd.[60]

But the same reasoning applies to average wages.

In other words, looking at the last thirty-odd years—and factoring out substantial non-wage compensation—it means that since 1980 the U.S. economy has not only been able to raise average wages slightly, it also has absorbed millions of immigrants. These people aren't plot-points; they're flesh and blood individuals, many of whom faced terrible odds to get to this country and are generally among America's lowest-paid workers. But low as their wages are, these wages are princely compared to what these same immigrants would expect to earn in their home countries. Despite serious problems, America is still the land of opportunity. If you're being honest, it's hard to put a pessimistic spin on that and yet, simply by omission, that's what Reich does.

Munger Games

Duke University political economist Michael Munger adds an important point to the discussion about wages: Things keep getting better.

> By most measures, real wages are up slightly since 1976. If anything, these measures understate the actual increase in consumption by a lot. How much did your hipster OWS kid's MacBook Pro cost in 1976? How about his iPad? How about his MP3 player? (Hint: infinity, infinity, infinity). Stuff has gotten WAY better, and cheaper at the same time. Attempts to control for hedonics, quality change, and innovation are notoriously difficult. How would you build Moore's Law into a CPI adjustment, when it implies prices of computer power are constantly falling at a rate of more than 25% per year? But these clearly lead toward understating the effective real wage increase. Even if I only have a minimum wage job, I can save up and buy an iPod. In 1976, I could not.[61]

Better, faster, cheaper. You'll find no shortages of mobile phones, even in the inner city.

Though he has long sung the wage-stagnation song, Paul Krugman seems to agree with Munger when he writes, "Think about the early 1970's, no personal computers, no Internet, no personal faxes ... we're an enormously more productive, richer economy than we were in the 1970's."[62] Is this not also true for the lower-income quartiles?

Back to Reich: Munger not only cottons onto the problem of healthcare benefits soaking up much of the gains of economic dynamism since 1980, he questions Reich's assumptions about what people *ought* to earn when they're first starting out.

> It really is absurd that people think wages have not gone up, for

John Smith the worker, hired in 1976. He makes a LOT more now (though he may have lost his job, which is a DIFFERENT problem than the one pointed out by Dr. Reich). Wages rise with job tenure, they just do. John Smith makes pretty good money now. The new guy just being hired, sure, he doesn't make much more than John Smith did in 1976, adjusted for inflation. Not sure why that is surprising, or even bad.

The relevant questions for Munger, I take it, are about income mobility and consumption power.

So here's the problem in a nutshell. Neither Meyerson nor Reich (nor Krugman) are *lying* exactly; it's that they are using discreet statistical artifacts that give a false impression. They want you to think that matters are much worse than they are. The question is why.

HOUSEHOLD INCOMES

Another major canard is "average (or mean) real household income." This statistic is similar to that about average wages, but invites a different sleight of hand. The great Thomas Sowell dispels this black magic: "It is an undisputed fact that the average real income ... of American households rose by only 6 percent from 1969 to 1996. ... But it is an equally undisputed fact that the average real income per person in the United States rose by 51% over that very same period. How can both these statistics be true? Because the average number of people per household was declining during those years."[63] Indeed, that people can afford to live with fewer people in a household is an indicator that we are wealthier, yet it's not uncommon to see spin doctors drag these data out every so often.

Instead of relying on these more manipulable stats, why not just simplify matters and look at improvements in per capita compensation and wages? Here are the data up to the 2006, prior to the Great Recession. I consider this to be a good picture of the last 30 years:

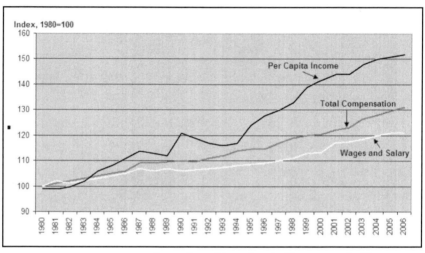

Source: Steven Moore, from his "Prosperity in Peril" presentation

As with other data, these are subject to interpretation in the same way a Gestalt picture is. But when we take a look at what has happened to the U.S. middle class…it's stretching!

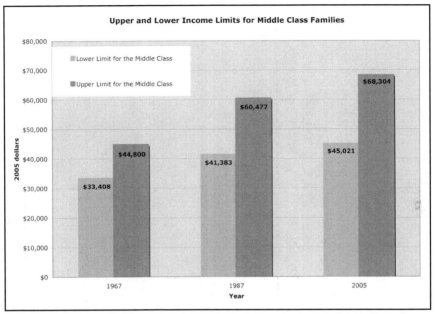

Source: Census Bureau

Here again, these data do not include pre-tax contributions to health insurance and tax-deferred investments.

NICE CURVES

To get a better idea about this wealth "stretching" phenomenon, allow me to share thoughts from my friend, social entrepreneur Gerry Ohrstrom. Ohrstrom asks us to imagine a bell curve with the y-axis representing population and the x-axis representing the amount of wealth each person in that population controls. Assume that money has fallen from the sky, resulting in a normal bell curve distribution:

The wealth could be generated by smarts, hard work, or innova-

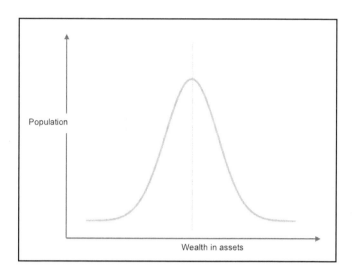

tion. For the sake of discussion, the wealth is manna from heaven. What's important for the exercise is to assume that the wealth is randomly distributed. Also, let's ignore any issues (such as inflation) that might arise. We're only looking at the distribution of real wealth.

What happens to the bell curve when the new wealth is randomly distributed? Well, random doesn't mean equal. Some people will be luckier than average, and others unluckier than average. Some people will be better at grabbing the manna. The society as a whole is wealthier than before, so most of the bell curve moves to the right along the x-axis. But because you'll randomly have some very lucky people and some very unlucky ones (just like random clusters in coin-flipping or cancer incidence), the bell curve will also fatten/broaden. So, the two tails of the bell curve are now farther apart than they were before in the destitute society, meaning a "wealth gap" has formed. As more wealth is randomly distributed the bell curve just gets broader as the wealth gap gets bigger.

These curves show that inequality is going to be present in

any such distribution when we assume a "black box" view of function—that is, when we ignore how the wealth distribution came about and assume it's just random. As we get richer, the curve of the bell piles up and stretches out but *the distance between rich and poor naturally widens.* That doesn't mean we're less rich; quite the contrary, it means we're moving the "bell" of the curve to the right (getting richer) while thinning out the poverty tail. Whatever you think about the manner and means of alleviating poverty, one thing seems clear: The "gap" is just not an important idea unless you make envy some sort of moral axiom. The question, with a nod to late philosopher John Rawls, is not "How well do the rich make out?" but rather "Does the lot of the poor improve?"

Now, even if we find Ohrstrom's stretching curve intuitive, we will of course want to talk about how the distribution came about. That's where the rubber hits the road, as we discussed in the How Wealth Works chapters. If we're going to talk about the gap without talking about function, the stretching curves example helps us appreciate how everyone can be better off even as the gap between the richest and poorest increases.

BAKING PIES AND HOUSEHOLD INCOME

Imagine that you're a freshman at a frat party. Your fraternity orders small pizzas, and you're given four pieces. The next week, the fraternity poobahs order extra-large pizzas and give you only three pieces. Would you complain? Not if the three extra-large pieces were larger in total than the four small pieces.

Likewise, the income share of the bottom 20 percent of households shrank from 4.1 percent in 1970 to 3.4 percent in 2006. Should we care? After all, that is 3.4 percent of a pie that's three times bigger as the economic pie of 1970. If one adjusts for growth in the number of households, the average inflation-adjusted income of households in the bottom quintile has risen by 36 percent since the era of Nixon. This means the poorest Americans are richer than they used to be *and* they're among the richest poor people in the world.[64]

It should be clear by now that household income is a poor measure for comparing 1970 with more recent times. As we suggest, the average number of people in a household has shrunken by one-fifth since then. Furthermore, 27 percent of households today are one-person households, up from 17 percent in 1970. And, as it happens, a disproportionately large number of people in the lower quintile now live alone.

Of course, not all of the folks in the bottom quintile of income (under about $18,500 per year) are living in hard economic times. This group includes millions of young people starting their first jobs who will earn more as they grow older. It includes retirees with lots of assets but little income. And, as we said, it includes millions of low-skilled immigrants. Yes, there are chronically unemployed people—since 2007 there are likely many more of them—but in looking at a picture of over thirty years it's hard to argue that most of the benefits of economic prosperity have accrued only to the wealthy. Indeed, we will look beyond quintiles to see just how much things have improved for the poorest.

ON THE (SPIRIT) LEVEL

Some equality fetishists have taken a different tack, however. Instead of looking at the data within, say, the United States, they ask, "What if we were to compare countries with varying levels of inequality on measures of health and well-being?" When I set out to write this book, a few people told me someone had constructed such an argument backed up by data. It was supposed to be the gold standard for the case against wealth inequality. Despite my bias—i.e. setting out to write a book urging people not to worry about the gap—I wanted to be fair-minded. So I bought the book.

Turns out I'm not one of those convinced by Richard Wilkinson's and Kate Pickett's case in *The Spirit Level*. In the foreword to that 2009 book, former labor secretary Robert Reich (again) avers:

> *The Spirit Level* looks at the negative social consequences of wide inequality—among them, more physical and mental illness not only among those at the lower ranks, but even those at the top of the scale. The authors find, not surprisingly, that where there are great disparities in wealth, there are heightened levels of social distrust. They argue convincingly that wide inequality is bad for a society, and that more equal societies tend to do better on many measures of social health and wealth.

This was the introduction. I was already finding more red flags here than in Tiananmen Square.

PROBLEMS IN PARADISE

The Spirit Level is a bad theory grasping for facts. The authors pack so many disassociated data around their theory that it reads like a Theory of Everything for the social sciences. The trouble is inequality ends up looking a lot more like miasma, the idea that discrete individual diseases were caused by a mysterious essence. It turns out cholera, chlamydia, and the Black Death were caused by distinct pathologies. Likewise, proponents of *The Spirit Level* hypothesis believe everything bad that ever happens in the world can be attributed to the fact that people are economically unequal. Mental health problems? That's "anxiety" that comes from worrying about your station. Drugs? If Bill Gates weren't so rich, you wouldn't use them. High murder rates? Its has nothing to do with gang warfare and drug prohibition. From pseudo-psychology to tortured data, you'll find it in the work of Wilkinson and Pickett. But let's take a step back.

First, it's not clear that the pathologies Wilkinson and Pickett identify don't result from different things, including the welfare state itself. We discuss many of these problems elsewhere and even among countries with robust welfare states, some score better along various dimensions of social health and well-being. So does this mean that the most equal societies do a better job on these dimensions *because* they are more equal?

The most unavoidable problem with Wilkinson's and Pickett's case is that correlation is not causation. When it comes to "the evidence," they arrive at their conclusions about poverty and trust by comparing aggregated data from different countries. Norway, Sweden, and Japan, for example, represent the "more equal" group; countries like Portugal, the United States, and New Zealand are "less equal." They argue that this former group fares better than the latter group on a number of dimensions (which they treat as a cluster they call "Health and Social Problems")[65]:

- Life expectancy
- Infant mortality
- Homicides
- Imprisonment
- Teenage births

- Math and literacy
- Trust
- Obesity
- Mental illness and addiction
- Social mobility

Using this list, we can start to call Wilkinson and Pickett out for rigging the evidence. When you break up these data, there are simply too many strong alternative explanations for each social problem taken individually.

For example, when we factor out homicides and traffic fatalities, which have almost nothing to do with healthcare system outcomes, the United States immediately jumps to number one in the world for life expectancy.[66] When we correct for the way stillbirths and live births are counted in different countries, the infant mortality picture changes, too. In the United States, for example, doctors have made phenomenal strides in saving premature babies. In many countries, if a premature baby doesn't survive, it's not even counted as a live birth[67], but in the United States it is.[68] World health non-governmental organizations conveniently ignore this counting discrepancy. As John Steele Gordon notes: "France, the Netherlands, and other European countries don't count as live births babies who weigh less than 500 grams or had less than 22 weeks of gestation. They are, instead, counted as stillbirths. Japan and Hong Kong, it seems, count babies that are almost a year old when they die as having lived a year and, thus, not an infant mortality."[69]

What about imprisonment? It's true the United States has far, far higher rates of incarceration than Sweden does. But, for example, Sweden has far less draconian drug laws than the United States. A little over half of the U.S. prison population is incarcerated due to drug-related offenses. By contrast, non-violent offenders in Sweden simply don't end up in jail as often, but this is a factor of drug policy, not of income or of economics in general. I could go on but the point is, when scrutinized, most of the dimensions from which Wilkinson and Pickett extrapolate are consequences not of inequality but simply of a series of local and national laws specific to the countries they have chosen to highlight for their own purposes.

If inequality itself cannot be causally connected to any one of the social problems Wilkinson and Pickett discuss in *The Spirit Level*, it certainly can't explain them all together. Their methodology is specious at best.

INEQUALITY OR POVERTY?

Inequality seems to be an awkward and imperfect way for Wilkinson and Pickett to talk about poverty. We have already established that one problem we should worry about is absolute poverty, not inequality. We can imagine a wealthy country in which everyone has his basic needs met, either through ultra-low unemployment, a policy of redistribution, or something else. If we stipulate that this country had the richest bottom quintile in the world, would it matter that there is a cadre of super-wealthy elites in the top quintile—people who made Warren Buffett look middle class? Of course not. There may be some "keeping up with the Joneses" behavior, but that sounds more like an argument for quelling our envy instincts than taking other people's money.

Finally, when looking at measures of inequality in modern, industrialized countries around the world, we find wildly different outcomes on any one of these well-being dimensions, and wildly different levels of absolute poverty. Again, we should never conflate inequality and absolute poverty.

WHY LESS INEQUALITY AS OPPOSED TO FULL EQUALITY?

It's interesting that egalitarians have gone soft since the fall of the Berlin Wall. Wilkinson and Pickett don't hold up the *most egalitarian* countries as health and well-being utopias. Perhaps that's because they are not. When we look at countries like North Korea and Venezuela, whose Gini indices (measures of inequality) reveal flat societies of human ants directed by tiny and wealthy government elite, things aren't so great.

So why don't Wilkinson and Pickett think increases in well-being will be proportional to increases in equality? They seem to be trying to find a sweet spot in countries that eat the rich to some degree, but leave their middle classes largely intact. I suspect they recognize there is something to the maxim about the geese and the golden eggs. I would also surmise that the authors—even if they harbor deep egalitarian instincts—understand the degree of totalitarianism required to bring about equality on par with that found in countries like North Korea.

THE FRENCH REVOLUTION

In the introduction to his TED talk on inequality in July 2011,

The Spirit Level author Richard Wilkinson said, "I think the intuition that inequality is divisive and socially corrosive has been around since before the French Revolution."

As I argue elsewhere in this volume, inequality has been around much longer (i.e. since the Stone Age). The problem with any egalitarian ethos is that we live in very different circumstances than we did when we were hunter-gatherers. It turns out we can live better lives if we accept the existence of income inequality in a system that rewards high performers from whom we can benefit by trading.

In 1989, the great doomslayer Julian Simon said that "200 years ago, in France, the chance that a person who was born of living beyond the age of 30 was just about fifty/fifty. That is to say, the life expectancy of a person in the richest country in the world was less than thirty years. And it had been less than 30 years for 10,000 years…a very, very long time. Very little had happened over the whole history of the human enterprise. And then, just in the past 200 years—a mere blip in history—life expectancy at birth has gone up to well over 70 in the rich countries of the world."[70]

This massive increase in life expectancy is a staggering achievement for the human race, whatever the relative inequalities might be among the richest nations of the world. When we put things into this perspective—realizing all the while that most of the major advances that improve life expectancy happened in countries in which a higher degree of inequality was tolerated—we get a better picture of what inequality actually means. We start to see inequality not as a cause of human misery, but a consequence of human material and social progress. In fact, if we look at Singapore and Hong Kong, the two areas with the greatest economic inequality as measured by the United Nations, *they perform well under almost every criterion.* And yet *The Spirit Level* thesis predicts that these countries should perform worse. (Conveniently, Wilkinson and Pickett leave these nation-states out of the book.)

TRUST

Let us linger for a moment on the idea of trust and the related concept of social capital. Wilkinson and Pickett claim that more egalitarian societies have higher trust. It's not always clear in *The Spirit Level* what they mean by that. People have certain degrees of trust in the government, trust in their neighbors, and trust in any given member of society they might encounter. Wilkinson and Pickett write that "inequality, not surprisingly, is a powerful social divider, perhaps because we all tend to use differences in living standards as markers of status differences. We tend to choose our friends from among our near equals and have little to do with those much richer or much poorer."

Some of that is true, of course, though it's not clear how massive, continuous, and coercive wealth transfers from the more productive members of society to the less productive would help people "identify with and empathize with other people."

But when we look at the countries Wilkinson and Pickett hold up as exemplars of high trust and social cohesion, other plausible explanations recommend themselves. Is it so shocking, for instance, that ethnically homogenous societies like Japan and Sweden might be quite trusting by comparison to ethnically diverse countries? Indeed, when we look at more ethnically diverse countries like France and the United States, the trust score falls. Robert Putnam of *Bowling*

Alone fame has studied the issue recently and found that social cohesion and trust capital tend to fall the more open a country's immigration policies become—casting doubt on some of his own earlier suggestions in that seminal work. This seems plausible. For example, although France has far greater income equality than does the United States, the latter scores *higher* than France on trust dimensions.[71]

The truth is, while Japan may tax and redistribute more than the United States, it has a far stricter immigration policy and hoary ideas about ethnic purity. Scandinavian countries, while they are far more tolerant toward immigrants than the Japanese, also have strict immigration policies when compared with the United States. Whatever you think about immigration, doesn't cultural and ethnic homogeneity really engender trust? If so, this reality thins out the notion that income inequality results in greater levels of distrust.[72]

Trust in Politicians and the Political Process

Suppose we look at trust a little differently—i.e. in terms of perceptions about corruption and the strength of institutions. New Zealand, a more "unequal" country, ranks number one in the world on Transparency International's Corruption Perceptions Index.[73] So even though Wilkinson and Picket think inequality attenuates trust, New Zealand citizens have a high degree of trust in their major institutions both public and private. It is therefore doubtful that greater reliance on government largesse engenders a spirit of community. As we discuss elsewhere, the welfare state has done much to destroy the deep communities Alexis de Tocqueville observed in that young America he found in the early nineteenth century.

Perhaps more importantly, Arnold Kling reminds us that:

> In the case of government, there is good trust and there is bad trust. Good trust is trust in processes that promote public service. Bad trust is trust in the virtue of leaders or the wisdom of voters.

> If you can trust the processes of government, then that is a good thing. Good trust in government is based on processes that provide for accountability, checks and balances, equal protection, and punishment of official corruption.

> Trusting the virtues of government leaders is a bad thing. It leads one to cede rights and powers to government that are easily abused.[74]

Kling argues that trust in the "will of the people" is also a bad thing. Democratic majorities can and do support bad policies, violations of people's rights, and even genocide. Democracy is useful as a check on power, but "not as a tool for over-riding the principle of individual liberty." And here's where elites' concept of trust sounds a lot like "government as God." Kling remarks:

> My idea of a high-trust society differs from that of many elites. Elitist journalists think that a high-trust society is one where we trust the mainstream media. Elitist politicians and activists think that a high-trust society is one where we trust legislators, regulators, and experts to exercise broad authority. In contrast, I believe that a high-trust society is one in which processes ensure that elites are subject to checks and accountability. It is particularly important for legislators, regulators, and experts to have their authority limited and their accountability assured.

If anything, the United States has become a place where the political class is less and less accountable to the general public. According to the Edelman Trust Barometer, a survey that examines trust in four key institutions (government, business, media, and NGOs), more Americans now mistrust said institutions than trust them.[75] As of 2011, only 40 percent trusted the government. Perhaps they learned some lessons trusting government with so much in the years before, only to witness so much of what the government did end up in failure.

And yet many Americans continue to show boundless faith in government, especially when it comes to ending economic inequality. But let me not get too far afield. The New Zealand example shows that trust in institutions has less to do with inequality and more to do with unrelated factors. We'll leave the Wilkinson and Pickett analysis behind for now. Suffice it to say it does not hold up under scrutiny.

INCOME MOBILITY

Income mobility is one of the two major indicators of economic success in prosperous societies. More recently, one of the most flagrant instances of statistical sabotage has come in the argument that the more egalitarian countries of Scandinavia have higher income mobility than the United States.[76]

There are two major problems with this claim: First, it's a misreading of the data based on comparing apples to and oranges; and, second, even if it were true, it would have little to do with relative levels of inequality and everything to do with policies that discourage upward mobility near the bottom. Let me take these points in turn.

Apples and oranges—Imagine you have two measuring sticks divided into fifths (or quintiles). One measuring stick reaches as high as the door knob. The other measuring stick goes up to the ceiling.

Now suppose a friend and I are having a jumping contest. Suppose also that my friend is a former college basketball player. If I'm using the door-knob measuring stick to measure my jumps, I am able to jump up into the fourth quintile! My friend, using the ceiling-length stick is only able to jump into the second quintile. Does that mean I jump higher than my friend? Of course not. It means we're using two different measuring sticks. People play the same kinds of tricks with data on income mobility.

"In Scandinavia, the income distribution is highly compressed," writes policy analyst Tino Sanandaji. "This means that even small and meaningless changes in income between parents and children appear as 'mobility.'"[77]

Lagging mobility?—A recent study by the Pew Foundation found that, whatever Scandinavian countries can boast in income mobility, the United States still has a lot to offer: "The vast majority of individuals, 71 percent, whose parents were in the bottom half of the income distribution actually improved their rankings relative to their parents."[78] The Pew study also confirms that any lagging mobility is caused more by ethnic disparities, education, and lack of skills development within certain groups. Pew confirms, for example, that American children from low-income families who excel in education have high income mobility. Thus, if the United States began to decline relative to other countries on income mobility, it would have less to do with inequality and more to do with policies that have the effect of removing the bottom rungs of the economic latter (policies like minimum wage laws, broken public school systems, and intergenerational cycles of welfare dependence come to mind).

As an elevated endnote, allow me to mention that the venerable

French economist Veronique de Rugy has looked at the Organisation for Economic Cooperation and Development OECD data and discovered something interesting: Not only do Scandinavian countries have more equality than the United States, they have more regressive tax codes! This fact is counterintuitive—so much so that left-liberal Jonathan Chait responded to it with ad hominem attacks on de Rugy.[79] But she is correct. Most European countries increase their tax revenues using consumption taxes in combination with income taxes. Consumption taxes, like value-added taxes (VATs), are far more regressive, meaning that when a poor person buys a loaf of bread, he pays as much in tax as a rich person.

De Rugy thinks we should care more about mobility than equality, and I agree. But for those who care more about equality, she cites an interesting related passage from the OECD paper:

> So while the U.S. tax system is progressive and reduces inequality, the U.S. welfare state is much less effective at reducing inequality. And because the U.S. has a very unequal distribution of income from capital and a much wider wage distribution than many other OECD countries, it ends up as a relatively unequal country after taxes and benefits.[80]

Why does the United States have an unequal distribution of income from capital? We discussed many of these reasons in "How Wealth Works: Rich People's Money," but one reason is that many Americans, from the time of the founding, think there is something unseemly about double taxation. So at least we do it to a lesser degree than other countries.

But let me not stray too far. The main points for us to remember are that despite serious policy problems that ought to be addressed, the United States still has very high rates of social mobility, and these rates are an important indicator of the success of any economic system. This brings us to the other important—though perhaps more elusive—indicator of an economic system's health: consumption power.

CONSUMPTION POWER

If ever there were a lesson to be learned about statistics, it is this: When it comes to the well-being of poor people, we need to look at consumption power. It's not an easy thing to measure, as there are many proxies, but if we all care about our neighbors climbing up Abraham Maslow's hierarchy of needs, we have to wonder how much consumption power they have.

In the chapter "Never Mind the Gap," we let *Rational Optimist* author Matt Ridley take us to France in the time of Louis XVI to illustrate how the poor among us enjoy prosperity on par with that of the Bourbon monarch. I found a similar passage from new institutional economist John Nye, which I cannot resist quoting at length. Nye describes a lavish American feast in about 1850:

> You had hot broth (consommé), roast beef, chicken, ham, lots of meats in aspic [i.e. salty Jell-O], maybe some fish or shrimp, various meat pies, stewed vegetables, a variety of breads and cakes, bread pudding, a few stewed or cooked fruits, and perhaps even an early sort of ice cream dish, along with coffee, tea, and fine wine. All the Brahmins of Boston and Swells of New York would have been suitably impressed by the variety and extravagance and would have been still further impressed had they been able to serve exotic out-of-season fruits like bananas or kiwi.[81]

Lavish indeed. Denny's, anyone?

I don't think I need to prod the reader hard to realize that (except for the wine) this is essentially the typical menu of your basic Midwestern, eat-all-you-can, $7.99 buffet. Indeed, the buffet would have more and better breads and fresher fruit and vegetables year round, while maintaining superior standards of hygiene in preparation and service. Compared to the fact that blue-collar workers can have such food today on a regular basis without much effort, is it really so much better for the rich to be able to afford $200-a-plate dinners or $400 bottles of wine? But if we judge inequality by what people can afford we will be blind to the fact that most of what ordinary people want to eat can be had for trifling sums and are therefore ignored. Indeed, progress at this level might be seen to count against the poor.

Nye goes on to say that a nation with inexpensive basic food leads to a situation in which food is effectively subtracted from the equation when we consider differences between rich and poor. He's right, of course. Now, the narrative is that poor people can't afford nutritious food or fancy food, so turn to cheap, fast food. Guilty elites focus on the enormous differences in going to, say, cheap buffets versus elegant restaurants. Nye cautions that "the relative price difference might be growing while the quality differential might actually be shrinking." It would be difficult, he says, to widen the real food gap "no matter how much money the rich could afford to spend or throw away on meals."

People in 1850 Western Europe could only count on eating meat once a week. There were often insufficient supplies of basics like potatoes. Spices like vanilla and pepper are now so trivially cheap that we forget people got rich "importing such treasures to the West." We take for granted the innumerable things ordinary people can afford because they have become so cheap and "fixating on monetary income will always overstate these differences," Nye says.

> Thus, whatever the measured gap between the rich and the poor in to-day's world—the real (utility-adjusted) gap in incomes and wealth is liable to be substantially smaller than that of a century or so earlier, even when monetary measures tell us otherwise. While the losses, or at any rate, the relative losses are liable to be felt more keenly by the rich.

A loss of consumption power at the bottom is thus what we should all be worried about if we care about the condition of the poorest among us. And to be fair, people with a redistributionist bent are concerned about the affordability of things we think are rather basic. As we've suggested, the big three are healthcare, education, and energy.

Is it any accident that the areas with which the government interferes most are areas in which our consumption power is currently being reduced?

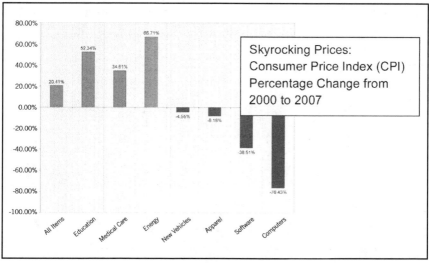

Source: BLS

THE SPECTER OF INFLATION

Without launching into a major diatribe about a gold standard or the Federal Reserve, I would be remiss in failing to mention the specter of inflation. In other words, policies that increase inflation hurt the poor the most and can have the effect of transferring wealth to the rich. Monetary policies like restoring liquidity (printing money) that increase inflation are considered by many economists to be a necessary evil, especially in systems that rely on central banks and or a Federal Reserve-type system.

While we cannot spare the space that would be required to launch into a debate about our monetary system, we must admit that measures taken within the current system can cause boom/bust cycles. Efforts by central bankers to smooth those cycles can result in weakened currencies and in inflation. These consequences have the most profound effect on the consumption power of the poor, even as the system benefits politicians and the politically connected temporarily. If, for example, you can convince a central bank to inflate a bubble via artificially low interest rates or currency manipulation, such policies have the short-term effect of getting politicians to the next election cycle. It can harm the economy in the long run because it can cause more severe crashes and/or make your dollar buy you less.

BILL AND ME

Taking a leaf from Don Boudreaux's ledger, I want to talk about just how good we all have it. This thought experiment is designed to help us appreciate our unprecedented consumption power, even if we have to appreciate it intuitively.

If you believe *Forbes* magazine, Bill Gates is worth about $61 billion.[82] By comparison, I'd guess my family's net worth is about $61,000—give or take—once you factor in some outstanding liabilities, such as my wife's student loans and a car note. I hate to admit it, but it might be less. Let's just say for argument's sake I'm close. Lord help, I'm no math whiz. But if I divide Bill Gates' net worth by mine, it means he's about a million times richer than I in terms of his net *monetary* worth. But when it comes to the things that matter, is Bill Gates a million times richer—where "rich" is defined in something close to consumption power?

Bill Gates surely enjoys levels of convenience, comfort, and luxury I can only dream of, but can Bill Gates:

- Consume a million times more calories than I?
- Fly a million times more miles—or a million times faster—than I?
- Drive a million times more miles than I?
- Marry a million-times-better-looking woman than I married (no way!)?
- Sleep in a million times bigger, better, or more comfortable bed?
- Read a million times more interesting books?
- Play a million times more interesting games?
- Have a million times more enjoyable vacation?
- Get a million times more valuable education for his children?
- Get a million times higher quality medical treatment?
- Buy a million times more happiness than I?

I'd say no to all of the above.

Consumption power and, generally, a steadily increasing standard of living for people over the long term is a consequence of economic growth. For much of that growth, we have Bill Gates to thank.

Happiness

Happiness is important, and unlike many scholars who find it fashionable I don't want to place too heavy a premium on so-called "happiness research," as happiness is a highly subjective phenomenon that is hard to parse with statistics. That said, we don't want to throw the baby out with the bathwater.

Carnegie Mellon University economist Allen Meltzer sums up the results of a 2003 OECD study, which include surveys of people in the United States and various European countries:

> Americans worked more hours, experienced substantially lower unemployment rates, and lived in houses with nearly twice the space. The Europeans had much more extensive welfare states, but the Americans were far more satisfied with their lives. When asked: "How satisfied are you with your life?" 57 percent of the Americans answered "very."[83]

In France, Germany and Italy, only 14 to 17 percent gave that answer.

I don't want to fall into the trap of pegging the results of any happiness research to any policy or set of policies, but happiness is, in some sense, at least as important as resources. Such results certainly track with our intuitions about living a purposeful life. I don't know how much empirical research can yield on questions of work, dignity, and happiness—these questions very well may invite purely philosophical answers—but they should hover close by when we start to consider related questions of whether or not to redistribute income.

STATISTICS

I wouldn't want you to go away thinking we have all the answers when it comes to statistics on wealth and poverty. I'll be the first to admit that we don't. I'd rather leave you with a healthy skepticism about statistics.

Numbers are tools. They can be used to build up a case and to tear it down. They can sketch a picture or obfuscate an entire scene. Numbers have the power to help us understand aspects of our world that our five senses cannot. And yet they are limited. When we use statistics to get a better idea about some aspect of the world, we have to be careful about our biases and the biases of others. We also have to remember that statistics are like the hands of the proverbial blind men touching a very, very large elephant.

9

GOVERNMENT AS GOD

Democracy is also a form of worship.
It is the worship of Jackals by Jackasses.
– H. L. Mencken

When I was a kid, you could almost always find a televangelist on the air. There was the ever-entertaining Jim and Tammy Bakker who cried black tears near my hometown of Charlotte, N.C. Don't forget Robert Tilton with the car salesman's coif—a huckster who would say long, weepy prayers and gibber in tongues intermittently. There was the ever-creepy faith-healer Morris Cerullo, who was always ready to lay hands. And Jimmy Swaggart's fall reminded us that the flesh can be weak.

What united all of these characters was that they got rich by convincing people that all you had to do to sow the seeds of abundance in your life was to give *them* a little bit of your money. This was sort of like an investment, only carried out through one of God's brokers. You didn't have to trust the fickle market or count only on the meager rewards of work. The Lord would reward you with prosperity for being a good TV tither—all without having to put on your Sunday clothes.

By the 1990s there was almost universal antipathy for the TV preacher. Most were found either to be frauds, philanderers, or both. They did a good job of preying on the gullible and the desperate. They took advantage of innocent people and yet people like my grandmother would argue that these preachers, despite their sins, "brought a lot of people to the Lord." My grandmother is no dummy, so maybe she's right. Me? I doubt God uses snake-oil salesmen as instruments of His will. I prefer the idea that if God exists he would work through people by giving them the talents, skills, and common sense to do good. A doctor who administers antibiotics, for example, is more likely to heal a child than the parent who foregoes medicine and prays really, really hard.

If you're a religious reader, don't close the book. None of what I'm about to write is meant to disparage faith or the faithful. Even if you still think there are some earnest televangelists out there with good hearts, or that God can work miracles, I hope you'll agree that when it comes to the secular religion known as politics a lot of people have replaced God with government. Politicians are perhaps the worst form of televangelists.

THE COSTS OF BELIEF

When the costs of believing something false are fairly low and not directly borne while the benefits of holding the belief are fairly high by comparison, there's a good chance a lot of people will believe it and support it. They may even vote for it. In that sense, most politics and political programs are the products of irrationality. I don't mean that people are crazy (although that can certainly be true). What I mean is that if most people took the time actually to look at the data or investigate an issue they might not support many of the causes and policies they believe make us better off. But they don't. That's one reason why it's so easy for bad policies to get passed. Then, of course, once they're passed, special interests accrete around those policies like a husk. So the policies stick around.

Take, for example, policies that originate in what economist Bryan Caplan calls the anti-market bias, or "the tendency to underestimate the economic benefits of the market mechanism. The public has severe doubts about how much it can count on profit-seeking business to produce socially beneficial outcomes."[84] Allow me to quote Caplan at length:

> People focus on the motives of business and neglect the discipline imposed by competition. While economists admit that profit maximization plus market imperfections can yield bad results, non-economists tend to view successful greed as socially harmful per se.
>
> Joseph Schumpeter, arguably the greatest historian of economic thought, matter-of-factly spoke of "the ineradicable prejudice that every action intended to serve the profit interest must be anti-social by this fact alone." Anti-market bias, he implied, is not a temporary, culturally specific aberration. It is a deeply rooted pattern of human thinking that has frustrated economists for generations.

There are a lot of variations on the anti-market bias, Caplan says. Probably the most common, he says, is to conflate transactions with transfers, which means ignoring the incentive properties of either. A transfer is a no-strings-attached movement of wealth from one person (or group) to another. In the world of politics, all that matters is whether you happen to empathize more with the recipient of the transfer or the one from whom it was taken—and that usually ain't the rich businessperson.

A lot of people think of profits as inadvertent gifts to the rich. "So unless you perversely pity the rich more than the poor," Caplan says, "limiting profits seems like common sense." But appearances can be deceiving.

> Yet profits are not a handout but a quid pro quo: If you want to get rich, you have to do something people will pay for. Profits give incentives to reduce production costs, move resources from less-valued to more-valued industries, and dream up new products. This is the central lesson of *The Wealth of Nations*: The "invisible hand" quietly persuades selfish businessmen to serve the public good. For modern economists, these are truisms, yet teachers of economics keep quoting and requoting this passage. Why? Because Adam Smith's thesis was counterintuitive to his contemporaries, and it remains counterintuitive today.

So if people are normally beset with biases and biases don't have direct costs to the holder of those biases, dogmatism can spread like a deadly virus.

Dogma

Philosopher Michael Huemer reminds us that people can be victims of dogmatism.

"If you have strong opinions about a subject before acquiring the relevant empirical evidence," Heumer says, "you might be irrational." Worse, he adds, if you're confronted with data and refuse to re-evaluate your opinion in light of it, you might be a dogmatist.[85]

Any time you encounter someone who might be a dogmatist, ask them: "Is there any information or data that, if it were made available to you, would convince you otherwise?" If their answer is no, it's very likely they are fixated on an irrational belief system.

Now, that may not be true in all cases. Some people might have views that settle in a principle, but to be fair it can sometimes be difficult to tell the difference between principle and dogma. By and large, people hold irrational beliefs because there are very few direct consequences for holding that view. In other words, most of the time we're not having a "rational discussion," we're talking to cocoons of irrationality.

PARALLELS

Government offers a lot of what a hungry spirit requires. Consider the parallels (X = God or government):

1. In times of crisis, people turn to X to give them comfort and pray X will solve all their problems.
2. X possesses special knowledge about the affairs of ordinary people, which these ordinary people do not possess.
3. X has a special power to intercede in their affairs to positive effect, as long as they are faithful and obedient.
4. Forces beyond anyone's control can be tamed by the will of X.
5. X can work through proxies and agents to exert its will. The agents and proxies are anointed by X.
6. X requires sacrifice, whether in tithes (taxes) or submission to its will.
7. Such sacrifices to X are rewarded tenfold by X, because X has infinite resources.
8. People organize and evangelize to their fellow men in order to convert them to belief in X.
9. Raids and crusades have been justified in the name of X, particularly during times of crisis.

10. X is personified in the form of a messiah (at least in the year 2008).

But there's a problem. Madison reminded us over 200 years ago that men are no angels. Government is neither omniscient nor omnipotent.

Market Failure and Deus Ex Machina

One of the grand old canards of government as God is the idea of 'market failure.' It's rather a catch-all term. Market failure can refer to some individual instance in which voluntary exchanges are said to bring about some unwanted social byproduct. Other times there are just problems "the market" can't solve. The term can also refer to the very idea that voluntary exchanges result in inequality. Whatever the intended sense, adherents to the idea of market failure usually conclude that government, by dint of largesse and power, can correct for these failures. And it's from this idea that so many of government's faith-based initiatives originate.

Market failure becomes the diagnosis for virtually everything. While some such diagnoses may be correct, the antidote of government may be "naïve and inappropriate," according to Nobel Laureate Gary Becker.

> The reason is that actual governments do not necessarily do what economists and others want them to do because there is "government failure" as well as market failure. Before recommending government actions to correct market failures, one should consider whether actual government policies would worsen rather than improve private sector outcomes. Since many factors often make for considerable government failure, considering such failure is crucial and not just a theoretical fine point.[86]

Becker points to failures such as Fannie Mae and Freddie Mac—"government-sponsored enterprises" (GSEs) designed to get more people into home mortgages, especially poor people.

What has happened since is now all too familiar. These behemoths enjoy lavish profits in the boom times, but when things go wrong (like a cascade of mortgage defaults), the losses get socialized. As of this writing, the GSEs have been hooked to the taxpayer I.V. since the mortgage crisis of 2008—a crisis Freddie and Fannie had a very big hand in creating (in collusion with their "government sponsors"). The result has been that the road to home ownership, while paved with good intentions, ended up where most good intentions do.

So I'll do Professor Becker one better. Whenever the government gets away from basics—police, roads, and justice—governments almost always fail. Here's why, according to F. S. McChesney and W. F. Shughart II:

> Homo politicus and homo economicus are the same. The critical implication of this assumption of universal self-interest is that the observed differences between public choices and private choices emerge not because individuals adopt different behavioral objectives in the two settings, but rather because the constraints on behavior are different. Different outcomes emerge not because public choices are guided by motives different from those guiding private choices, but rather because in private markets self-interested voters and politicians make choices that mainly affect themselves, while in political markets self-interested voters and politicians make choices that mainly affect others.[87]

If McChesney and Shughart are correct, government is bound to fail. Government, down to the system level, is one big "principle-agent" problem. In other words, there ain't no such thing as "the public benefit." There are only special interests, constituent groups, politicians, and bureaucrats. All of these groups have something in common: the benefit they receive from government spending other people's money.

Milton Friedman wisely reminded us that:

> There are four ways in which you can spend money. You can spend your own money on yourself. When you do that, why then you really watch out what you're doing, and you try to get the most for your money. Then you can spend your own money on somebody else. For example, I buy a birthday present for someone. Well, then I'm not so careful about the content of the present, but I'm very careful about the cost. Then, I can spend somebody else's money on myself. And if I spend somebody else's money on myself, then I'm sure going to have a good lunch! Finally, I can spend somebody else's money on somebody else. And if I spend somebody else's money on somebody else, I'm not concerned about how much it is, and I'm not concerned about what I get. And that's government. And that's close to 40% of our national income.

The more government spends money in that latter category, the more difficult it is for the beneficiaries of such spending to stop craving it. Federal dollars are like crack to the body politic, and they are certainly addictive to the dependent class.

Democracy

Another golden calf of government worship is faith in democracy. I know, I know, voting is the only game in town. But when we really start to scrutinize the system, many of us would see just how much faith we put into this majority-rule business.

"Democracy is another way to allocate resources," writes Carnegie Mellon economist Allen Meltzer. "Generally, those who succeed in the marketplace favor allocation by markets, not governments. Those who do not succeed favor government redistribution, joined by those who dislike capitalism or prefer collectively mandated 'social justice' over market efficiency. Actual social outcomes are a compromise between the two."[88] So what's wrong with that compromise?

The great political economist Gordon Tullock says democracy is overrated. "It's said you're more likely to get in a car crash on the way to the polling place," Tullock says, "than to affect the outcome."[89] Presumably, the point of voting is to change things you don't like or to make the world a better place by electing the "right" people, but the likelihood that your vote will affect the outcome of an election is vanishingly small.

Consider that it takes about 3,633,600 drops of water to fill a 40-gallon bathtub (90,840 drops per gallon). Considering that 122,394,724 people voted in the 2008 election, your vote is like a single drop in 33 bathtubs. What are the odds that your drop will fill the thirty-third tub?[i]

And yet democracy is the only game in town. Now that constitutions don't seem to be worth the parchment they are scribbled on, suffrage has become the secular religion. It's as if we've got a system that depends pretty much on getting a whole lot of people to do something irrational—at least from the standpoint of effecting change. It's a hive's rationality, perhaps. You have to be willing to waste your time for the "greater good." Just as the absence of a single worker ant won't make or break the construction of the mound, there is a point at which the colony would suffer without the contri-

---

i   This is more or less for a presidential election in the United States. Your odds improve by degree for your congressman or local government officials. Ironically, people participate less in local elections.

butions of many acting in concert. I guess that offers some comfort to us as we go to the polls.

So how might we better rationalize democracy?

Well, we could expand our definition of the voting "preference function" to include:

1. Getting all puffed up with a feeling of civic participation.
2. Getting a free "I voted" sticker.
3. Getting to be involved, in some insignificant way, in the process of turning out a scoundrel.
4. Getting, in some sense, to "cheer for your team" or express yourself.
5. Knowing that your individually irrational behavior resulted in a positive outcome (provided your team wins and you don't become disillusioned soon after your team takes office).

Ain't democracy grand? Despite all this, your humble author will probably drag himself to the polls next election. Honestly, though, I'm not sure I can explain why.

VOTER PARADOXES

There are a number of voting paradoxes, but we'll credit the Marquis de Concordet and Kenneth Arrow. Irrational results follow from majority-rule voting. For example, imagine you're the owner of a small business. You need to make a decision about the business, so you decide to let your three top employees vote on the following three choices:

1. Hire more people, including more managers;
2. Keep the status quo; or
3. Lay off employees and managers.

Your CFO prefers 1 to 2 and 2 to 3. Your HR manager doesn't want to make any waves: He prefers choice 2 to either 1 or 3, although he prefers 3 to 1. The production manager doesn't care whether you hire or fire anybody. She prefers 3 to 1 and 1 to 2.

When the three vote between 1 and 2, they vote in favor of 1—to hire more—because the CFO and the production manager outvote the HR manager. When the three vote between 2 and 3, 2 wins. But when they vote on 1 and 3 a problem arises: 3 wins! But if 1 beats 2, and 2 beats 3, how can 3 beat 1? It's a perverse result when we consider people's actual ordered preferences.

The same problem applies in elections. Here's a hypothetical election with three candidates: Rand Paul, Michael Bloomberg, and Hilary Clinton.

Voter	First Preference	Second Preference	Third Preference
Voter 1	Rand Paul	Michael Bloomberg	Hilary Clinton
Voter 2	Michael Bloomberg	Hilary Clinton	Rand Paul
Voter 3	Hilary Clinton	Rand Paul	Michael Bloomberg

If Hilary Clinton is chosen the winner, it can be argued Michael Bloomberg ought to be president based on actual voter preference rankings—namely that two voters prefer Michael Bloomberg. Only one voter prefers Hilary Clinton to either of the others. Because our democracy doesn't include such preference rankings, we can get results that really don't track with a majority's actual desires.

CLUSTERING

But things get still worse for democracy. When you vote for a candidate, you're not really voting for one thing but a cluster of things. It's sort of like going to the supermarket and instead of filling the shopping cart with the items you want, you have to choose from among three pre-filled shopping carts. You get to take that cart if you're not outvoted; otherwise you have to take another pre-filled cart based on the preferences of others. Either way you'll pay for it.

Making matters worse, by the time you get home with your choice of cart (the contents of which aren't everything you wanted), you are probably going to get less of the things you chose at the store. This is because by the time you get home, the gremlins we'll call "special interests" have already switched out many of the items you liked in your chosen basket for items they want and you don't necessarily like. In other words, your preferences are further attenuated by the preferences of people who have a far more direct stake in what's in your cart. They lobby to get what they want. So it's not just that you can't pick out your own groceries, it's also that the cluster of groceries you thought you were getting is an illusion because politicians almost always compromise away their promises.

TYRANNY BY THE MANY

Paradoxes aside, let's suppose there is some magic about majority rule that manages more or less to capture people's preferences.

That leaves us with a deeper problem. Without sufficient checks on democracy, a majority can take advantage of a minority.

- Non-smokers outnumber smokers in a municipality. The town holds a referendum and votes to limit smoking in private establishments such as bars and restaurants. What's wrong with that? Bar and restaurant owners have property rights, which include a right to decide their own smoking policies. A restaurant or a bar is, after all, not public property.

- Less-productive voters outnumber more-productive voters. They decide the more-productive citizens should subsidize their less-productive lifestyles. They raise taxes on the more-productive voters and redistribute the proceeds among themselves. The trouble is, the more-productive voters claim certain rights and don't want to be treated as being subject to the whim of the majority.

- A majority of people with fair skin color decides through majority rule that they will have property rights over other people, namely people with darker complexions.

In each case, don't members of these minorities have rights? We might refer to these examples as instances of "diffuse benefits, concentrated costs." Economist and economic historian Lawrence Reed reminds us that "those democratic elements of our republic should be given their due. Elections are a political safety valve for dissident views, because ballots not bullets resolve disputes. But the saving grace of democracy is not that it ensures either good or limited government; it is nothing more than that the system allows for political change without violence—whether the change a majority favors is right or wrong, good or evil."[90]

Tyranny by the Few

While the minority is getting screwed under representative democracy, the majority often gets screwed, too. Political scientist Mancur Olson figured out the problem of concentrated benefits, dispersed costs; that is, small interest groups are nimble, vocal constituencies with direct interests in the outcome of this legislation or that (our grocery gremlins again). The rest of us stand to lose fractions on the dollar, pound, kroner, or yen, so we have comparatively less incentive to advocate vociferously for this bill or that, much less pay attention to whether or not it's on the House or Senate floor. In such a case we get "concentrated benefits, dispersed costs." But all these dispersed costs add up over time in the form of higher prices, higher taxes, and general economic malaise. Most of what Congress doles out, after all, creates no economic value per dollar spent—except, of course, to special interests who almost always win.

"There is nothing sacrosanct about majority rule," economist Walter Williams says in an archived video conversation with James Buchanan (which I poached from Bob Chitester's Idea Channel archives). It can be a form of tyranny, after all, and the tyranny is compounded when moneyed interests are involved. When the state and business get in bed together, citizens lose. Democracy becomes but a shroud of sanctimony that obscures the loss of freedom and prosperity. And, of course, this state of affairs makes it more and more difficult to tell the difference between the rich parasites and real entrepreneurs.

Faith-based Initiatives

Faith in politicians and government bureaucrats is bad enough, but it gets worse when that faith replaces the trust bonds we have in each other. Mencken puts it best:

> What is any political campaign save a concerted effort to turn out a set of politicians who are admittedly bad and put in a set who are thought to be better? The former assumption, I believe is always sound; the latter is just as certainly false. For if experience teaches us anything at all it teaches us this: that a good politician, under democracy, is quite as unthinkable as an honest burglar.[91]

We place too much faith in experts, too, as we'll see. As we'll discuss later, the intellectuals in the media and in academia act as a kind of priest class for the church of state. The university system has all the trappings of a cloister, and the media act as a fifth column.

MARKET FUNDAMENTALISM

Without a trace of irony, those who see government as God often refer to those committed to free enterprise as "market fundamentalists." The implication is that faith in market processes is like faith in six-day creation, nothing deeper. As popular as the barb has become in the titter-factories of the leftish blogosphere, it misses the marrow. It's not that advocates of free enterprise don't believe in "market failure." Indeed, far from being dogmatic about the power of markets to solve every problem under the sun, it's that we're skeptical about government power to solve any such problem. Prior to that, we start by asking, "What did the market fail at?" If we can agree on X and on the criteria for the success or failure of X, we want to then talk about alternative means—particularly those that involve the Rube Goldberg apparatus of state bureaucracy.

Free-market types know that because perverse incentives, power brokering, and principal-agent problems are a given when it comes to any state action, government failure at X is almost a foregone conclusion, particularly when it comes to matters of economics. What can we say about the wisdom of a cadre of elites whose political interests are almost never aligned with the "public interest?" Mencken is funny, but he ain't that funny.

When reflecting on the rush to "stimulus" in the years after the 2008 financial crisis, I am reminded of a passage from *New Scientist* magazine:

> While many institutions collapsed during the Great Depression that began in 1929, one kind did rather well. During this leanest of times, the strictest, most authoritarian churches saw a surge in attendance.

> This anomaly was documented in the early 1970s, but only now is science beginning to tell us why. It turns out that human beings have a natural inclination for religious belief, especially during hard times. Our brains effortlessly conjure up an imaginary world of spirits, gods and monsters, and the more insecure we feel, the harder it is to resist the pull of this supernatural world. It seems that our minds are finely tuned to believe in gods.[92]

The author of the preceding might have asked some simple anthropological questions about the American church community in 1920. He might have found that people in hard times turn not just to God, but to each other, and they find each other at church. But assuming he's at least partially right there are modern analogs. For today, the phenomenon is largely the same only now people flock to the church of state. All those who would invest their faith and hope into a technocratic elite may find things continuing to worsen.

SCIENTISM

Politicians promise they'll "create" jobs; their political lives depend on it. They use the bully pulpit to propose "jobs" bills, which will include stimulus spending on anything from university studies to infrastructure. Journalists want to know what these bills will do, so they turn to economists.

These experts, armed with the most sophisticated methods available, give the journalists what they need. In turn, the journalists—armed with what they uncritically accepted as good information—return with coffee to their keyboards and report.

Here's an example:

> Mark Zandi, chief economist at Moody's Analytics, is frequently the go-to guy for both parties when it comes to analysis of various jobs proposals. So, what did he think of [the president's] speech last night? Here's the report: "The plan would add 2 percentage points to GDP growth next year, add 1.9 million jobs, and cut the unemployment rate by a percentage point."[93]

Who are the willing consumers of this information? People looking for reasons to be hopeful. People looking for certainty. Who can blame them? Times are tough.

But this sort of reporting is scientism on display. The great Friedrich Hayek, in his Nobel Prize speech, warns about scientism (which we might define simply as "physics envy"):

> It seems to me that this failure of the economists to guide policy more successfully is closely connected with their propensity to imitate as closely as possible the procedures of the brilliantly successful physical sciences—an attempt which in our field may lead to outright error. It is an approach which has come to be described as the "scientistic" attitude—an attitude which, as I defined it some thirty years ago, "is decid-

edly unscientific in the true sense of the word, since it involves a mechanical and uncritical application of habits of thought to fields different from those in which they have been formed."

I'm not alone in this line of thinking. Economist Russ Roberts, reacting to reporting in the *Financial Times*, writes: "Really? That's what they found? [The journalist] treats it like a discovery of fact. As in '[Alan] Blinder and Zandi weren't sure of the distance between the earth and the sun but when they measured it, they found it was about 93,000,000 miles.'"[94]

Roberts knows economists aren't capable of auguring such things because when it comes to national-level prediction and forecast, macroeconomics has all the reliability of a *Farmer's Almanac*. And that's being charitable.

CERTAINTY FOR SALE

Here's the problem: Economists such as Mark Zandi belong to a great power nexus that relies on scientism for its very existence. To repeat: People crave certainty and politicians crave power, so the latter have to provide the former with at least the illusion of certainty to stay in office. But they can't do it alone.

Economists—especially those who tend to get tapped by the media or by Washington elites—are the ones willing to strut around on the national stage showing their predictive plumage. Journalists, no experts themselves, report what they're told (and few try to spot the turkey behind all that peacocking).

A nexus of politicians, economists, journalists, special interests, and a desperate lay public can hardly be virtuous. This industry enables peddlers of scientism to hock their wares in a world full of uncertainty. Indeed, a pseudo-certainty creates the circumstances under which great wishes can father great lies.

Since Hayek's death, a growing movement of smart folks working across disciplines warns us to mind our wax wings.

CHAOS RULES

In 1961, Edward Lorenz discovered the "butterfly effect." Ironically, when he figured out that tiny changes in initial conditions could mean seismic shifts in the rest of a system, he was studying weather and climate. I won't discuss the irony here. Suffice it to say Lorenz is the one who taught us that complex systems—whether the climate, an ecosystem, or an economy—can also be chaotic systems. "I realized," said Lorenz of his then-obscure finding, "that any physical system that behaved non-periodically would be unpredictable."

Although "chaotic" eludes strict definition, the term usually refers to a system that is sensitive to changes in initial conditions, shows order without regularity, and is immune to prediction and forecast.

In his still-vibrant *Chaos* (1989), James Gleick tells Lorenz's story, including the latter's discoveries and the implications of chaos. "Forecasts of economic growth or unemployment were put forward with an implied precision of two or three decimal places," Gleick writes. "Governments and financial institutions paid for such predictions and acted on them, perhaps out of necessity or for want of anything better. [...] But few realized how fragile was the very process of modeling flows on computers, even when the data [were] recognizably trustworthy and the laws were purely physical, as in weather forecasting."

Little has changed.

AGGREGATES, AGENTS, AND ANTS

I think the failure of macroeconomics can be boiled down to this: Macroeconomics deals primarily with aggregates, or macro-level trends. But to be truly accurate the macro level would have to be explained in terms of the micro—that is, individual agent behavior. Micro behaviors give rise to macro trends. Another way of putting this is that macro trends are dependent on micro behaviors. The trouble is, individual agents interact with, and react to, one another in diverse, complicated ways.

Similarly, it's impossible to predict exactly what an ant colony will do when confronted with two picnics at equal distances from the colony. In that famous experiment we might be able to predict a single ant's behavior if we have lots of local information about its pheromone-secretion algorithms and such. However, relative to each food source it would be impossible to predict the behavior of the colony as a whole. Such is life at the edge of chaos.

A BLIND SPOT

Now of course we have processors that can crunch tons of data. We have a new breed of mathematical wizards in the tradition of Paul Samuelson who can write whole tracts with as many equations as words. And we have whole new constituencies of politicians, pundits, and people ready to believe them. So are we finally living in a time when macroeconomics can tell us all we need to know about unemployment in a year, just as Newtonian mechanics tells us when Halley's Comet will arrive?

Alas no, says mathematician William Byers. In his excellent *The*

Blind Spot, Byers makes an audacious argument for humility in the sciences—both hard and human: "Human beings have a basic need for certainty. Yet since things are ultimately uncertain, we satisfy this need by creating artificial islands of certainty. We create models of reality and then insist that the models are reality. It is not that science, mathematics, and statistics do not provide useful information about the real world. The problem lies in making excessive claims for the validity of these methods and models and believing them to be absolutely certain."

Interestingly, Byers also picks up on the idea of selling certainty. Whether he's talking about the complicated financial instruments that obscured the problems leading to the financial meltdown or the schematics for all the Keynesian fixes that followed, models are the conduits of pseudo-certainty. "The more complex the package and the more arcane the mathematics, the better," Byers says. "What was being sold was the faith that the complex, human, world of economics and finance could be made over in the image of science, could be made objective and predictable."

Byers goes on to explain that there is a kind of quantification bias at work. That is, if you can describe things in mathematics, you are in some sense speaking the language of nature. But drawing the world in numbers has its limits, especially since so many of the important aspects of science are subjective and so many aspects of nature are, well, uncertain. Numbers, Byers argues, are our attempt to create the illusion of objectivity where objectivity is thought to be the very stuff of certainty. But "science does great damage when it turns into ideology, when it begins to worship certainty."

HERETICAL THOUGHTS ABOUT SOCIAL SCIENCE

Eminent physicist Freeman Dyson is no market fundamentalist, but his call for humility in science extends to economics, too:

> The politicians and the public expect science to provide answers to the problems. Scientific experts are paid and encouraged to provide answers. The public does not have much use for a scientist who says, "Sorry, but we don't know." The public prefers to listen to scientists who give confident answers to questions and make confident predictions of what will happen as a result of human activities. So it happens that the experts who talk publicly about politically contentious questions tend to speak more clearly than they think. They make confident predictions about the future, and end up believing their own predictions. Their predictions become dogmas which they do not question. The public is led to believe that the fashionable scientific dogmas are true, and it may sometimes happen that they are wrong. That is why heretics who question the dogmas are needed.[95]

So if Dyson is right about the need for heretics, are those skeptical of macroeconomics heretics or "market fundamentalists?"

People who understand markets know they can't do everything under the sun. Yes, markets can and do work wonders. But most truly liberal thinkers start with a particular kind of skepticism:

- Knowledge is dispersed, not centralized. Planning or tweaking by central authorities is a fool's errand and results in perverse effects. (Skepticism of grand designs.)
- Centralized power tends to corrupt people. Coalitions of interests, bureaucrats, and moralists form to transfer resources from the masses or from competitors to the pockets of coalition members. (Skepticism of power wielded for the "public good.")

- Value is not objective but rather subjective. This not only makes market exchanges possible, but makes it difficult for any central authority to claim it is operating in the name of a universal good. (Skepticism of claims to objective value.)

I could go on but the long and short is this: To be a market liberal is to be a heretic, and for heretics skepticism is a prime virtue. Yes, we tend to admire the market process but unlike those who prostrate themselves before the golden calf of aggregate demand or government as God, we are skeptics first and foremost.

SOOTHSAYERS AND CHARLATANS

When it comes to heresy in economics, Arnold Kling comes to mind. Writing in *The American*, the economist says: "I think that if the press were aware of the intellectual history and lack of scientific standing of the models, it would cease rounding up these usual suspects. Macroeconometrics stands discredited among mainstream academic economists. Applying macroeconometric models to questions of fiscal policy is the equivalent of using pre-Copernican astronomy to launch a satellite or using bleeding to treat an infection."[96] Damn!

Kling says economists should be more honest about their limitations. He thinks the Congressional Budget Office, with all its scoring, can do little to predict the effects of various policy scenarios, such as taxing and spending: "The CBO adds value to policymakers by 'scoring' the impact of policies on the budget. However, the 'scoring' of policies in terms of GDP growth or jobs saved is of no value. The CBO should simply refuse to do it, and the consulting firms that purport to provide such estimates should be regarded as the charlatans they are."

The great expert on experts Phillip Tetlock agrees. In his 2005 book *Expert Political Judgment*, Tetlock writes:

> [N]o matter how unequivocal the evidence that experts cannot outpredict chimps or extrapolation algorithms, we should expect business to unfold as usual: pundits will continue to warn us on talk shows and op-ed pages of what will happen unless we dutifully follow their policy prescriptions. We—the consumers of expert pronouncements—are in thrall to experts for the same reasons that our ancestors submitted to shamans and oracles: our uncontrollable need to believe in a controllable world and our flawed understanding of the laws of chance. We lack the willpower and good sense to resist the snake oil products on offer. Who wants to believe that, on the big questions, we could do as well tossing a coin as by consulting accredited experts?[97]

When the shaman of the pundit classes (experts) and the priests of intellectual class (ideologues) serve the high priests in the legislature (politicians) in the great church of state, the people have something to believe in.

Though the methods used by these macroeconomists are no more reliable than "soothsaying or entrail reading," they belong to that great nexus of power, which creates incentives for folks to step right up for more of the same elixir.

Sadly, there is no competing power nexus and yet people are growing increasingly suspicious of these nostra. Just as Americans have grown weary of intervention in foreign affairs, they're growing weary of intervention in the economy, too. Call it what you like—stimulus bills, jobs plans, back-to-work schemes, or whatever—fiscal interventionism is not producing the desired effect and people are getting wise to it. In the old days they ran the charlatans out of town.[ii]

PLANNING FOR UTOPIA

When it comes to the subject of inequality, those who believe the state is all-knowing and all-powerful believe that the state can redesign society. We might call this a fallacy of "intelligent design." The whole idea of fixing an economy or building a Utopia rests on the idea that if the right smart guys are at the buttons, the economy can be ordered by people. But there are no buttons. There are no controls. Neither central bankers nor government bureaucrats can fly in like a *deus ex machina* to correct things. Why? Because knowledge, Hayek reminds us, is not concentrated among a few technocrats, it is dispersed among billions of people. Society is too complex to be designed. It is dynamic and inequality is a feature of dynamism.

Of course those looking for a more equal world might argue that reducing inequality doesn't mean we need to have central planning, make-work programs, or experts to justify it all. Reducing inequality requires only taxation and redistribution. Suppose we granted that, as well as the assumption that such policies have few perverse effects and that capitals can be staffed with white knights. We then have to return to those core questions of value, right, and wrong. They're always there.

---

ii   Part of this chapter was used in *The Freeman* magazine, in an article titled "Scientism and the Great Power Nexus."

I'm reminded of Plato's *Euthyphro* in which Socrates asks Euthyphro, "Is the pious loved by the gods because it is pious, or is it pious because it is loved by the gods?"[98] To restate the question in our weary analogy: Is forced redistribution (theft) justified because the state does it, or does the state redistribute (steal) because it is justified?

10

THE INTELLECTUALS

The fight is being waged on all fronts, and the most insidious idea employed to break down society is an undefined equalitarianism. [...] Such equalitarianism is harmful because it always presents itself as a redress of injustice, whereas in truth it is the very opposite. I would mention here the fact, obvious to any candid observer, that "equality" is found most often in the mouths of those engaged in artful self-promotion.

– Richard Weaver, from Ideas Have Consequences

The first thing a man will do for his ideals is lie.

– Joseph Schumpeter

About ten minutes away from our apartment here in Austin, professor Daniel Hamermesh keeps an office at The University of Texas. Hamermesh found fame recently in a Warhol sort of way when he suggested that attractive people have advantages over ugly people, so deserve to be a protected class.

Does he have a point? Shouldn't the fruits of good looks be redistributed among the less attractive? Looks (good or bad) are arbitrary. Here's Hamermesh writing in *The New York Times*:

Ugliness could be protected generally in the United States by small extensions of the Americans With Disabilities Act. Ugly people could be allowed to seek help from the Equal Employment Opportunity Commission and other agencies in overcoming the effects of discrimination. We could even have affirmative-action programs for the ugly.[99]

Hamermesh's fifteen minutes was magnified by his appearance on Comedy Central's *The Daily Show.* Correspondent Jason Jones had fun discussing "uglo-Americans." Jones walked around with Hamermesh on UT's campus rating co-eds on a scale of one to five. What was so funny about this segment? A lot. But somehow the funniest thing was that Hamermesh took his idea very seriously. One's looks, after all, are something you win in the "natural lottery." You don't do any work to be cute and sexy. Why do you deserve all that your cuteness and sexiness yields?

I used to use the example of looks to expose the absurdity of wealth redistribution. "[P]eople use their natural endowments to gain advantages in individual acts of consensual exchange in both dating and trading," I wrote in 2010. "Such results in natural inequality in the distribution of sex and money. The distribution is such that ugly people normally get dates with other ugly people if they get dates at all. Sexy people get dates with sexier people—and more of them. I think we can agree that it would be wrong to suggest 'redistribution' based on any abstractions like the *distribution of dates among the sexy and the ugly.* So why is this different for other outcomes of consensual exchange?" I guess I was too clever by half. Leave it to the intellectuals to double down on any absurdities you might expose.

The point here is not so much to join *The Daily Show* in poking fun at Daniel Hamermesh. He is only a tiny plot point in a pointillist's painting—one among millions of intellectuals eager to justify taking the earnings of the successful. It's perhaps unfair of me to frontload one of the stranger proposals but as we'll see, the idea that natural attributes are arbitrary keeps resurfacing. Once we explore reasons why so many intellectuals have these left-authoritarian leanings, we will return to some of the redistributionist ideas that have actually gained some traction (or at least, didn't end up on Comedy Central).

INTELLECTUALS AND REDISTRIBUTION

If academia is a purgatory of strange ideas about redistributing wealth, it should invite us to ask: Why do so many intellectuals advocate redistribution? A lot of really smart people support the idea. There are so many, in fact, that if you're half-way intelligent and you don't support soaking the rich you might start to gaze at your navel. *How could such smart people be in the grip of groupthink? Could people like me who don't support redistribution be missing something? Are smarter people morally enlightened in ways the rest of us are not?*

When it comes to asking why most intellectuals are socialists of some stripe, there are a few giants on whose shoulders we can stand. That is, even though they are in a minority, some scorching non-socialist intellectuals have asked similar questions about the connection between smarts and socialism. Their answers are fascinating.

Before exploring their theories, I admit that I don't think matters are simple. Any of the following hypotheses could be partially correct and work in combination with the others. I wish I could offer a single, sweeping thesis—such as this one:

A pair of sociologists think they may have an answer: typecasting. Conjure up the classic image of a humanities or social sciences professor, the fields where the imbalance is greatest: tweed jacket, pipe, nerdy, longwinded, secular—and liberal. Even though that may be an outdated stereotype, it influences younger people's ideas about what they want to be when they grow up.[100]

Perhaps, but let's see what else we can see.

SECONDHAND DEALERS IN IDEAS

The great F.A. Hayek was one of the most important thinkers to discuss "the intellectuals and socialism". And in the famous 1947 article of the same name, Hayek observed:

> In the light of recent history it is somewhat curious that this decisive power of the professional secondhand dealers in ideas should not yet be more generally recognized. The political development of the Western World during the last hundred years furnishes the clearest demonstration. Socialism has never and nowhere been at first a working-class movement. It is by no means an obvious remedy for the obvious evil which the interests of that class will necessarily demand. It is a construction of theorists, deriving from certain tendencies of abstract thought with which for a long time only the intellectuals were familiar; and it required long efforts by the intellectuals before the working classes could be persuaded to adopt it as their program.[101]

When Hayek refers to "recent history," he no doubt means the National Socialism of Germany, Stalinist Russia, Fascism in Italy, the U.S.'s New Deal, and the then-rising Fabian Socialism of postwar Britain—the latter of which Hayek saw firsthand as he wrote. Intellectuals around the world were dazzled by redistribution and planning at that time. Hayek commented that "intelligent people will tend to overvalue intelligence." This was not a casual observation for the Austrian; this was the intellectuals' "fatal conceit," which would lead them (erringly, he thought) to conclude that societies and economies were things that could and should be designed, planned, and implemented by intellectual elites. After the horrors of the early 20th century, Hayek thought a little humility was in order.

The intellectuals ignored Hayek and their enchantment with redistribution persisted for forty more years. But then something happened: The Berlin Wall fell. Communist dictatorships in Eastern Europe toppled like dominoes. The Soviet Union broke apart. It should have proved once and for all that socialist ideals were not sustainable if they were realizable at all. Reality had finally answered the intellectuals but their academic papers, their tenured professorships, and their very identities were bound up in those failed theories.

Authoritarian socialism might be disproved by history but to accept market capitalism was beyond the pale. Instead of abandoning socialism, they concluded it needed tweaking and rebranding. So for the next twenty years the intellectuals set out to tweak and rebrand. Phrases like "social justice," "distributive justice," and "progressivism" found new life. Some intellectuals flocked to the environmental movement, which gave central planning a green veneer. Others sought to develop milder forms of socialism that would, unlike communism, preserve the geese that lay the golden eggs—but take every second egg for the state. Indeed, many held up Scandinavian models of democratic socialism, which tosses much of the central planning but preserves redistribution. The academics moved their trenches and regrouped around ideas that tempered, hid, or ignored the brutality of purer socialisms past. In their place, they would erect massive welfare states. European welfare statism would become the new morality of the academic priest class. It still is.

Centralized Meritocracy

Before his death in 2002, Harvard philosopher Robert Nozick wrote: "Not all intellectuals are on the 'left.' Like other groups, their opinions are spread along a curve. But in their case, the curve is shifted and skewed to the political left." Boy, Nozick wasn't kidding.

In a comprehensive study of California universities in 2006, Christopher Cardiff and Daniel Klein found that Democrats outnumber Republicans five to one among faculty.[102] But Nozick didn't want to overstate the case: "By intellectuals, I do not mean all people of intelligence or of a certain level of education, but those who, in their vocation, deal with ideas as expressed in words, shaping the word flow others receive. [...] The wordsmiths are concentrated in certain occupational sites: academia, the media, government bureaucracy."[103] Nozick, a libertarian, was rare among his colleagues in the humanities.

Few question the observation that academia, media, and government are dominated by the left, but Nozick wanted to know why. This was the crux of his hypothesis:

> In an open capitalist society, the pupils are not resigned early to limits on their advancement and social mobility, the society seems to announce that the most capable and valuable will rise to the very top, their schools have already given the academically most gifted the message that they are most valuable and deserving of the greatest rewards, and later these very pupils with the highest encouragement and hopes see others of their peers, whom they know and saw to be less meritorious, rising higher than they themselves, taking the foremost rewards to which they themselves felt themselves entitled. Is it any wonder they bear that society an animus?[104]

In other words, the smart liberal arts kids were rewarded with praise and grades until they got to the job market. Once there, they are often consigned to coffee-shop limbo and saddled with thousands of dollars in federally subsidized student loan debt. (Only a select few would ever make it into the ivy halls, the newsrooms, or into Washington's marbled rotunda.)

Either way, once they finished their degrees, they saw C-students who had gone to B-schools end up making six-figure salaries. Philosopher Edward Feser points out wryly that those in the academy realized that if "P. Diddy's album sells millions of copies and Prof. Doody's magisterial five-volume history of Liechtenstein sells precisely 106 copies, Prof. Doody begins to wonder whether a free market is the fairest way of distributing economic rewards."[105]

Our public education system creates a centralized meritocracy whose closest approximation after graduation is higher education. But markets are a de-centralized meritocracy—if they're a meritocracy at all. That is, people out in the real world reward each other for giving them things they want or need. That's very different from the Skinnerian reward structure of our education system. I'm not alone in this observation. In *The Secret Knowledge*, playwright David Mamet describes the system as only he can:

> "George Washington, Father of our country—have a pellet of food [...] Thomas Jefferson, third President, but owned slaves and kept a mistress—have an appointment as a graduate instructor." Light comes on, pull lever, get the pellet of food. This is fine for the rat, for the rat lives in the lab. In the wider world, however, the path to food is more demanding and its signals cannot be learned inside the lab.

The wider world is tough on the ill-prepared liberal arts kid. So that world becomes an object of scorn.

People working in a marketplace have to learn to be *other-centered*. If you don't figure out how to serve others better, you won't be successful. Meanwhile "higher education is selling an illusion" continues Mamet, "that the child of the well-to-do need not matriculate into the workforce—that mastery of fungible skill is unnecessary."

By contrast, intellectuals who remain in the guild are protected by it. They need not be particularly other-centered, however. Higher education is notorious for backbiting and politics. Students don't pay professors for good teaching, either; they pay the institution for an expensive signaling mechanism (and parties). The often incestuous publish-or-perish system that paves the way to tenure can end up rewarding bad teaching.

Intellectuals who purport to be compassionate and socially conscious often use the lowest-cost ways to signal their altruism—that is by writing about it, talking about it, or voting. Rarely do they live their rectitude, say, by volunteering or giving more to charity (or the IRS). What better way to engage in moralistic peacocking than to trot out a Marxist pony in the lecture hall? What better way to puff yourself up on rectitude than to pen an op-ed about inequality in *The Los Angeles Times*?

But when it comes to paychecks and pensions, the intellectuals are as selfish as the next guy. Lillian Taiz, president of the California Faculty Association, the union that represents professors in that state's bloated university system, refuses to budge on budget cuts in that bankrupt state. "These are institutions that we call the people's university," Taiz said at a University of California, Davis campus demonstration, "but all of us who are in it have just watched this thing collapse on itself, being starved for resources year after year."

Starved of resources? The average salary for an associate professor in the University of California system in 2008 was $80,177. For a full professor? A whopping $114,287.[106] As of 2012, the national average salary for a full professor was $197,800[107] and these figures don't include pensions and healthcare benefits. The hoary guild structure makes parasites out of smart people.

"So let us vote for higher taxes on business," writes Mamet in character, "although if we look around, California, with the highest taxes in the country, is broke, having taxed business away."

THEORIES ABOUND

Philosopher Edward Feser has a number of hypotheses for why the professoriate is dominated by the political left. I'd like to paraphrase a few of them:

1. *Survival of the Left-est*—Despite all the talk about diversity, universities tend to take on colleagues who are in broad agreement with themselves where matters of politics, morality, and culture are concerned. Since professors tend to be left-of-center, those noticeably right-of-center will tend to get "selected out" when hiring and tenure decisions are made. This prompts the question, of course: How did the higher education come to be saturated with leftists to begin with?

2. *Philosopher Kings*—An enlightened elite ought to be running the show and running the show means redistributed resources in enlightened ways. If the great unwashed is allowed too much freedom, things won't be properly administered. "Experts in running human affairs ought to be found to direct their lives for them. The intellectual, fancying himself

to be just such an expert, selflessly volunteers to do the job." The intellectual is in the thrall of the idea that things would be better if everybody went along with the vision he and his peers have "hashed out over coffee in the faculty lounge."[108]

3. *Heads in the Clouds*—Many layfolk think the intellectual simply has his head in the clouds; the cottony confines of the ivory tower exist far way from the realities of the real world. A little common sense would do the intellectuals good, but since most of their ideas are contrary to common sense it's no surprise intellectuals are drawn to them. It's fashionable for an intellectual to define himself against common sense. Of course, common sense is not always correct, but the intellectual takes absurdity and calls it nuance. Perhaps this theory of the intellectual finds no greater support than in the intellectual's reliance on the theoretical model, which is conveniently immune to facts and feedback from the real world.

4. *Everyone Ought to Live Like This*—Despite intellectualized envy directed at businesspeople and professionals, academics live rather comfortably and may feel a little guilty about that. "He may teach two or three courses a semester, come in to work only three days a week, and have summers off," Feser writes. Not to mention he has grad students in his thrall. "If he's got tenure, he's got it made: good health care and other benefits, the occasional sabbatical, and job security for life." It makes sense that if taxes were raised high enough and regulations were introduced, everyone else could live that way, too. The intellectual fails to realize that

the "specific economic forces that make his cozy lifestyle possible are isolated, highly idiosyncratic, and artificial; parasitic upon a larger economic order."

5. *Interest Group*—Under this theory, the intellectuals are little more than yet another special-interest group "struggling alongside the other herd animals of the welfare state for access to the governmental teat." Being more articulate, and thus more effective than the others at nosing aside the competition, they masterfully mask (or rationalize) their true motive, which is to belly up to the trough. Thus "it presents itself as a new priesthood, whose socialistic religion offers the state a justification for its existence in return for permanent employment in the state's propaganda factories—'public' schools and universities—and the opportunity to create the plans the state's officials will implement, fresh off the intellectuals' drawing board." Feser warns this explanation can be taken too far and devolve into ad hominem. Yet it has its merits.

But let us not pick on just the professoriate. There are other areas in which intellectuals heavily favor redistribution.

IN-GROUPS, OUT-GROUPS AND TRIBES

John Tierney, one of the few non-leftist columnists for *The New York Times*, recounts a talk given by social psychologist Dr. Jonathan Haidt who spoke about ideological diversity at a 2011 psychology conference in San Antonio. Haidt polled the audience at the convention center there, asking how many of his colleagues considered themselves politically liberal.

"A sea of hands appeared," Tierney writes, "and Dr. Haidt estimated that liberals made up 80 percent of the 1,000 psychologists in the ballroom."[109] When Haidt asked for centrists and libertarians, he got fewer than three dozen hands. Conservatives? A grand total of three.

"This is a statistically impossible lack of diversity," Dr. Haidt concluded, noting polls showing that 40 percent of Americans are conservative and 20 percent are liberal. In his speech and in an interview, Dr. Haidt argued that social psychologists are a "tribal-moral community" united by "sacred values" that hinder research and damage their credibility—and blind them to the hostile climate they've created for non-liberals.

The idea of a tribal-moral community is not entirely new. Anthropologists and sociologists have gone very far in unpacking the idea of group identification and tribes. Social identity, according to British social psychologist Henri Tajfel, is a person's sense of who they are based on their membership in a group. Tajfel thought identification with a group is an important source of pride and self-esteem. Tajfel performed a series of experiments in the 1970s on teenage boys, the results of which supported his theory.[110]

Whether it's where you're from, your favorite team, or your nationality, groups can give us a sense of social identity, of belonging to some social sphere. Sometimes people increase their sense of group identity through discriminating against those perceived as being in the "out-group." We thus divide people into "us" (Tajfel's in-group) and "them" (Tajfel's out-group). Social identity theory says people will discriminate against or negatively stereotype the out-group to enhance their self-image and sense of belonging to the in-group. A quick scan of the comments on the DailyKos.com or Big Government.com reinforces this idea.

It's no wonder, then, that intellectuals have coalesced around a certain set of ideas about redistribution. These mores are a part of their in-group categorization scheme and there are high costs associated with rejecting the mores of your in-group, including the self-esteemed one derives from it, not to mention a sense of belonging to the group. Peer pressure, it turns out, is a potent driver of opinion. People want to reduce the costs of membership once they see themselves as members of the tribe, and disagreement is one such cost. What better way to lubricate interaction within your group than to adopt the morality of the tribe? Such may or may not be a conscious process.[i]

So, can intellectuals look outside of their in-group? Can social scientists, like the ones at Haidt's conference in San Antonio, open up to outsiders' ideas? The answer is blowing in the wind. But if the ideas on redistribution coming out of the academy are any indication, I suspect the intelligencia will be trapped in their in-group for a long time to come.

HAPPYNOMICS

Again, there are all sorts of fashionable theories about redistribution floating around. One of the more modish ideas is called the economics of happiness, sometimes referred to as "happynomics."

The bones of philosopher Jeremy Bentham may be locked in a case at University College London, but Bentham's ghost is flying

---

i   While I think there is a very large genetic component to political orientation, genetics may give you a "first draft" of your dispositions. The rest is epigenetics. As NYU research psychologist Gary Marcus said: "The initial organization of the brain does not rely that much on experience. ... Nature provides a 'first draft,' which experience then revises. 'Built in' does not mean unmalleable; it means 'organized in advance of experience.' "

around universities and government buildings, animating nice people. Bentham is the fellow who, in the 1700s, set out the philosophy of "utilitarianism." That's the moral theory that basically says the "good" or the "moral" is whatever action or policy contributes to the greatest total happiness in society. Bentham thought you could devise a "hedonic calculus," a measure of aggregate happiness. It's no accident that some forms of welfare economics grew out of his idea. In fact, some consider Bentham to be a founder of modern economic science. People on both the left and right have used variations of utilitarianism since its full articulation in John Stuart Mill.

But be warned: Utilitarianism is a bankrupt idea.

The theory is full of problems, but the main problems are:

- It's impossible to measure happiness or well-being (despite lots of questionnaires);
- Happiness is fundamentally personal—that is, subjective;
- Attempting to aggregate happiness means thinking of "society" as having happiness;
- Policies derived from utilitarian thinking tend to ignore individual rights;
- It opens doors to those who claim to know how to make "society" happier, given power; and,
- Proponents usually jump to conclude that wealth redistribution satisfies the utility principle, whether or not the methodology works.

There are more, and putting new clothes on these problems doesn't change much. Happiness research and "happynomics" are pretty much just mainstream utilitarianism wrapped up in surveys and questionnaires. That's why we should be suspicious from the start.

UTILITARIANISM WARMED OVER

Take Kentaro Toyama's pitch for happynomics in *The Atlantic* magazine. In "The case for happiness-based economics," the Berkeley information scientist concludes:

> Building a public policy on the foundation of happiness research would be controversial, to say the least. Critics, especially on the right, might accuse Washington of using wishy-washy assumptions about money and happiness to guide our tax and welfare policy. To be sure, causal relationships between income and happiness are still not established, and we care about values beyond income equality. But, focusing on the logarithm of income might make us pay a little more attention to that third pursuit Thomas Jefferson hailed in the Declaration of Independence.[111]

Before doing anything else, we ought at least to defend Thomas Jefferson. The whole point of that "third pursuit" (the pursuit of happiness) is that it is a right to *pursue*, not to an outcome. Welfare economics and so-called "happiness-based" policies are not concerned with pursuits at all. In fact, the whole point of utilitarianism is that it is concerned with consequences—e.g., the measure of happiness in a population at some slice in time.

Similarly, redistributing wealth is about the goal of reducing wealth inequality. Jefferson meant something very different when he wrote the declaration, however. Jefferson wasn't concerned about whether or not you *became* happy or rich, but that you had the freedom to pursue happiness your own way. Jefferson sought basic rules that respect diverse means to achieving diverse ends. I don't know which is more troubling: confusion about the term "pursuit of happiness" or conflation of the phrase "all men are created equal" with worries about income.

Eudaimonia

Utilitarians like Toyama rarely bother to ask the eudaimonaic questions, such as: Would one be happier working toward income or being the passive recipient of it? Is there any dignity on the dole? What about having wealth makes people happy: having it, earning it, or both?

Don't be afraid of the fancy Greek word. Aristotle described a form of happiness that comes from living a purposeful, contemplative life. Happiness researchers would do well to look back at his work, as well as the positive psychology of Mihaly Csikszentmihalyi, who has modernized the idea of happiness-in-pursuit.

If you think I'm being unfair to Toyama, consider this passage:

> [Recent happiness research] also emphasizes something that most economists are less eager to discuss. Central to Stevenson and Wolfers' analysis is the use of a logarithmic scale to relate happiness to income. What correlates with a fixed increment of happiness is not a dollar increase in absolute income (e.g., an additional $1,000), but a percentage increment (e.g., an additional 100%). So, going from a $5,000 annual income to $50,000 links with as much additional happiness as going from $50K to $500K, or from $500K to $5 million, or even from $5 million to $50 million.[112]

What in blazes does a "logarithmic scale" tell us about the happiness of an individual living a purposeful life? About the joy of making one's own way? About individual incentives, or those incentives created by the institutions around us? About the trade-offs we have to make to increase well-being when living among family and neighbors making similar trade-offs? A logarithmic scale tells us nothing meaningful about these questions and neither does the research to which Toyama appeals. It is the granularity and peculiarity of context that will forever elude happiness researchers, but in which real answers about happiness are found.

But here's the passage that really shows Toyama's redistributionist bent:

> Still, if policy makers were serious about utility, they could take the logarithm of personal wealth and sum over all citizens for an estimate of national welfare. Though this would overlook other components of well-being, it would immediately focus more attention on *income inequality*: Ten people each earning $100,000 would have much greater total happiness than nine people earning $10,000 and one person with $910,000, even though each group earns the same $1 million. [Emphasis mine.][113]

That is Toyama's punch line: *Happiness is wealth redistribution.*

How does he know these folks would be happier? What does he mean by "earn?" Does he consider that stewardship might be an important factor in maintaining wealth, as these kinds of lottery stories suggest? A connection between assets and happiness can't be made simply by juxtaposing them. Again, the circumstances of arriving at your wealth are key factors in explaining happiness.

Utilitarians are far too busy deriving grand pronouncements from statistical abstractions, a problem which crops up again and again among the intellectuals. It appears they're also too busy worrying *what* group has *what* assets while trying to connect that information with something that is fundamentally personal. By simplifying things this way, happiness researchers are able to use the so-called "gap" between rich and poor as an instrument with which to beat up the rich.

The trouble is the rich are usually productive. Productivity is the key determinant of economic growth, which increases well-being on a number of dimensions. If you tax productivity and reward less work, you're likely to get what you pay for. No matter: circumstances of time and place are irrelevant to most intellectuals. Unintended consequences, far from being indicators of a bad theory, are at worst setbacks wise elites can legislate away at some point.

SALARY AND HAPPINESS

Toyama ain't done yet. He finds an "ah ha" moment in a study of income:

> To put it another way, as income rises, every additional dollar represents a smaller increment of happiness. At one level, this is perfectly obvious. The first increase of $45K—from $5K to $50K—would take a family from hunger and homelessness to being well-fed in an apartment, probably with a TV to boot. An additional $45K of income to $95K might allow for a few luxuries, but certainly nothing close to the difference between starvation and the middle class![114]

Fine, it's probably easier to be happy if you can afford to eat and have a roof. This intuition resonates with affluent readers of *The Atlantic* who imagine how unhappy they'd be suddenly making $17,000 per year, so we really didn't need a logarithmic scale to prove that intuition (though it's not clear that there aren't meaningful counterexamples).

Perhaps we can also agree that income above $45,000 may only make us marginally happier compared with going from starving to middle class. Most people have a lower bound and upper bound for happiness that's considered a natural range, which has to do with biological conditions like levels of neurotransmitter in the brain. These are insights of brain sciences more than of economics, so if our political leaders really wanted to be utilitarian, they might just put Prozac in the water supply and not worry about inequality at all. But we recoil at that brave new thought because we know that at some level our emotions connect up with our circumstances and, I dare say, with our pursuits.

So, the fundamental point is even if someone really does become happier when they go from, say, $50,000 to $500,000, and that happiness is sustained over one's lifetime (doubtful), the income boost tells us little about why they became happier. In other words, it's quite possible these individuals became happier because of their journey, not just their destination.

Remember, much of this happiness data comes from surveys. Did someone in the sample of people filling out Stevenson and Wolfers' bubble sheets leave a boring desk job to work on a successful business? Did one go back to college to learn a trade that paid more and made them more fulfilled? Is someone finding a sense of purpose in the work that yields more income? Did they find joy in the opportunity to give away much of the wealth they acquired? Or did they simply win the lottery? In short: Why are these people happier? Correction: Why is each individual happier? The wonks can't tell us because, as Toyama admits, the "causal relationships between income and happiness are still not established."

And they never will be.

Income's diminishing marginal utility has nothing to tell us about the mechanisms by which people might most effectively and sustainably get from $0 to $45,000. That is, there are functional aspects to wealth creation and upward mobility that have little to do with happiness *per se*. These functional aspects have a lot to do with why redistributionist policies fail. Consider, for example, that welfare economists have been behind foreign aid efforts—that is, redistribution from rich countries to poor ones—in Africa for more than 50 years. It's not clear it's done very much good. Some would argue it's done a lot of harm and the harm has come not just to the well-being of Africans, but to the processes that would improve well-being that foreign aid keeps from springing up.

THE BIRD'S EYE VIEW OF HAPPINESS

In a similar vein, *New York Times* columnist Roger Cohen writes wistfully from London:

> I was thinking about some recent moments of happiness in my own life. One came walking across Regent's Park, my skin tingling at the first brush of spring. Another came kissing my daughter goodnight as she slept and seeing how peaceful she was.[115]

Cohen is writing about highly personal moments and, oddly, he was also writing in defense of "happynomics" and of Prime Minister Cameron's proposal for a British "happiness index." But far from supporting a happynomic agenda, Cohen's examples illustrate just how far away from government policy happiness really is.

Far from being a humane way of understanding people, happiness economics is a way of lobotomizing them. When people become abstractions, it becomes easier to be a utilitarian. It thus becomes easier to justify the redistribution scheme du jour. As one takes on the bird's eye view, the faces become fuzzy. Each person becomes devoid of identity, perspective, circumstances, or, indeed, of his or her own story.

My perspective, my life, and my pursuit of happiness are what make me human. Imagine policymakers trying to measure and develop policies to enhance spiritual awareness or religiosity. Luckily, we have constitutional limitations on this sort of thing, but the idea should strike us as absurd, even if we're not all that religious.

More to the point: Who is better equipped to find happiness, you or the government? I know what my answer is and it is in this spirit that Jefferson would have agreed with the most famous utilitarian of all, who said:

> [L]et not society pretend that it needs, besides all this, the power to issue commands and enforce obedience in the personal concerns of individuals, in which, on all principles of justice and policy, the decision ought to rest with those who are to abide the consequences. Nor is there anything which tends more to discredit and frustrate the better means of influencing conduct, than a resort to the worse. If there be among those whom it is attempted to coerce into prudence or temperance, any of the material of which vigorous and independent characters are made, they will infallibly rebel against the yoke.[116]

John Stuart Mill realized that there are a great many people for whom freedom and dignity are more important than someone else's notion of happiness or the good. Put another way, freedom and dignity are features of happiness not easily captured on pseudo-scientific questionnaires. There is just no such thing as a hedonic calculus. (Sorry, Bentham.) There is just no way to get "beyond" freedom and dignity. (Sorry, Skinner.) And there is no way to fuse the ideas of Skinner and Bentham to make anything practicable. (Sorry, Toyama.)

ON THE VERY IDEA OF AN IDEAL WEALTH DISTRIBUTION

Happynomics isn't the most pervasive of the ideas currently on offer. When it comes to theories of "distributive justice" the big dog is the late philosopher John Rawls, whose 1971 *A Theory of Justice* has had more influence than probably any theory since Marx. You might say Rawls literally wrote the book on mild egalitarianism.

There is much to admire in *A Theory of Justice*. Indeed, whatever your political orientation, intellectual honesty demands you read the book. It is the standard by which other egalitarian theories are measured and is why I'm discussing it here. I'll do the book very little justice with a brief summary, but word count constrains me.

The basic objective of *A Theory of Justice* is to reconcile some individual liberty with some equality of outcome, giving us "mild" egalitarianism. Rawls sets out to do this in three basic ways: *The Original Position*, *The Liberty Principle* and *The Difference Principle*.

The Original Position is based on a cluster of concepts at whose core is the idea that justice is impartial. According to Rawls, the way to get to impartiality is to think of yourself as being in a kind of pre-birth state. You don't know what circumstances you'll be born into or what your natural endowments will be. Crudely put: *You might make a crappy spin on the wheel of fortune and the natural lottery may deal you a shitty scratch card; or you might be born with a silver spoon, good looks, and talent.* Given that you don't know what life will be like, what would you, as a basically self-interested person, want justice to look like when you come into the world?

Of course, there is a lot of really interesting methodological stuff in Rawls's *Theory* but the punch line is that people reasoning behind this pre-birth "veil of ignorance" will arrive at the latter two principles.

The Liberty Principle says you have an equal right to the most extensive set of basic political liberties, such as freedom of speech, assembly, property, and protection from arbitrary arrest (compatible with a similar liberty of others). Rawls makes clear that, though this principle is primary, it doesn't always extend to economic liberties.

The Difference Principle says that social and economic inequalities are to be arranged so that a) they benefit the least-advantaged members of society; and b) that offices and positions must be open to everyone under some concept of equality of opportunity.

When you see how elegantly Rawls weaves wildly different intuitions about the nature of justice into a single, consistent worldview, you cannot help but admire him as a theorist.

Admiration for Rawls's mind notwithstanding, the voice of Hayek echoes profoundly. Again, from "The Intellectuals and Socialism," Hayek writes:

> In some respects the intellectual is indeed closer to the philosopher than to any specialist, and the philosopher is in more than one sense a sort of prince among the intellectuals. Although his influence is farther removed from practical affairs and correspondingly slower and more difficult to trace than that of the ordinary intellectual, it is of the same kind and in the long run even more powerful than that of the latter.

Hayek could easily have been talking about the impact of Rawls.

> It is the same endeavor toward a synthesis, pursued more methodically, the same judgment of particular views in so far as they fit into a general system of thought rather than by their specific merits, the same striving after a consistent world view, which for both forms the main basis for accepting or rejecting ideas.

Holistic elegance has drawn a number of intellectuals to Rawls's theory or variations on it. In the years following the publication of *A Theory of Justice* we saw book after book that was essentially a response to Rawls—augmentations, variations, and critiques. Rawls had started a decades-long conversation that is still going on today.

I won't spend time here recounting those responses or offering my own critique of Rawls. Instead, I want to focus on some of the recent messes the intellectuals have made using Rawls, for there is Rawls and there are those who would hitch their wagons to Rawls with what might somewhat indelicately be termed pseudoscience. As Hayek warns, the "popular influence of the scientific specialist begins to rival that of the philosopher only when he ceases to be a specialist and commences to philosophize about the progress of his subject and usually only after he has been taken up by the intellectuals for reasons which have little to do with his scientific eminence."[ii]

THE INTELLECTUALS: PREDICTABLY IRRATIONAL

Everyone knows the social sciences are fuzzy. Economists, political scientists, and anthropologists bring their moralistic baggage into the ivory tower as soon as they decide what to study and what not to. Social science is value laden, but there is baggage and there is a naked agenda. In the first case you might be a victim of selection bias or other unconscious human processes that skew your data. In the latter case you start with a political agenda and with its (usually faulty) premises.

Michael I. Norton of Harvard and Dan Ariely of Duke (and famous for the book *Predictably Irrational*) fame are in the latter category. In a 2010 study, Norton and Ariely appear to be engaging in democracy by proxy. They claim that Americans really want

---

ii   The first time I read this passage from Hayek, I immediately thought of Noam Chomsky who is great at linguistics, but his political philosophy leaves something to be desired.

more "wealth redistribution" and they have the evidence to prove it. Here's their own description of the findings from their *Los Angeles Times* piece "Spreading the Wealth."

> We recently asked a representative sample of more than 5,000 Americans (young and old, men and women, rich and poor, liberal and conservative) to answer two questions. They first were asked to estimate the current level of wealth inequality in the United States, and then they were asked about what they saw as an ideal level of wealth inequality.

> In our survey, Americans drastically underestimated the current gap between the very rich and the poor. The typical respondent believed that the top 20% of Americans owned 60% of the wealth, and the bottom 40% owned 10%. They knew, in other words, that wealth in the United States was not distributed equally, but were unaware of just how unequal that distribution was.

> When we asked respondents to tell us what their ideal distribution of wealth was, things got even more interesting: Americans wanted the top 20% to own just over 30% of the wealth, and the bottom 40% to own about 25%. They still wanted the rich to be richer than the poor, but they wanted the disparity to be much less extreme.[117]

What should we conclude from this? Norton and Ariely did succeed in proving that Americans don't know who has how much money.

Strangely, Norton and Ariely proceed to ask the same Americans who are ignorant about the current wealth distribution what their "ideal" distribution is. Those surveyed then dreamed up what they thought would be a good breakdown, even though no such ideal exists in that great Tablet in the Sky. From all of this surveying they conclude something that cannot readily be concluded:

[O]ur results *suggest* that policies that increase inequality—those that favor the wealthy, say, or that place a greater burden on the poor—are unlikely to reflect the desires of Americans from across the political and economic spectrum. Rather, they *seem* to favor policies that involve taking from the rich and giving to the poor. [Emphases mine.]

Notice "suggest" and "seem." You see, Norton and Ariely can't claim those surveyed favor coercive redistribution. They merely infer it—and in dubious fashion. Absent any context, the most ardent libertarian surveyed might wish that poor people had more resources and yet not support forced redistribution. I know I do. But even if they learned most people favor redistribution at some point, we cannot conclude such desires *justify* forced redistribution, much less prove that redistribution is a good thing. This is where Norton and Ariely's malpractice really begins.

Academic socialists with bees in their bonnets are eager to point out which quintile has what at every turn, as if concern for the poor somehow translates automatically into worries about the assets of the rich. One reason they do that is they believe layfolk are ignorant. If they were enlightened, they would change their tunes and want to alter the distribution.

Somehow, though, this self-same group of distribution-ignorant Americans—when polled about a complete abstraction like the distribution of assets over quintiles—suddenly becomes endowed with a magical insight. Again, Norton and Ariely want us to think this special insight provides justification for redistributionist policies. But why should we think that Americans factually ignorant in one area would have some sort of mystical authority on the timeless and intractable questions of justice? In other words, Norton and Ariely conclude that asking Joe Sixpack, Jill Accountant, and Barb Waitress their thoughts about an abstraction like national income quintiles limns some great truth about right, wrong, and the good. Even the venerable soft egalitarian John Rawls would likely have bristled at this, for it is an intrusion into a discipline (philosophy) that demands more than what amounts to the naturalistic fallacy[iii] dressed up in finery of Gallup and Zogby.

I wonder: Did any of the respondents have the option of saying, "I don't think there is such an ideal distribution?" To me the whole exercise is as meaningful as asking people what should be the ideal distribution of vehicle types. Suppose for simplicity there are five categories of vehicle: cars, pickups, buses, local trucks, and transfer trucks. Someone with no concept of the *function* of each vehicle might say each category should have 20 percent of all vehicles—i.e. 20 percent are cars, 20 percent are trucks, 20 percent are buses, and so on. But once we start to think about what each vehicle does, we might conclude that it makes sense for there to be a different, rather unequal, distribution. Similarly, the distribution of assets in quartiles just doesn't tell us anything substantive about the function of wealth (e.g., opportunities, quality of life, desert, upward mobility, or what is likely to make any given person better off). The "ideal distribution" is meaningless because it is completely divorced from much more important questions about the *way wealth works*, which may have much more to do with human well-being than some distribution at some slice in time.

---

iii   David Hume said you cannot derive a value from a fact—or an "ought" from an "is"—and yet Norton and Ariely dance that two-step. From the "fact" that a statistical cluster of people have a loosely similar abstracted idealization of how assets should be distributed, they are led to the "value" that wealth ought to be taken and parsed out by state coercion. This is the kind of thing students quickly learn to dispatch with in Philosophy 101.

Now, speaking of Rawls, Norton and Ariely actually start their paper by claiming their study is Rawlsian: "We take a different approach to determining the 'ideal' level of wealth inequality: Following the philosopher John Rawls (1971), we ask Americans to construct distributions of wealth they deem just."[118] People may have good reasons to disagree with the late Rawls, but as we've suggested, his theory is elegant and sophisticated. Norton and Ariely have no business hitching their wagon to Rawls's *A Theory of Justice*.

Rawls's theory was a product of a philosophical reasoning. His theory requires people to think about what sort of society they would want to be born into if they didn't know what their own circumstances would be. Rawls thought people would want a high degree of political freedom, but also security; they would want the least well off to be cared for lest they themselves be born as the least well off. Most importantly, perhaps, Rawls's theory, right or wrong, was a product of philosophical deliberation, not about opinion polls in which people simply come up with a distribution and have academics point to the results as utopian. When it comes to Rawls, one can only conclude that Norton and Ariely are shrouded in a veil of ignorance.

Norton and Ariely also never consider the possibility that some of their respondents might want to see a different wealth distribution carried out through means other than forced redistribution by the state.[iv] For example, might we rid government of all the fa-

---

iv   Even if we went back and asked all these folks if, given their ideal distribution, they would support policies of forced redistribution and 90 percent said "yes," it wouldn't make it just. Heaven forbid, we learn this in Logic 101, too. Ever heard of fallacy *ad populum*? The gist is: Just because a bunch of people believe or claim it, doesn't make it so. Norton and Ariely's entire thesis seems to be that because a bunch of people believe something, it ought to be policy. If that were the case, we'd have to agree that popular support for Jewish pogroms justified policies put in place during 1930s Germany. Or we might agree that Christianity is the one true religion because there are more Christians.

vor-seeking schemes that protect the assets of banking CEOs and agribusiness and shift costs onto consumers? If people had greater information about the circumstances of time and place—like the effect of taking X dollars from businessman B means B can afford to hire fewer people—would they think differently about matters? Ask people for idealized abstractions and you'll get idealized abstractions. After all, aren't people "predictably irrational?"

MASLOW'S COVERED

In his own critique of Norton and Ariely, George Mason University economist Don Boudreaux reminds us that money ain't everything:

> That Americans "drastically" underestimate the wealth of "the very rich" compared to the wealth of "the poor" reveals that the difference in the number of dollars owned by "the very rich" compared to the number of dollars owned by "the poor" translates into a much smaller—that is, far more equal—difference in living standards. In other words, differences in monetary wealth are not the same as differences in living standards.

Indeed, maybe the reason Americans misjudge the actual wealth distribution is that most consider themselves wealthy in Boudreaux's sense—at least when it comes to the things that matter.

As far as "the gap" is concerned, one of the major themes of this book has been: If your goal is to alleviate poverty or perhaps to raise the baseline for what constitutes a minimum level of income that would allow most everyone to escape distress, that's something reasonable people can talk about. But that is not the same thing as worrying about what assets the wealthy control.

Suppose you asked the same Americans in the Norton-Ariel study, "If you could guarantee that every poor person in America had their basic needs met, would you agree to abandon your 'ideal' wealth distribution?" Their answers might surprise you. That's because many people conflate wealth distribution and concern for the poor. Indeed, we don't find any upper limit on income anywhere in Rawls, either. Rawls's only criterion was that the least advantaged benefit from inequality (The Difference Principle).

WHY ARE THERE SO MANY SOCIALIST INTELLECTUALS?

We could go on endlessly treating the various arguments for "social justice." I chose only a couple to illustrate just how pervasive this sort of thinking is. But we should return to the question with which we started: Why are there so many socialist intellectuals? Or, why are most intellectuals socialist?

We would be remiss if we did not look to answers from economist and philosopher Thomas Sowell.

> Whether in war or peace, and whether in economics or religion, something as intangible as ideas can dominate the most concrete things in our lives. What Karl Marx called "the blaze of ideas" has set whole nations on fire and consumed whole generations. Those whose careers are built on the creation and dissemination of ideas—the intellectuals—have played a role in many societies out of all proportion to their numbers. Whether that role has, on balance, made those around them better off or worse off is one of the key questions of our times. The quick answer is that intellectuals have done both. But certainly, during the 20th century, it is hard to escape the conclusion that intellectuals have on balance made the world a worse and more dangerous place.[119]

Today's intellectual would cry out that this is not the 20th century. They want a gentler socialism. They just want to be like Italy or France. They just want everyone to have a "living wage" and "free healthcare" and "tuition debt forgiveness" and "mortgage assistance" and, and, and…the kinds of things that are threatening to push Europe over a cliff because the utopians forgot there's no free lunch.

I have no central, definitive theory for why so many intellectuals are consumed with the idea of using naked coercion to strip resources from the wealthy, but I think Thomas Sowell offers us a clue in the quotation above.

The blaze of ideas is most common among people who have the luxury in living in a world of abstractions. Marx himself had that luxury and never worked a day in his life. It is no accident that most social intellectuals are children of the rich. The blaze of ideas drives them. Could it also be that the blaze of ideas is fueled by something deeper within? Guilt? Envy? Indignation? Ideas without passion, after all, are like toys on a planet with no children. And as I'll argue, this guilt-envy-indignation trinity lies within all of us to varying degrees because we're human. But why is the mind of the intellectual such ready tender for certain ideas and passions? Groupthink? Genes? A herd mentality from years spent grazing on the quad?

Perhaps it's simply a desire to see the world be a better place, coupled with a failure fully to reckon with the steps and tradeoffs required to get to that place. Sowell calls this the "unconstrained vision." In his landmark *Conflict of Visions*, Sowell writes:

> Without the underlying assumption that man's deliberate reason is too limited to undertake comprehensive social planning, an entirely different set of conclusions emerges in field after field. If, for example, effective rational planning and direct control of an entire economic system is possible, then it is clearly more efficient to reach desired results directly in this way, rather than as the end result of circuitous and uncontrolled processes.[120]

Robert Nozick, you'll recall, said that most left-liberal intellectuals were scribblers and artists. That could explain a lot since scribblers and artists rarely think about the steps required to get to some end, much less the costs or the unintended consequences. They begin and end with the vision, which means they generally leave off the economic way of thinking. This goes back to Feser's "head in the clouds" thesis.

So how do you explain someone like Paul Krugman, an economist?

That is, perhaps, a book unto itself. It's no wonder, though, that Krugman comes from the sub-discipline known as macroeconomics, which tends toward generalizations, abstractions, and heavy reliance on economic models. But in Krugman's case, a lot can be chalked up to who pays the bills and who constitutes the adoring readership. To echo a father of American conservatism, Richard Weaver: "I would mention here the fact, obvious to any candid observer, that 'equality' is found most often in the mouths of those engaged in artful self-promotion."[121]

Krugman is a very high-ranking member of what we have called the intellectual priest class. He would be a fool to embrace intellectual honesty at this stage, even if he could somehow turn off Marx's blaze of ideas. "What a vision may offer, and what the prevailing vision of our time emphatically does offer," Sowell writes, "is a special state of grace for those who believe in it. Those who accept this vision are deemed to be not merely factually correct but morally on a higher plane."[122] They are The Anointed. Only they have replaced God with government.

11
The Origins of Envy

When Envy breeds unkind division: There comes the ruin, there begins confusion.

> – Shakespeare, Henry VI

Man will become better when you show him what he is like.

> – Anton Chekhov

They're the 99 percent. They have a set of demands as clear as the streets they occupy. They'll hold a vigil for Steve Jobs, throw pies at Bill Gates, and may just vote reflexively for someone who has come to represent much of what they claim to loathe. But what underlies their demands? What really motivates the Occupiers? Is it injustice? Perhaps. Maybe it's an idea of injustice wrapped around something they just can't put their fingers on. Something deeper.

Consider this scene:

The guy is wearing Hugo Boss. His Mercedes S-class is parked in front of a restaurant you can't afford. Remember that pair of boxer-briefs you just bought at Target? He's the guy on the package. And on his way to open the car door for the best-looking woman you've ever seen, Johnny Moneybags ignores the outstretched hand of a homeless guy. Between Johnny and Ms. Candypants, a lot of people will find something to dislike.

For many of us, the emotional response to this scene is not a decision. It's a reflex. The bile duct secretes. If Johnny were to run his Mercedes into a hydrant, launch the airbag, and spill latte all over his soft leather interior, we'd feel better somehow. In the fairer sex, Johnny may inspire other emotions. Still, female readers may want to see Ms. Candypants and her Coach handbag covered in Johnny's latte. This emotion can be so strong for some that they would rather see the couple be ugly and broke than trade places with them.

It's not hard to find examples of this very human emotion creeping into other aspects of life. It can leech into our conscious thoughts, even masquerade as morality.

Economist David Henderson recalls a time in his childhood when he shared his father's deep resentment of people who had more than his family: "And given that about half the families in Canada had an income higher than ours, I had a lot of resentment. I adopted, subconsciously at least, my father's view that those with much more than us had come by it dishonestly. I had no evidence, of course. Sure, I had a few stories about wealthy people who had taken advantage of others, but I had no basis for my grudge against the millions of people I resented. Because I couldn't have some of the material possessions other kids had, I felt left out, and that was enough."[123]

Henderson is not alone. He recounts meeting Will Herberg at a conference in 1969. Herberg had been a prominent American communist in the 1930s and '40s, but later became a strong anti-communist. Henderson asked Herberg how he came to be a Marxist in the first place.

"Immediately, his eyes lit up," Henderson writes. "He told us of his intense resentment of the fact that he was smart and had nothing, while they were dumb and had a lot. 'That,' he said, 'is how I became a Marxist. I hated the rich.'"

The liberal blogger Matthew Yglesias channels his inner egalitarian when he admits he thinks "the world would be a better place if Americans were less polite about the obscenity of superwealth in terms of individual morality. Rich people who don't want to have their funds taxed away ought to be shamed into showing they're able to use individual ethical action to help ameliorate serious local and global problems."[124] Yglesias will be neither the first nor the last to wrap this inborn indignation in a moral-political mantle. Charles Dickens made quite a good living spinning tales of villainy out of the cognitive dissonance created by the contrasts of the Industrial Revolution. Even some superwealthy people like Warren Buffett say "tax me more." Guilt is the other side of the egalitarian coin, as we'll see.

THE 'ENVY GENE'

Those who've never felt such emotions of envy may belong to a rare breed that simply lacks the gene. The inimitable H. L. Mencken insists:

> My distaste for democracy as a political theory is, like every other human prejudice, due to an inner lack—to a defect that is a good deal less in the theory than in myself. In this case it is very probably my incapacity for envy. That emotion, or weakness, or whatever you choose to call it, is quite absent from my make-up; where it ought to be there is a vacuum. In the face of another man's good fortune I am as inert as a curb broker before Johann Sebastian Bach.[125]

Mencken is at least cooler than most of us. And although he was a heathen, many Christians would consider Mencken a saint in this department. Envy, after all, is a deadly sin to many. Aquinas said, "Envy according to the aspect of its object is contrary to charity, whence the soul derives its spiritual life. … Charity rejoices in our neighbor's good, while envy grieves over it."[126] That should have given ol' Mencken a couple of cosmic points, at least.

In an important way, though, envy is beyond good and evil. It is a link in the nexus of egalitarian feelings that originate in our DNA. Evolutionary fires forged these feelings over millions of years. For most of those years, after all, our forebears were grubbing around in the bushes trying to survive on a never-ending camping trip without marshmallows or coolers. So our brains evolved to survive not in climate-controlled shopping centers, but within kinship groups in unforgiving wilds. You needed your clan and your clan needed you.

Thus, the feelings that accompany that tribal interdependency—including envy—are "hardwired" and we've not had enough time in civilization to rewire them. "Natural selection, the process that designed our brain," writes Leda Cosmides and John Tooby, "takes a long time to design a circuit of any complexity. The time it takes to build circuits that are suited to a given environment is so slow it is hard to even imagine—it's like a stone being sculpted by wind-blown sand. Even relatively simple changes can take tens of thousands of years."[127]

Hardwired

Max Krasnow, a postdoctoral researcher at the Center for Evolutionary Psychology in Santa Barbara, Calif., explains that egalitarian emotions made good sense for our forebears. I contacted him at his office in Southern California to get a better idea about the origins of our envy.

"Under a loose meaning of the term 'hardwired,' all emotions are hardwired by evolution," Krasnow said. "We have the particular constellation of emotions we have because of our evolutionary history. Dung beetles go gaga for feces, but we generally have the opposite reaction." Krasnow went on to explain that evolution is the only way for any emotion to exist at all. But that's not to say our emotions are not malleable. "We apply them in all kinds of strange ways," Krasnow said. "For example, we direct parental emotions toward our pets, which are highly unlikely to be their usual adaptive targets."

Krasnow defines an emotion as "the coordinated response of diverse psychological and physiological systems to a class of stimuli." This is a fancy way of saying that your mind and brain react to things in the world around you. But neither your mind nor brain has any way of learning the right responses from scratch—for example, when responding to inequality of resources in various contexts. As Krasnow and his mentors Cosmides and Tooby explain, there's no way for our onboard cognitive systems to learn the associations necessary to produce an emotional response in the "right" circumstances.[128] We have to deal with a kernel of emotion pre-built into the system. For example, snake-like shapes in our visual field trigger a neural response that goes straight to our limbic system. This response bypasses object recognition processes and activates the sympathetic nervous system so as to mobilize the body. That is, you start, jump, and dash before you have a chance to reflect. Most of our emotional propensities come from similar innate kernels. "A kernel may be elaborated upon or modified throughout one's life," Krasnow adds.

The range of egalitarian emotions we're focused on here relates to a class of stimuli we might call *who has what and how much*. Let's travel a little further into our human past and see what we can find out.

THE STONE AGE TRINITY

I call envy, guilt, and indignation the "Stone Age Trinity" of primary egalitarian emotions. These three are connected as facets of the same socio-biological function. To get a better sense of this connection, let's break them down as follows:[i]

- If in comparing myself to you I find you have more, I may feel envy.
- If in comparing myself to you I find you have less, I may feel guilt.
- If in comparing someone to you I find you have more, I may feel indignation.

For Paleolithic Man, this was not just some errant feeling. It provided the basis for survival logic in a mostly zero-sum world. That logic worked for a time and place in which survival depended on sharing and close cooperation. Og's story will help us unpack this idea.

Og lives in a small group of hunter-gatherers on the steppe. He is a hunter. His sister Igg is a gatherer and her two girls go with grandmother to fetch water. Og ventures out frequently with two other men in his tribe, Zog, and Drog, to track food. It's usually guinea fowl, but they find wild boar on occasion. Og, Zog, and Drog are pretty equally matched as hunters. Though Og is a little better at throwing spears,

---

i   A more nuanced version of this to a scientist like Max Krasnow might be something like: "I feel envy when you have more than I AND my mechanisms perceive that I can cheaply take some of it from you. But I may not feel envy when you have more than I and my internal mechanisms suggest that there is nothing I can do about it."

Zog and Drog are faster runners. Together, they are a formidable team out on the hunt. Depending on what sort of animals they're tracking, it sometimes makes sense to work closely as a team. Other times, it makes more sense for each to go out and hunt alone so as to cover more territory.

In the short term, Og could benefit from killing and hoarding some food. Likewise, Igg could pluck and eat her way to a gatherer's feast of berries. Luckily, both have inherited the Stone Age Trinity. Over time, each is better off if both share what they hunted or gathered. Nuts, berries, and grubs provide certain kinds of nutrients, such as vitamins and carbohydrates. Meat provides iron, fat, and protein. (And nothing hoarded has a very good shelf life.) When both parties share, each gets a more balanced diet. If any individual member were to hoard, the relationship in the tribe would begin to break down, cutting off the benefit stream of cooperation. Tomorrow's hunting partners might be undernourished. Mothers might have difficulty providing fat for growing babies. Persistent malnutrition and lack of social cohesion in the harsh environment of the steppe meant certain death. By evolutionary logic, individuals disposed to share and cooperate lived to pass along their "selfless" genes. In other words, because Og feels guilt, envy, and indignation, he has increased the odds that he will pass his genes along to the next generation.

A critical mass of individuals lacking the Stone Age Trinity within a group meant that group did not survive the winter. With group members dividing labor and sharing the proceeds, survival was possible. But this "logic" was not developed through deliberation. It is a dynamic of emotions originating in genes that were selected due to environmental pressures.

Krasnow sums up the whys rather tidily:

> In an environment where resource acquisition involved a great deal of luck, and where individuals had to buffer this uncertainty by sharing when they were lucky, that would mean that, at least in some circumstances, those in need would feel entitled to the production of others, and others would feel guilty for not giving it to them. From the evolutionary standpoint, individuals who had such emotional adaptations would maintain a more steady flow of resources (and thus survive to reproduce) than would those who didn't.[129]

In *The Origins of Virtue*, Matt Ridley argues that aspects of Og's story can be seen in tribal societies today: "Private property or communal ownership by a small group is a logical response to a potential tragedy of the commons, but it is not an instinctive one. Instead, there is a human instinct, clearly expressed in hunter-gatherers, but present also in modern society, that protests any sort of hoarding. Hoarding is taboo; sharing is mandatory."[130]

In most situations there were diminishing returns for hoarding resources. For example, the benefit of going from no fruit to one fruit was bigger than the benefit of going from 100 fruits to 101 fruits. So those more in need would value any hoarded resources more highly than the hoarder. If the needy person could inflict harm through violence, in some circumstances, it would pay for the needy to try to take the resource from the hoarder (especially if the alternative was starvation). Strangely, it often made sense for the hoarder to tolerate it. After all, the cost of violence is usually greater than the benefit of keeping the extra fruit. In the academic literature, this is referred to as "tolerated theft" and describes a lot of food transfers among diverse animal species, including our forebears. (Could this help explain some of the attitudes towards higher taxation by wealthy elites?)

Finally, we suggest Og survived in a place where there were more opportunities to benefit when he worked with others. There also was a limit to the number of high-benefit opportunities Og could capitalize on by himself. So, individuals like Og might also have competed for access to the best cooperation partners. For those in the know, this is referred to as competitive altruism.

"Individuals broadcast their quality as a cooperative partner by means of good acts meant to signal good intentions," Krasnow explains. "Many egalitarian motives could be a product of this signaling competition, as well: *He thinks he's a good person because he cares about the poor. Well, guess what? I care about the poor and the rainforests too!*"[131] Reporter John Cloud describes the phenomenon in *Time*:

> Evolutionary psychologists have a cynical term for cooperative, pro-community behaviors like buying a Prius or shopping at Whole Foods or carrying a public-radio tote bag: competitive altruism. Cynical, but accurate. As several studies [such as this one[132]] have shown, altruistic people achieve higher status, and are much more likely to behave altruistically in situations where their actions are public than when they will go unnoticed. Competitive altruism explains why soldiers jump onto grenades during war (their clans will reap the rewards) and why vain CEOs build hospital wings (they enjoy the social renown that they could never acquire from closing another big deal). In many hunter-gatherer societies, including some Native American tribes in the Pacific Northwest, prominent families have staged elaborate ceremonies in which they compete to give away possessions.[133]

This reminds me of Warren Buffett's rather public displays of philanthropy (not to mention sanctimony about higher taxes).

INEQUALITY, IRRATIONALITY, AND THE ULTIMATUM GAME

It's one thing for evolutionary psychologists to theorize about the origins of the Stone Age Trinity, and even if we agree we inherited this cluster of emotions from our ancestors, who is to say these emotions are appropriate or inappropriate in the context of modern society? To get some idea, I asked an experimental economist.

Bart Wilson, of Chapman University in Orange, Calif., studied under Nobel Laureate Vernon Smith, who is considered a founding father of this relatively new sub-discipline, which combines economics with observation in controlled settings. Wilson gets to use his students as guinea pigs for many of his experiments. These usually involve computer simulations and cash prizes but with some experiments, Wilson doesn't even need a computer.

"What we find from running experiments on fairness in the laboratory is that our notion of it varies pretty substantially depending on the circumstances," Wilson explains. "People are very sensitive to the social context in which they're making their decisions."[134]

One classic experiment is the Ultimatum Game, variations of which Wilson runs on college kids using beer money. This simple experiment involves only two participants, the Proposer and the Responder, who are chosen at random. The "game" mechanics are simple. The Proposer gets a certain amount of money, say $10. He can offer the Responder as much of it as he likes. If the Responder accepts the offer, then the Proposer has benefitted by whatever's left over. If the Responder rejects the offer, *both get zero*. Either way, the game is over. If we're being "rational" in economic terms, anything is better than zero. A robot programmed to accept any benefit will choose even $1 over zero dollars. Not people. The amounts vary, but most Responders will usually not accept an offer of less than $3 out of a Proposer's $10. Somehow it offends their sense of fairness.

In a variation of the Ultimatum Game called the Dictator Game, the Proposer can't lose all the money. If the Responder rejects the amount offered, the Proposer keeps it all. If the Responder takes what's offered, the Proposer keeps the rest. Predictably, the Proposer makes smaller offers because he has no fear of losing the money. Still, Proposers often worry about getting a reputation for being stingy, so the offers are usually more generous than they need to be, perhaps in case the tables are ever turned. And in the "double blind" version, in which all the Proposers are anonymous, people are exceptionally stingy.

But things got really interesting when Bart Wilson put a meritocratic spin on these classic Ultimatum Games.

"If you just bring people in and randomly assign them to be the Proposers and the Responders, the modal offer is about half the pot—$5.00. But if you first bring in people and give them a quiz—and the people who score best on the quiz get to be the Proposers—the offers are much lower *and they're accepted.* The rejection rates don't go up. All of a sudden what's 'fair' now is different. The modal offer is shifted down. 'Fairness' is still involved, but it's not about equity anymore."[135]

It's about fair play.

In this situation, Responders were far likelier to accept lower offers than in the first version because of some concept of desert. Knowledge that a Proposer came to be such due to his or her performance usually muted the Responder's sense of being entitled to an equal portion. Wilson found the Responders seem to *respect* the outcome a lot more than in cases where the money is not associated with the participants' relative performance. I cannot say whether this more meritocratic response is mostly inborn or learned, but the idea of rewarding good performance in the clan group does have its own logic. It would mean communal living with performance bonuses—and that means inequality.

"Fairness means a lot more than equity," Wilson finds. "It's also about the rules of the game."

INVISIBLE BANDS

Sharing among members of communal groups is known in academic literature as 'reciprocal altruism.' Interestingly, the very idea of reciprocal altruism has some built in Adam Smith-like aspects. More to the point: Altruism is one thing, reciprocity is quite another. You might be willing to make a sacrifice now, but only if others in the group are willing to make them later. That is why we might prefer the term 'delayed trade' or 'slow trade.' The system only works if most of the folks are willing to return favors and contribute their part.

Although in these systems the benefit to oneself may be on a giver's terms, the arrangement works pretty well in a small group of specializers. Fleet-footed stalkers, hawk-eyed gatherers, agile spearmen, gifted diviners—all bring their abilities to the whole cooperation project. You might say that *it is not from the benevolence of the hunter, the gatherer, or the diviner, that we expect our dinners, but from their regard to their long-term interest.* Adam Smith would have been proud.

I realize this may not sit well with those who have apotheosized the Stone Age Trinity, but as Steven Pinker points out in *The Blank Slate*, "The real alternative to romantic collectivism is not 'right-wing libertarianism' but a recognition that social generosity comes from a complex suite of thoughts and emotions rooted in the logic of *reciprocity*."[136]

Before turning to other matters, we should point out a complication. The Stone Age Trinity doesn't show up in every caveman with the same intensity. It shows up by degrees from one caveman to the next. So in whatever population we're talking about, we are likely to find a mixture of dispositions, just as we find a mixture of abilities, aptitudes, looks, and other characteristics. Such a mixture creates its own dynamic.

"One exception to the rule that selection reduces variability arises when the best strategy depends on what other organisms are doing," Pinker notes. "The child's game of scissors-rock-paper is one analogy, and another may be found in the decision of which route to take to work." In evolution, "frequency-dependent selection can produce temporary or permanent *mixtures* of strategies." Over time, whether the strategy is unitary or a mixed set, a period of stability eventually follows. It's no wonder then that we find a mixture of dispositions today, which could go very far indeed toward explaining differences in political orientation, party affiliations, and other moralistic tribes.

So evolution, far from being a source of moral content, doesn't really give us moral imperatives at all. It gives us different people with different dispositions. So it's not that people who express the Stone Age Trinity are enlightened and those who think hoarding is okay are benighted (or vice versa), rather it is that some strategy (or set of strategies) worked in some environments of the past. Otherwise evolution is as indifferent to morality and politics as a deck of cards is to poker players. The evolutionary question is always: Does your strategy allow you to pass along your genetic material in a certain milieu? (As opposed to: Does my strategy make me a good person?)

HUTTERITES, SHIRKING, AND SCALE

Let's suppose that, based on the application of some slow-trade strategy, your small group is successful. What if, over time, the strategy starts to make your group a victim of its own success? What if, as your numbers grow, cooperation falters and your group strains available resources?

In his landmark book *The Tipping Point*, Malcolm Gladwell picks up on the question of scale by looking at a religious people who still live largely according to a slow trade ethos:

> The Hutterites (who came out of the same tradition as the Amish and the Mennonites) have a strict policy that every time a colony approaches 150, they split it in two and start a new one. "Keeping things under 150 just seems to be the best and most efficient way to manage a group of people," Bill Gross, one of the leaders of a Hutterite colony outside Spokane [Wash.] told me. "When things get larger than that, people become strangers to one another." The Hutterites, obviously, didn't get this idea from contemporary evolutionary psychology. They've been following the 150 rule for centuries. [...] At 150, the Hutterites believe something happens—something indefinable but very real—that somehow changes the nature of community overnight.[137]

Some observers have compared the splitting of Hutterite colonies to cell mitosis.[ii]

Nearly 30 years before Gladwell shared his insights on Hutterites, two colleagues were looking at the political economy of Hutterite communes in Montana. Richard Stroup and John Baden, an economist and a political scientist, respectively, found the group to be an exemplar of small group dynamics. Writing in the spring 1972 edition of the journal *Public Choice*, Stroup and Baden conclude:

> In a relatively small colony, the proportional contribution of each member is greater. Likewise, surveillance of him by each of the others is more complete and an informal accounting of contribution is feasible. In a colony, there are no elaborate systems of formal controls over a person's contribution. Thus, in general, the incentive and surveillance structures of a small or medium-size colony are more effective than those of a large colony and shirking is lessened.

A less sophisticated way of putting all this is members of the group are a lot less likely to slack off if they can keep an eye on each other.

Hutterite colonies offer clues about the dynamics Paleolithic peoples had to face. Clans and other communal groups reach a critical mass not only because it's difficult to account for each member's contribution beyond a certain size, but because slow trade becomes more and more impersonal—"strangers" as Gladwell puts it. So even if we're evolved to cooperate in small groups, information flows and feedback loops get disrupted in larger ones.

---

ii   Eliot Sober and David Sloan Wilson have a tidy description of splitting process: "Like a honey bee colony, Hutterite brotherhoods split when they attain a large size, with one half remaining in the original site and the other half moving to a new site that has been preselected and prepared. In preparation for the split, the colony is divided into two groups that are equal with respect to number, age, skills and personal compatibility. The entire colony packs its belongings and one of the lists is drawn by lottery on the day of the split. The similarity to the genetic rules of meiosis could hardly be more complete."

Stroup and Baden's work reveals something pretty important: Communism works, but only if the commune is small. As a commune grows, free-rider problems infect the labor pool. The commune becomes a "paradise for parasites," a former resident of a kibbutz told Steven Pinker. These inefficiencies cause breakdown in the colony. Among people for whom failure means famine, ensuring the colony doesn't get too big literally becomes a rule to live by. After all, slow-trade yields pretty slim margins of benefit. As the group grows, these margins get slimmer. The group has to change or die.

Interestingly, a group very similar to the Hutterites chose a different path in the early 1600s. They did something rather taboo. They institutionalized hoarding:

> All this whille no supply was heard of, neither knew they when they might expecte any. So they begane to thinke how they might raise as much corne as they could, and obtaine a betercrope then they had done, that they might not still thus languish in miserie. At length, after much debate of things, the Govr (with ye advise of ye cheefestamongest them) gave way that they should set corne every man for his owne perticuler, and in that regard trust to themselves. [...] And so assigned to every family a parcell of land, according to the proportion of their number for that end, only for present use (but made no devission for inheritance) and ranged all boys and youth under some familie. This had very good success; for it made all hands very industrious, so as much more corne was planted then other waise would have bene by any means ye Govr or any other could use, and saved him a great deall of trouble, and gave farr better contente. The women now wente willingly into ye feild, and tooke their little-ons with them to set corne, which before would aledgweaknes, and inabilitie; whom to have compelled would have bene thought great tiranie and oppression.

These are the words of William Bradford, governor of the original Pilgrim colony in Massachusetts. As more people arrived and the colony grew, Bradford opted for a change in the rules—the institution of private property—over dividing the colony. When it comes to group dynamics, then, the Hutterite and Pilgrim experiences show that success (growth) can only be managed by changes to the internal rules of organization. In order to get from small colonies to large-scale civilization, you have to adopt new institutions.

Much of history is a story about changes in the rules and these rule changes can sometimes insult our more clannish instincts. As with other Stone Age kernels like sex and violence, having civilization means we sometimes have to check our emotions. Attitudes about property, hoarding, and exchange come to mind. People will start to engage in more direct trade, and they'll start to specialize more.[iii] Add currency and a system of prices to the mix and things really start to take off. In the language of complexity, we undergo a series of "phase transitions," but contrary to the forces of the Stone Age Trinity, when those transitions happen, inequality is a foregone conclusion.

CAVEMAN ETHICS TODAY

What can we conclude from this handful of insights about the Stone Age Trinity?

First, the rules, mores, and dispositions ideal for living in civilizations could be very different from the rules, mores, and disposi-

---

iii This is a grossly simplified version of institutional economics. For a much richer and more detailed treatment, see the work of Douglass North, e.g. *Structure and Change in Economic History*, New York, 1981. The emphasis on changing the institutional rules rooted in Coasean "transaction costs" is the thrust of my argument here, while North's lens for viewing history goes much deeper in terms of its explanatory power.

tions for surviving in Paleolithic clans.

Second, if our ancestors spent 99 percent of their species history out on the African steppe or foraging near caves, they did not spend very much time in large-scale civilizations or even small city-states. That means our species has not had time to evolve all the dispositions that might have made us better suited to civilization.

And finally, acknowledging our Paleolithic brains may help us take a more detached view of the Stone Age Trinity. We can start to look at wealth disparities not so much through the lens of guilt, envy, or indignation, but through the lens of function, form, and fair play. When we do, ethical systems designed to redirect some of our baser instincts will emerge. We may even do well to listen to curmudgeons like H.L. Mencken, who claimed, "The fact that John D. Rockefeller had more money than I have is as uninteresting to me as the fact that he believed in total immersion and wore detachable cuffs." Entertaining counterintuitive ideas such as those offered by bourgeois economists couldn't hurt, either.

Let's pause briefly to think about the phrase "better suited" in the second point above. Interestingly, "better suited" has no evolutionary content. That we are alive is enough for any evolutionary criterion, as the process is relentlessly binary: Either you live to pass on your genes or you die trying. "Better suited" means that in some world we might have evolved stronger dispositions towards life in crowded civilization, such as a stronger disposition to be peaceful, greater toleration for others who are not like us, appreciation of differences in ability, and any of the other Western "bourgeois virtues."[138] And yet, we are flexible and smart enough as a species to work on these.

WHEN THE STONE AGE TRINITY IS OUT OF PLACE

In both the Paleolithic context and in the modern context, inequality can indicate an overall benefit to a group. Sometimes, for example, it benefits everyone to reward high performers. Such is the paradox of prosperity. I won't try to convince you here that accepting the paradox of prosperity should lead us to celebrate wealth disparity. My goal is merely to convince you that it is at least possible that our egalitarian feelings are not always appropriate in the context of the modern world because in doing so, I think we can go very far toward isolating the critical difference between concern for the poor and antipathy for the rich.

While nature can lead any one of us to become an individual moralizer about inequality, it does not reveal in any universal sense how much inequality should be tolerated in society at large. In other words, there is no great survey in the sky.[139] In fact, nature reveals no moral-political truths at all. Nature just is. Sometimes it makes us "red in tooth and claw." Other times it makes us better cooperators. Still other times it just gets in the way of progress.

Mother Nature's lack of direction has led brilliant philosophers like John Rawls and Immanuel Kant to spin elegant theories that originate in something *other* than our DNA. Others, like Sam Harris and Jeremy Bentham, look for moral truth in human nature itself. Yet both of these approaches come up short. Why? Because we can no more escape our emotional "kernels" than we can ground morality in them.

So, maybe those unlikely bedfellows Mencken and Aquinas are on to something. Our inborn caveman ethos is not always appropriate in the context of the modern world. We sometimes have to put it in check, albeit with the clumsiness one might expect from hunter-gatherers living in suburbia.

Economist Bryan Caplan argues, for example, that "'Hardwired' does not mean fixed. All humans may feel these emotions to some extent but there's plenty of room to maneuver. You can become less envious than you are. Make an effort to monitor your thoughts and behavior. Count your blessings. Give credit where credit is due. Focus on improving yourself instead of comparing yourself to other people. Spend more time with less envious people."[140]

Steven Pinker says the "science of the moral sense also alerts us to ways in which our psychological makeup can get in the way of our arriving at the most defensible moral conclusions. The moral sense, we are learning, is as vulnerable to illusions as the other senses. It is apt to confuse morality per se with purity, status, and conformity. It tends to reframe practical problems as moral crusades and thus see their solution in punitive aggression. It imposes taboos that make certain ideas indiscussible. And it has the nasty habit of always putting the self on the side of the angels."[141]

Any human emotion can become destructive by degree. Economist Young Back Choi thinks that envy is particularly destructive because it "is man's desire to eliminate others' relative gains even if he would become absolutely worse off in the process."[142] We see this in the original Ultimatum Game and we see it in the brutal consequences of Stalin and Mao. "Because a certain degree of self-less behavior is essential to the smooth performance of any human group," writes Natalie Angier in *The New York Times*, "selflessness run amok can crop up in political contexts. It fosters the exhilarating sensation of righteous indignation, the belief in the purity of your team and your cause and the perfidiousness of all competing teams and causes."[143]

Understood this way, envy, despite its evolutionary rationale, does not seem very sane. Perhaps we should hope that any given person is likely to be a little better off over time, even if some are a lot better off (even if this goes against the emotional grain). Alas, a positive-sum orientation is neither a feature of the egalitarian ethos, nor any politics of envy and this is just one aspect of the trouble with the Stone Age Trinity as it gets institutionalized. "Envy is appeased only at equality, regardless of the absolute level of consumption," adds Choi. "'Only those societies that have been able to develop sufficient means to mitigate the destructive forces of envy have been able to build civilizations and prosper. Anthropologists have documented that two of the most distinguishing features of poor societies are the relative free expression of envy and the universal fear of envy on the part of those who come to have above-average gains."

Envy can creep into both our politics and our personal lives. So also can envy's sister emotions: guilt and indignation. All three are facets of a brain that was sculpted by millennia in a mostly zero-sum environment. But now we can live in a positive-sum world.

I wonder how the Wall Street Occupiers would have made out on the African Savannah around 10,000 B.C.[144]

12

SUPERPHILANTHROPY

The Americans make associations to give entertainment, to found seminaries, to build inns, to construct churches, to diffuse books. ...Wherever at the end of some new undertaking you see the government in France, or a man of rank in England, in the United States, you will be sure to find an association.

– Alexis de Tocqueville

Charity is injurious unless it helps the recipient to become independent of it.

– John D. Rockefeller

You are reading this book right now thanks to the generosity of others. It's a sign of the times.

That is, philanthropy brought you this experience. There is the philanthropy of Tom Phillips, a man who started a media empire out of his garage with a $1,000 investment. Phillips's foundation awards the Robert Novak Fellowship, of which I am a recipient.

Second, and perhaps just as importantly, you're reading this because of a clever team of innovators who created Kickstarter, an online crowd-funding tool that allows writers, artists, filmmakers, and dancers to raise capital more easily. This was a good avenue for me because I wanted to publish my own book, in my own way and at my own pace. A couple of hundred people on Kickstarter—some generous friends and family, some strangers—enabled me to do just that. Many are in the same financial situation as I (which is to say not rich). But crowd-funding changes the game. It's what Glenn Reynolds has called "an army of Davids," only they have giving spirits not hurling slings.

It is only fitting then that I devote this chapter to superphilanthropy.

Please understand, though, this is no extended acknowledgements page. My experience provides one small example among many, building up to a new age. This volume, whether I sell one hundred copies or ten thousand, will be read by *somebody*, thank goodness. Had I written it just ten years ago, it might have gone to that great graveyard of literary efforts having never stirred a human soul. But times are changing.

As we move further into this century of possibility, we must not let go of what is beautiful and foundational about our past. We stand on the shoulders of giants.

The Greatest Generation

Dr. Dwight B. "Whitey" Hord, DDS—my grandfather on my mother's side—never retired. For years he was pretty much the only dentist in Upper Cleveland County, N.C. A lot of people depended on him. When he was about forty, his joints started giving him problems due to a severe case of rheumatoid arthritis. His fingers were so gnarled he couldn't straighten them. But it never disabled him. He scaled back his practice when he got into his late 70s but he knew if he ever stopped practicing, he would wither. So he never stopped and he never withered.

Eventually he succumbed to complications of pneumonia but he practiced dentistry right up until he died. Even as his hands became utterly crippled, he would simply position the dental instruments between the knobby joints so he could work. And work he did.

Whitey was one of the Greatest Generation. I used to wonder about that term. I understood that living through the Depression and World War II would qualify someone for a nice designation. But it's only as I've gotten older that I've begun to appreciate the contrasts between his generation and my own: the way they thought, the way they behaved, what they built. We've inherited the country and some of the riches but as that generation passes, they take some of their greatness with them. (Let's just hope it's not irretrievable.)

Whitey was no different. After WWII he returned from the Pacific to create a life for himself back in his hometown of Lawndale, N.C. When the local high school failed to renew his teaching contract for having taught evolution, he went back to Chapel Hill to study in UNC's first dental class. He might have gotten richer setting up a dental practice in an area with more people but he set up near his parents who had taken in ironing and worked longer hours at the mill—all so he could study dentistry.

Not too long after starting up his practice, Whitey became a man of means. By today's standards we might not think as much of his home atop the pine-covered hill there in sleepy Lawndale but to the people of the time, it must have been like Monticello. Whitey was a county patriarch, a community pillar, and a deacon of the church. In Upper Cleveland County, he was among the "one percent." Doing well for oneself in small-town America is not always about becoming wealthy. There are tacit exchanges and deep responsibilities that go beyond money.

Strange Produce and Mysterious Letters

Soon after Whitey got his practice going, he started coming home with strange things. At first it would be corn or just a bag of apples. Another day it might be a giant head of cabbage, a jar of chow chow, or block of liver mush. The kids never thought much of it—that is, until years later when even stranger things started showing up.

"A year or so before he died," my Aunt Jean recalled, "he showed me a letter he received in the mail from someone who sent him a $10 bill in an envelope. The unsigned note included that this was for services from many years before that the person couldn't afford to pay at the time. Daddy didn't know who sent it. The truth is, it could have been countless people and that was the beauty of it."

Whitey was known for being private about financial matters.

"I recall him being surprised once when someone asked how much he paid for a car," my Uncle Ed said. "He gave a vague response that politely drew a line. I suspect he extended that courtesy to his patients and their affairs."

What Whitey did for the people in his community was really nobody's business and yet in some way everybody knew about it. How else would he have ended up with so much strange produce and mysterious letters? And how are his children still hearing things, years after his death, about what he did for people?

Within the family, stories of his frugality tend to outnumber stories of his generosity. My Uncle Ed admits these tales are "well documented in family lore." That's pretty typical of families. We don't take the time to familiarize ourselves with good things about our loved ones when they're alive. Likewise, because we enjoyed all the advantages of being the children and grandchildren of a successful dentist, we occupied ourselves with Whitey's parsimony. Turns out his children and grandchildren were well taken care of and he was wise not to spoil us. We're all better for it.

No Charge

The first amazing thing about Whitey as a dentist is that he never charged a penny if he didn't have to do any work. No cavities meant no charge. While an exam cost him another opportunity or some free time, perhaps Whitey felt a good checkup deserved a reward. Can you imagine a dentist not charging for a visit today?

Many summers, Whitey would spend Thursdays doing dental work for low-income kids. For many of those children, it would mean multiple visits to fill multiple cavities. They all left with a new toothbrush, a tube of toothpaste, and whiter smiles—for which Whitey never received a dime.

He also used to pack his tools and do a "house call" every year to a young woman with cerebral palsy. My Aunt Jean, the youngest, used to assist him.

"I remember being with him as he tried to clean her teeth and do repair work while she twisted and jerked involuntarily," Aunt Jean said.

And, of course, there are those bills that should have been coming due. In a small town, they're probably people you know. My Aunt Ellen (third-born sibling) helped out in the dental office many times over the years.

"When I was helping Daddy with his office affairs," Aunt Ellen recalled, "he wouldn't let me send second notices to patients. He told me that they knew they owed him and they must not have the money to pay. He didn't want to embarrass them by sending additional notices." Embarrass them? That seems like such a distant consideration in an era of collection agencies. Yet in a genuinely bottom-up community, looking out for the dignity of every member is essential to its cohesion.

Black and White

My mother, Ann (the second of Whitey's four children), told me she once tried to shame her father about having had a segregated waiting room. Her grilling came at a time when the national mood had finally turned away from Jim Crow. My mother's youthful indignation was peaking. Whitey patiently explained to her that some dentists in rural North Carolina wouldn't even put their hands into the mouths of black patients back in those days. My mother realized her Dad had probably been the only source of dental care for blacks in the area. When it dawned on her that he rarely ever charged his poorest patients (most of whom were black), she also saw that Whitey could have provided no service to anyone at all had he tried completely to buck the system. Things are rarely so black and white.

Right Back Where It Started

Whitey was realistic about wealth accumulation, too. As most North Carolinians were in those days, Whitey was a lifelong Southern Democrat and yet my mother once asked him why—given all the suffering and inequality in the world—didn't 'we' just redistribute all the wealth so that everybody could have equal portions. That seemed like the fair thing.

"Before too long, it would end up right back where it started," he said. The great philosopher Robert Nozick couldn't have said it any better.

THE OSEOLA MCCARTY ETHIC

Maybe you've heard of Oseola McCarty. She's the woman who took in laundry and ironing to eke out a living in Mississippi. She scraped, saved, and lived austerely for most of her life, starting when she was teenager. That is, until 1995. That was the year she gave her life savings, $150,000, to the local college, Southern Mississippi University. Since she could remember, she had always wanted to be a nurse. So her whole life savings went to setting up a scholarship fund so that young women would be able to study nursing.

When McCarty gave her gift, she didn't just give it to anyone, anywhere. She gave locally. She gave based on what she knew and what held meaning for her. She also gave in a way that would help young women pull themselves up by the bootstraps, rather than offering the money as a handout. If she'd wanted simply to give her money away, she could have simply divided it into envelopes and stuffed it into the mailboxes of people along a poor street in Hattiesburg, Miss., but her ethic said otherwise. She wanted to give wisely by investing in Hattiesburg's human capital.

"Contributions from more than 600 donors have added some $330,000 to the original scholarship fund of $150,000," writes Rick

Bragg in *The New York Times*. "After hearing of Miss McCarty's gift, Ted Turner, a multibillionaire, gave away a billion dollars."[145]

Oseola McCarty had not only left a legacy, she had started a movement. But what does her gift mean? It's certainly about dying knowing you've lived a life of meaning, whatever your means. It's also about leaving a trace. Some people believe that a life of meaning is about posterity—leaving the world somehow better than you found it. Oseola McCarty certainly did but her gift is also about community—real community.

ADJACENT OPPORTUNITIES

Ms. McCarty's ethic is admirable but so also is her method. You see, McCarty sought out what social entrepreneurship guru Ron Schultz calls "adjacent opportunities."

Recall that the adjacent possible are phenomena that emerge locally. For example, the adjacent possible in entrepreneurship is about having what the great Austrian economist Israel Kirzner calls an "alertness" to opportunities in the marketplace, which reduces the margins of a competitor and brings value to customers. This alertness is almost always having sensitivity to that which is already familiar to you. In the social entrepreneurship space, adjacent opportunities are those that emerge as you interact with people in your community. Your sensitivity to such opportunities is a kind of mindfulness. It's not always about radical localization of your philanthropic instincts, but it *almost always* is (or perhaps, should be.) Why would people like Ron Schultz suggest localizing social entrepreneurship?

The closer you are to the action, the better equipped you are to determine whether your gift is needed and the results of your giving are good. It's simply easier to be mindful if you know the people and the terrain. As Schultz puts it:

> In practicing this level of engagement, we discover that something rather unexpected happens. When we operate from a mindful image of the world we encounter, we see things we might previously have missed. We still bring our causal chain of experience with us, but as we break through the patterned behavior and habitual responses that have influenced it in the past, and add a new and more present way of looking at the world we encounter, the possibility space surrounding us enlarges and we see more within it with greater clarity, so that when something does appear that we hadn't seen before, we recognize it before it hits us on the side of the head or passes us by.[146]

Mindfulness—especially when it comes to those affective bonds we can form with our family, friends, and neighbors—changes the dynamic; it changes the *karma*. Thus, mindfulness will be the first virtue to embrace in restoring those bonds of community required to usher in an age of superphilanthropy.

Digital Opportunities

Of course, adjacent opportunities may not always be local, especially in the digital age. This book was funded by people all over the world who had some contact with my work. Weirdly, as I wrote the previous sentence, I got a Facebook note from a Chicago-based friend. It read:

> I'm raising money for the organization at which I tutor a ninth-grader named Davion who goes to Lincoln Park High School. I've been working with him since September and he's really now coming out of his shell. Just yesterday we talked for two hours about Homer's Odyssey. We discussed Odysseus' trials and whether his actions were those of a good leader. Davion thinks he is a good leader and is writing an essay about it now.

If you are so inclined, please donate to Cabrini Connections through the link below.

Normally I might reserve my five-dollar micro-gift for something or someone I know a little more about, but in this case I know my friend in Chicago. Not only is he getting results with the young man, but I was able to follow up and do a little more digging. Now it has become personal. I consider that an adjacent opportunity to give even if it was discovered through digital means. Of course, the Web can allow us to be careless with our giving, but if the Web connects us with knowledgeable people on the ground, that's a good thing because in the end high-quality knowledge is *local* knowledge.

RUGGED COMMUNITARIANISM

Due to more than half a century of the welfare state in the United States, part of what we're losing is not just rugged individualism, but rugged communitarianism. These are the bonds of community for which America was once known. The state has helped to unravel them.

It may sound paradoxical, but strong community does not simply arise out of repeated interactions with people you know, say, down at the corner store or the church potluck dinner. Community often arises out of need. When Ralph Nader said, "A society that has more justice is a society that needs less charity," he got it mixed up. *A society that has more justice is a society that has more charity but needs less of it.* Rugged communitarians don't see justice (or charity) as compulsory. They see it as flowing from the beating heart of community—which also means flowing from within oneself as a community member.

Left to their own devices, people will architect civil society from the bottom up. In other words, philanthropy and mutual aid are rarely, if ever, the artifacts of central planning. They are the way people solve problems, help each other, and guard against the uglier things life can throw at them. But these structures of civil society are fragile. As quickly as we construct them, we can lose them.

As of 1931, only 93,000 families received state assistance in the precursor to Aid to Families with Dependent Children (AFDC), according to David Beito in *The Voluntary City*. By contrast, in 1995, 17 percent of the U.S. population received analogous state assistance.

"Paradoxically, this rise in the welfare rolls has occurred despite a substantial decline in poverty rates," Beito writes. "This raises an obvious question: how were poor people once able to avoid dependence?"[147]

The answer, at least in part, is that they could turn to any one of thousands of mutual aid societies, lodges, or fraternal organizations that no longer exist today. (If they do, most of the organizations may exist in name only, as the missions will have changed.) Allow me to pilfer a quote from economic historian David Beito who uncovered this in his more diligent research. In 1934, a spokesman for the Modern Woodmen of America wrote (note: members are called "neighbors" and lodges "camps"):

> [A] few dollars given here, a small sum there to help a stricken member back on his feet or keep is protection in force during a crisis in his financial affairs; a sick Neighbor's wheat harvested, his grain haled to market, his winter's fuel cut or a home built to replace one destroyed by a midnight fire—thus has fraternity been at work among a million members in 14,000 camps.

These features of civil society were evident to visitors in these times. Tocqueville famously documented them in *Democracy in America* but their rich tradition extends back in time to pre-America Europe. The British-friendly societies are but one example. "Some organizations, such as the United General Sea Box of Borrowstouness Friendly Society and the Sea Box Society of St. Andrews, appeared as early as the 1630s and 1640s," Beito writes.[148] Friendly societies enjoyed robust growth as the British began to find their way to America.

Britain's mutual-aid traditions continued in New England. In 1733, the first Masonic lodge opened in Boston and Philadelphia's came next, but as with many new things these societies began among the elites. The American Revolution served to democratize the Freemasons. While the Masonic Lodge still catered to elites, the post-Revolution period was far less exclusive, according to Beito:

> By the 1780s, modifications began to be introduced to this [decentralized] system. The state grand lodges stabled charity committees to supplement (although never supplant) the local lodges. In 1789, the Pennsylvania Grand Lodge established a fund that was financed through annual assessments of sixty-five cents per member. That same year, the Connecticut Grand Lodge began to deposit three dollars of each initiation fee in a state charity fund.

These societies helped insure against sickness, burial, and all manner of misfortunes. As they developed, their internal rules and local flavors became more distinctive.

Aid to members was not a blanket policy. Applications for aid in most associations were considered on a case-by-case basis.

> The Scots Charitable Society, for instance, allocated funds for such diverse purposes as ship passage, prison bail and an old-age pension. It

> also paid regular stipends to a widow who had lost her husband at sea. [...] Extant records of these organizations invariably classify any case dispersals as "charity" and "relief" rather than "benefits."

All told, members were able to formulate internal checks to keep applicants from taking advantage—something the state has a very difficult time doing when distributing "entitlements."

According to Beito the 1800s saw a flowering of mutual-aid societies—from the Odd Fellows, a national insurance organization, to the Ancient Order of United Workmen. These were some of the more prominent societies. Hundreds of new organizations emerged as the nineteenth century unfolded; names like The Royal Arcanum, the Knights of Honor, and The Order of the Iron Hall, now almost entirely forgotten, were among those that sprang up around the country. "The ranks of fraternalism had become nothing less than an 'enormous army,'" writes Beito, citing a magazine of the time. "The foot soldiers were 'middle-class workmen, the salaried clerk, the farmer, the artisan, the country merchant, and the laborer,' all attempting to 'insure their helpless broods against abject poverty."[149]

WHAT BECAME OF THE MUTUAL AID SOCIETIES?

By the turn of the twentieth century, it would seem that the future of mutual-aid societies could not have been brighter. But the modern welfare state soon replaced great swaths of this robust sector. Voluntary association is often a creature of mutual human need. Government, for better or worse (and I think worse), undermined this by constructing a giant aid monopoly. Beito reminds us that "much that transcended money calculations was lost in the exchange. There has not yet to arise a modern analog to the fraternal society either as a provider of services, such as low-cost medical care, or as a device to encourage the spread of the survival values of thrift, neighborhood cooperation, and individual responsibility."[150] Mutual-aid societies were the natural product of Schultz's adjacent opportunities but the invisible threats that weave communities together cannot long withstand the weight of largesse.

Government, by its nature, produces no good from adjacent opportunities, which are decentralized and require local knowledge. Thus, the welfare state uses resources like a blunt instrument. The n'er-do-well who begs his fellows in the lodge for a handout may or may not get it, but either way he is likely to get wise council and correctives from his peers. The state with all its functionaries cannot hope to reproduce the profound connections created by local circumstances among real neighbors.

LIVING AND FEELING INVISIBLE STRUCTURES

My friend and fellow writer Michael Gibson shared with his blog readers a passage from a book by Jonathan Haidt called *The Righteous Mind*. In it, Haidt relates his personal story of coming to something like cultural relativism—a view that helped him become much more tolerant and far less dogmatic about his own secular American liberal sensibilities:

> On one hand, I was a twenty-nine-year-old liberal atheist with very definite views about right and wrong. On the other hand, I wanted to be like those open-minded anthropologists I had read so much about and had studied with, such as Alan Fiske and Richard Shweder. My first few weeks in Bhubaneswar [India] were therefore filled with feelings of shock and dissonance. I dined with men whose wives silently served us and then retreated to the kitchen, not speaking to me the entire evening.

I was told to be stricter with my servants, and to stop thanking them for serving me. I watched people bathe and cook with visibly polluted water that was held to be sacred. In short, I was immersed in a sex-segregated, hierarchically stratified, devoutly religious society, and I was committed to understanding it on its own terms.

It only took a few weeks for my dissonance to disappear, not because I was a natural anthropologist but because the normal capacity for empathy kicked in. I liked these people who were hosting me, helping me, and teaching me. ...Rather than automatically rejecting the men as sexist oppressors and pitying the women, children, and servants as helpless victims, I began to see a moral world in which families, not individuals, are the basic unit of society, and the members of each extended family (including its servants) are intensely interdependent. In this world, equality and personal autonomy were not sacred values. Honoring elders, gods, and guests, protecting subordinates, and fulfilling one's role-based duties were more important.

I had read about Shweder's ethic of community and had understood it intellectually. But now *for the first time in my life, I began to feel it.*[151]

This passage gives rise to a lot of interesting issues we'll have to pass over. In the context of this discussion, what's so powerful is not that one might come to appreciate some cultural norm that currently is repugnant. It is rather that the passage unpacks something *else* about those invisible structures that bind people together within communities and cultures. That there is so much variation among communities and cultures may be more than just an academic point.

I wonder what Haidt might have written had he traveled to 1950s North Carolina to work with my grandfather treating black patients *pro bono* after they had had to suffer the indignity of waiting in a blacks-only waiting room. I wonder what Haidt might have written if he'd traveled to 1890s and lived among the members of a single lodge in that "enormous army" of mutual associations that helped people survive and thrive in era before the rise of the welfare state. The point in letting one's mind wonder like this is not to apologize for injustice or justify cultural relativism. Rather it is to get us into habits of being that keep us mindful of the adjacent possible, that let us see the invisible structures of community, and that give us healthy skepticism about the centralization of, well, anything. Thanks to politics, we have replaced the generosity structures within a thousand communities with the Department of Health and Human Services. The government steamrolls over the shoots and saplings of emergent community.

Commenting on the passage, Gibson writes:

> No amount of arguing could have led Haidt to adopt these attitudes. No deduction from moral principles in a reflective equilibrium could have led to these intuitions. They had to be lived and then felt. Not that this suite of moral sentiments presents a better way of life. But it does show how people can change. In a world of robust competition between jurisdictions, we should see a variety of different ways of life. That variety is a good thing. But if anything like a free society can flourish amid the competition, it will be because people have opted into it and have grown accustomed to its norms and values. That will be the larger force for change. Arguing for people in Chicago or Los Angeles to adopt those attitudes today one by one doesn't stand a chance.

Analogously, we might wonder whether *in a world of robust competition between charities and communities of mutual aid, we should see a variety of different ways to lift each other up. That variety is a good thing, but if anything like a poverty-free society could flourish amid the competition, it would be because people have opted into it and have grown accustomed to its norms and values.*

POLITICS AS TUG O' WAR

Politics is like turf war. Tug o' war. King of the mountain. Politics is a game of winner-take-all that is balanced only by compromise, horse-trading, and the occasional threat of an electoral rout. At the end of the process, one single way of doing things gets set into motion, then that way gets institutionalized. The experimentation process made possible through variety, trial-and-error, and competition grinds to a stop.

Moreover, titanic election cycles mean we're sinking resources into deadweight activism. More and more resources are going into the promises of politicians who consistently let us down. The system is rigged—left, right, and center. Corporations are spending more time, energy, and money protecting their asses, colluding with politicians, or chasing the spoils of legislation instead of innovating.

Entrepreneurship, social or otherwise, is starting to languish. The resources we use to play political tug o' war don't get used on positive social change. As a result, we're increasingly disillusioned, polarized, and angry. Why can't we just abandon this paradigm?

It's a tit-for-tat struggle, which means each side seeks domination. If one side were to capitulate or redirect too many resources, the other side would seize the opportunity to gain power. It's not the worst of possible outcomes, but it's certainly not the best. One thing is clear: If we could find our way out of the political paradigm we could do better. If we could find our way to a transpartisan paradigm, we could unleash superphilanthropy.

DEADWEIGHT ACTIVISM

What does a transpartisan paradigm look like?

The potential of supercharged, distributed philanthropy could be unleashed if the state got out of the social change business. Right now, that doesn't seem likely. Understanding about the power of distributed philanthropy has not caught up with how people actually use it. For example, as we have suggested, a lot of giving and organization is wasted on electoral politics—i.e. who gets to run the show and what legislation will direct the government to take care of people.

Political tribalism drives our thinking. That tribal thinking often keeps us in the mode of dead-weight activism, which strengthens and reinforces the status quo. According to the Center for Responsive Politics, the 2008 presidential race cost an estimated $2.4 billion, about double that of 2004. The entire election cycle cost $5.3 billion.[152] What if every dime of that went to philanthropic organizations making real, positive social change?

Just think about what all the fighting is over: Entitlement spending alone accounts for about 10 percent of U.S. GDP.[153] One-tenth of our economy is going to bureaucratic means of "helping" people in various ways, from healthcare to welfare. What if just a quarter of those resources went to distributed philanthropy; that is, to a new, high-performance market of social values with its attendant experimentation and feedback loops?

Social entrepreneurship could not only be a powerful new sector, but it could unleash some of the value currently being pressed down by the monoliths of state bureaucracy. Social problems could be solved by the wisdom of crowds rather than the whims of legislators. We might disagree about the extent to which there is room for both public entitlements and private charity, but perhaps we can agree that there is considerable crowding-out of charity by the public sector. Government simply doesn't do "distributed" well.

Despite the fact that government consumes most of what could reasonably go to supercharged, distributed philanthropy, giving is alive and well. In 2008, people gave in excess of $307 million, despite a major recession.[154] That is a staggering amount. It may seem modest next to recent stimulus bills, bank bailouts, and industry nationalizations we were all compelled to pay for, but Americans are still generous by any measure. If this level of giving continues and these resources can become positively channeled using technology, we are likely to see unprecedented social change occur as the transaction costs for information sharing, coordination, and funding continue to fall.

PHILANTHROPY UNCHAINED[155]

Ronald Coase's seminal 1937 work *The Nature of the Firm* poses an important question: Why do folks organize into firms? Why isn't there a totally "free" market in labor? Or, more prosaically, why do organizations take on scales that result in relatively costly, hierarchical forms of order? Coase's answer is "transaction costs." The firm reduces the costs that would be incurred to continually coordinate actions among scattered people with disparate skill sets, all of whom would have to contract with one another, hammer out details of said contracts, and then get together somehow to divide labor and accomplish something profitable. So, up to a certain point, organizations arranged like hierarchies have been less costly to organize because it is usually cheaper for some people to give orders and some to take them (the former pay the latter for the privilege). But that is changing and fast.

Enter technology. Social media are lowering the costs of organizing and giving. Firms are still around, but these industrial forms certainly don't look like they did in 1937. Some people are starting to organize for certain things without organizations, from political activism to charitable giving. Clay Shirky describes the phenomenon well in his book *Here Comes Everybody*. He hits squarely upon the implications of these new media when he writes: "Groups like ex-Jehovah's Witnesses and the Pro-Ana [anorexic] girls no longer need social support to gather; they all operate under the Coasean floor, where lowered transaction costs have made gathering together so simple that anyone can do it."[156]

The big-picture implications of these media lag their mass utilitarian uptake. Your teen tweets and grandma stalks on Facebook without grasping the enormous social transformation of which they are a part. Philanthropy already figures into this dynamic; indeed, even if people gave less to charity in the future, we could do so much more with less due to the kinds of efficiencies distributed philanthropy will enable. We can look forward to Tocqueville's America on steroids, Coase's firm becoming less hierarchical, and Smith's invisible hand extending to help like never before.

EXPERIMENTATION

Competition is a loaded term. Its connotations could make us lose sight of its power in the voluntary sector. Let me borrow a sliver from Allen Meltzer and James Madison to put the idea into perspective:

Competition brings choice and improved relevance not only to commerce but also to religion. James Madison believed that competing churches would prove stronger than an established state church—because each would appeal to its members and try to attract others. Time proved Madison right. In Europe, the state supports established churches, yet organized religion is weak; the public rejects the state's religion monopoly by simply not participating.[157]

Religious freedom is guaranteed by the First Amendment to the U.S. Constitution but because Congress can make no law establishing a state religion, religion is a free-market phenomenon. There is no shortage of churches, temples, and places of worship, and there is tremendous variety. They compete for your attendance and your tithes. From old sects, new sects are born. The process is evolutionary. Some organizations change with the times and others find solace in old ways or traditional rules and liturgy, but there is tremendous experimentation in the market for religion due to competition among these places of worship.

The charity sector is no different. There is tremendous competition among groups vying for a piece of your giving spirit. Poverty relief, in particular, could use a lot more market discipline. Of course, non-profit organizations don't function, strictly speaking, within a profit and loss system. Figuring out better proxies for effectiveness, such as transparency and accountability mechanisms, will be a major aspect of superphilanthropy as it emerges.

When it comes right down to it, though, some organizations will live and some will die. Often in the non-profit sector, survival is not always about which non-profit is the most effective. Sometimes it comes down to brand recognition or effective marketing.

Still, that's why it is incumbent upon us to become more responsible philanthropists. We must do our due diligence and we must look for more adjacent opportunities as opposed grand designs because, ultimately, failure due to competition and experimentation is far preferable to a single monolithic failure.

THE FIRST STIRRINGS

The first stirrings of superphilanthropy are already with us. Take a look at the giving portfolio of Pierre Omidyar, the superwealthy eBay founder. You can see how much activity is already going on globally just in the area of microfinance:[158]

- Balkan Financial Sector Equity Fund
- BlueOrchard
- Boulder Institute of Microfinance
- BRAC
- Catalyst Microfinance Investors
- Consultative Group to Assist the Poor
- Elevar Equity
- Finestrella
- Global Commercial Microfinance Consortium
- International Association of Microfinance Investors
- Kiva
- LeapFrog Investments
- Mango
- MFX Solutions
- Microfinance Centre
- Microfinance Information Exchange
- MicroSave

- MicroVest
- Mobile Transactions
- Opportunity International
- Rêv
- Sa-Dhan
- SEEP Network
- SOLIDUS Investment Fund

If you've never heard of microfinance, it's based on the idea that what the world's poorest people really need is capital—that is the stuff of which ventures are made. But the reason that they're poor to begin with is that, despite smarts and a good work ethic, capital is very hard to come by in the developing world. Indeed, third-world banking systems are underdeveloped and many economic freedoms are curtailed by corruption and predatory governments. For example, if you can't own property, how can you use your property as collateral to get a small business loan? Most of the world lives in this informal sector and has no access to the legal structures we take for granted in the developed world.

So what do the superphilanthropists do? They circumvent these institutional problems by getting very tiny loans to people who will work hard engaging in small-scale entrepreneurship. In other words, microfinancing is not mere giving. It splits the difference between giving and investment by creating opportunities for sustained economic activity, however humble it may be.

Microfinance is not just for the developing world, either. Nobel-prize winning founder Mohammed Yunus, who founded Grameen Bank, now has a robust microfinance operation in the United States: Grameen USA. We should keep our eyes out for these new funding models. They could provide major opportunities for the working poor to pull themselves up by the bootstraps at home and abroad.

EDUCATION

In 2008, the last year *Fast Company* magazine put out its Social Capitalist Awards, one-third of the forty-five social philanthropies listed had been founded to address some aspect of American education. To my mind this is another among many indications that the government school system has failed.

Donor's Choose, one of the 15 school-oriented groups that made the list, allows teachers to sign up and ask donors for needed books, computers, or other classroom materials. However, Donor's Choose doesn't allow private schools to participate, which reflects a bias against private education—whether for-profit or non-profit. It also suggests just how many wasted resources are going into fixing a failed system. Consider that in Austin, Texas, the average per-student private tuition is about $8,000 a year. For the government schools? Cost per pupil is about $9,000 per student, even as it has dropped sharply from years prior.[159]

Given the poor performance of government schools (bankrolled through coercive taxation) and the lower-cost and higher quality of private schools, shouldn't we question all this philanthropic support for an expensive, dying system? Might we stop thinking in the public (good)/private (bad) duality and start thinking in terms of what is effective for teaching kids? Indeed, it may also be time to dispel the stereotypes of the non-profit versus the for-profit organization.

I'm reminded of a passage from Whole Foods CEO John Mackey in an essay called "Creating a New Paradigm for Business":

> A wall exists between the non-profits and the for-profits consisting partly of the stereotypes that exist in our society today. Non-profits are viewed as good because they have altruistic, idealistic goals. [...] [N]on-profits often believe that money "grows on trees," and because their ideals are altruistic, they are seen as "angels." Non-profits sponsor idealistic events like AIDS walks and they have an environmental consciousness. On the other side of the wall you will see the clear contrast with the for-profit sector of business. You see the stereotype of the greedy businessman with dollar signs in his eyes, grasping after money, and smokestacks popping up all around the world. The angel is transformed into a devil because again, the only goal is to maximize profits and that is seen as simply selfish and greedy.[160]

Mackey believes these stereotypes have outlived their usefulness; that the wall between non-profit and for-profit needs to be torn down and "the polarities integrated." He suggests that a more holistic model of the organization is due, that machine metaphors for organizations ought to be abandoned, and that profit is one side of a coin whose other face is what Mackey calls a "deeper purpose."

Private schools can absolutely be "deeper purpose" initiatives. Social entrepreneur Michael Strong, who has helped found four schools, writes:

> In each case the school was proprietary primarily in order to ensure founder's control. Often non-profit boards can drift away from founder's intent. Each proprietary school would have liked to have been profitable, but in the world of high-touch, high-quality education that I love, it is tough to make a profit.[161]

Strong's blunt assessment is interesting given that he is normally relentlessly optimistic. He does believe there is room for high-quality, low-cost education despite heavy state subsidies for state schools. But his realism goes to my point that people who love alternative education aren't necessarily in it for the money (as my wife and I can attest). It is a shame, though, that "edupreneurs" have to compete with a system of "free" government schools that exist in large part to enrich developers (who build Taj Ma-schools) and in large part to maintain an administrative apparatus that sucks resources right out of the classrooms without bringing much value to students.

Whatever you think about government versus private schools, there are bright spots in educational philanthropy that foreshadow an education revolution currently in the making: I'm thinking about Khan Academy, for example, which organizes lessons on an array of subjects across levels of ability. Anyone can access these lessons online at no cost to them. All you need is a computer and an Internet connection.

TOCQUEVILLE ON STEROIDS

What does all this mean for philanthropy? Decentralization due to social technology fundamentally changes the way we make the world a better place through giving. How? By lowering costs in three primary areas: acquiring information, coordinating action, and funding initiatives. Often, we give based on an organization's reputation and perhaps some anecdotal evidence of the good it does.

What if we had greater access to information about specific projects and the results of organizational activity? We'd be much smarter givers. Also, what if it was easier just to get people together and get them active, say, as community volunteers? Organizations or determined individuals would have greater access to human capital. Finally, what if it was simpler and more convenient to give even a small amount—$20, $5, even $1, all of which could add up for some worthy group (as long as said group has an army of givers)? These three factors alone will continue to transform the philanthropic sector in ways we cannot entirely predict.

IF WE MUST HAVE A WELFARE STATE

Political realities tend to quell idealism. So what if we could strike something of a great compromise? How might we have a welfare state that does less damage? This is a big, big question—one I could devote a whole book to. But I'd like to sketch out some ideas here. After all, the more government stays out of the business of "helping" people, the more robust that sector can become.

The Great Inversion—We alluded to the idea of competition and experimentation above. If there is anything to the idea that experimentation allows us more opportunities to yield good systems, we should ask is it better to have one welfare state or 50? I would argue for the latter. As F.A. Hayek once wrote, "The solution of the economic problem is a voyage of exploration into the unknown, an attempt to discover new ways of doing things better."[162] Nothing is exempt. Economics (including the giving economy) is a discovery process. So if we must have welfare systems, 50 welfare states would allow state legislatures and bureaucracies to try out competing systems. Hopefully, the welfare states that were effective—that is, created less dependency and didn't break budgets—would become models for the other states. This process wouldn't always play out. Politicians can live in denial but it would be more likely to happen than under a single scheme.

To be fair, states currently have some latitude with respect to the way they allocate federal welfare dollars. However, what I'm suggesting is that the federal government not be involved at all. Thus, the first order of business would be to devolve all forms of welfare to the states—*that means on both the taxation and distribution sides.* Congress might have to pass a law directing the states to contrive their own models, but otherwise the federal government would simply stay out of the way.

Minimum Income—Within some system, whether at the federal or state level, we should simply get rid of welfare bureaucracies and adopt something like a negative income tax as proposed by Milton Friedman. To adopt such a tax would mean not only that we scrap the welfare state bureaucracy but all forms of entitlement transfers. One such Friedmanite plan has been explored by the social scientist Charles Murray. I interviewed him about his idea back in 2006. He assured me that repositioning unproductive bureaucrats within the creative economy would be a happy byproduct of a negative income tax-type scheme. But ultimately, this is the point he wanted to make:

> We start with a country that is the richest country in the world, with most of its people having lots of money (compared to any historical standard), ample money to provide for their own retirements, medical care, and the rest of it. On top of this national wealth, we then add more than $1 trillion to help people provide for comfortable retirement and medical care, and so forth. And guess what? We still have millions of people without comfortable retirements, without adequate medical care. And only a government can spend that much money that ineffectually. *The alternative I suggest is give every adult American, age 21 and older, $10,000 a year. And let them run with it.*[163]

I think this is a strong proposal. When we consider Friedman's four ways to spend money, putting the money "in our hands" (which happens also to be the title of Murray's book[164]) makes much more sense that continuing with an administrative welfare state. Now, it would be hard to live off of $10,000 a year, but when life is easy under welfare, it keeps people trapped.

Now, we started this section by talking about a great compromise, but such is a bit pie-in-the-sky. As Murray explains:

> I start out ... by saying there would have to be a constitutional amendment. And I am not confident to frame that in legal language, but I can tell you the sense of it. And the sense of it is that—hence forth—no government program shall be used to transfer money directly from individuals or groups to other individuals and groups. You know, the programs that are legitimate for the government are ones that provide authentic public goods—such as police protection, the court system, and national defense. The one exception to all of this shall be the grant—the $10,000—that starts out at $10,000 a year on the opening of the program. And other than that, no transfers at all. And that includes corporate welfare and agricultural subsidies and all the rest. At the local, state, as well as federal level.[165]

Given what we understand about the Takers Nexus, this sounds like a plan that, despite imperfections, is way better than the system we have now.

> But here's what I think we have to talk about. [...] [T]he best solution of all is to leave all of this money in the hands of the people who started with it. And this would energize unimaginably effective, widespread, voluntary means of dealing with the problems we face.
>
> We cannot blink at the fact that there's so much money out there—and the impulse to use the government to redistribute is widespread. We are

not going to change that. For all time to come, governments are going to take in vast sums of money and redistribute it. And then the question for [us] becomes: if one accepts that it's going to happen, is there a way to do this which leaves people's lives in their own hands?

I acknowledge we are still a long way away from having any rational, national conversation on the subject, but we should aim to start one.

Voucherize—Now, if given political realities we couldn't get as far as we suggest above, how about means test and voucherize everything government currently meddles in? Healthcare? Education? Anything that is done in the name of the poor can be reserved for the poor. Voucherization will inject a sclerotic system with market dynamism.

Choice Within Coercion—I'm more tentative about this proposal but what if we created a system in which people could voluntarily redirect tax dollars that would normally go to some welfare/entitlement scheme to the philanthropy sector? In other words, suppose you really, really care about ensuring that poor kids get health insurance coverage. Instead of your tax dollars going to SCHIP (the children's Medicaid program) your tax dollars could go to, say, a non-profit consortium of health insurers that provides health savings accounts (HSAs) and high-deductible plans for children at reduced cost? Instead of your tax dollars going to NASA or NEA, a sizable portion of your tax dollars might go to a cancer charity, research non-profit, or a local arts co-op.

I realize there are a number of difficulties with this idea. First, it would be difficult to parse which groups get to count as eligible for these diverted tax dollars. Second, the scheme could end up corrupted. Finally, most people would argue that some tax revenue has to be reserved for what constitutes "basic government services." Of course, when you're in (or dependent on) a government agency, you almost always regard your own agency as basic. Nevertheless, even if we could divert much more taxed resources for state causes to charitable causes, such could go very far in supercharging the voluntary sector.

BUT CAN WE TRUST EACH OTHER?

When pressed, advocates of a more extensive welfare state often say we just can't trust our neighbors and greedy industrialists to be charitable. People are selfish, they argue, so an enlightened group of unselfish people must use coercive means to ensure social justice for the poor and disenfranchised. Curiously, this parallels arguments by those skeptical of government power. We argue that men, even bureaucrats, also are selfish—cut as we all are from Kant's crooked timber. So, if advocates of social justice and advocates of limited government can agree on the nature of man, then why are they so divergent on questions of how best to look out for the poor?

I believe we can cut this Gordian knot. There will be plenty of people who want to help their fellow man when they feel the onus of responsibility rests on them (as opposed to "society") and they are left with the means to do so. In the years after Charles Dickens's death, Britain was a nation of tithers, according to Richard Ebeling:

> By the 1890s [...] most middle-class British families devoted 10 percent
> of their income for charitable works—an outlay from average family
> income second only to expenditures on food. Total voluntary giving in
> Britain was greater than the entire budgets of several European govern-
> ments, and more than half a million women worked as full-time volun-
> teers for various charitable organizations.[166]

And we know that contemporary Americans are big givers.

Maybe we can trust each other here in the United States, too. Consider the latest available data (2010) from the Giving USA Foundation and its research partner, the Center on Philanthropy at Indiana University:

> [T]otal charitable contributions from American individuals, corporations and foundations were an estimated $290.89 billion in 2010, up from a revised estimate of $280.30 billion for 2009. The 2010 estimate represents growth of 3.8 percent in current dollars and 2.1 percent in inflation-adjusted dollars.

This despite 10 percent of U.S. GDP going to the welfare state.

Those who do not reach out to the most distressed among us might be considered "greedy." As long as they engage in honest entrepreneurship they are lifting people out of poverty through their effort. As Milton Friedman said before a packed crowd at Stanford University in 1978, "So far as poverty is concerned, there has never in history been a more effective machine for eliminating poverty than the free-enterprise system." Let us not forget that giving is a part of that system.

FREE TO GIVE

One of the simplest and most profound things we can take with us is this: Any value can be exchanged with almost any other value. I value my time and things I can buy with my money. Sometimes I'm willing to exchange my time and money for benefits to my family, my neighbors, and complete strangers. From these dynamic exchanges among values a new prosperity emerges.

But neither plain old entrepreneurs nor superphilanthropists can engage in free enterprise without the right kinds of institutions. Institutions are those laws and policies that tend to either raise or lower the costs of cooperation and exchange. Institutions considered more free actually lower the costs of cooperation and exchange; those considered less free raise those costs. In the least-free areas of the world, transaction costs can be insuperably high.

To get an idea of how powerful this truth is, consider the Economic Freedom of the World Index compiled by the Fraser Institute. Authors of the index rate countries around the world on five basic dimensions:

1. Size of government: expenditures, taxes, and enterprises
2. Legal structure and security of property rights
3. Access to sound money
4. Freedom to trade internationally
5. Regulation of credit, labor and business

As this study shows (and aggregate editions of data over time show) the relationship between economic freedom and prosperity is strongly correlated. This strong correlation tracks with our intuitions about the wealth of nations, too. Consider the 2009 Top Ten:

1. Hong Kong	6. Canada
2. Singapore	7. Chile
3. New Zealand	8. United Kingdom
4. Switzerland	9. Mauritius
5. Australia	10. United States

The Heritage Foundation compiles a similar index. In 2012, its Top Ten was strikingly similar:

1. Hong Kong	6. Canada
2. Singapore	7. Chile
3. Australia	8. Mauritius
4. New Zealand	9. Ireland
5. Switzerland	10. United States

Notice that the United States barely makes it into the top ten on both these most recent indices. That is because the United States has become less free on those vital dimensions the index measures. The least-free countries in the world are Zimbawbe, Venezuela, and Myanmar according to the Fraser Index; Cuba, Zimbabwe, and North Korea according to the Heritage Index (bearing in mind that the former doesn't collect data on Cuba or North Korea). These least-free countries are also some of the least prosperous in the world. Interestingly, they are also some of the most egalitarian. Their regimes have done away with virtually all of the institutions that give rise to wealth. And, of course, where there is very little wealth, there is very little philanthropy.

As I opened *Superwealth* with a narrative about my great grandmother, I realized that with every word I was giving Mama Borders
new life. Her existence meant something—not just to her children
and grandchildren, but to a few people in the future who would
never meet her. She had left traces and in some fundamental sense,
we all want to do that. We hope we can do something that will outlive our bodies.

Writing is an act of leaving traces. What traces do I want to
leave with this book? I realize it's not particularly artful to spell out
in stark letters what could be left in a reader's mind like a scent, an
echo, or a pleasant memory, but I'm going to: I would like to propose an ethic. Not pulpit bashing or finger wagging. A way to look
at life and to relate to each other.

I gave up professional philosophy long ago, so I'm not looking
for indelible ink with which to write the Book of Morals. To me, an
ethic is at best a set of tenets that—if we all kept tucked in our hip
pockets—we'd get along better. The least I can hope for is to leave
something to my child. I want shamelessly to do that here.

An ethic of wealth is a set of tenets that will help us navigate our
way into an age of abundance. Five is a good number for a set. Not
too many. Not too few.

1. *Resist envy*—It doesn't yield much good that I can see. Even if we try to dress up envy in the finery of justice, it's still envy. Most everyone is going to feel envy at one time or another but when we do, we should put it in its place—just as we do other urges that don't do us much good.

2. *Help others often*—Whenever we have an opportunity to help others, we should. That doesn't mean turn into Mother Teresa. It means that we look out for the most vulnerable people in the world, especially those who live closest to us. It means we take the time not just to assist the poor, but to mentor the young and look out for our friends and neighbors. It's not always about throwing money at problems, either. To help, sometimes it's about knowing when not to give.

3. *Create value*—Selfishly serving others means doing our very best to give people as much value as we can in any profitable exchange. Whatever the job, creating value means providing the best product or service while looking for the win-win. We should create value wherever possible and look for new opportunities to create value, which means understanding the needs and desires of others at the same time as we seek to understand our own.

4. *Be excellent*—Maybe I should say shoot for excellence. In whatever we do, we should try to do it with a view towards perfection. Of course, one shouldn't let the perfect be the enemy of the good; for example, by wasting time or learning to do useless things. But one should always strive for continuous improvement.

5. *Embrace change*—We should never be afraid to let things flow and unfold. As we enter a new age of abundance, we

should do so with eyes wide open. Some things will happen in fits and starts. It may all come across to us as a bit uneven, dare I say, unequal. This natural unfolding means that certain people will benefit early, while others benefit later. But things can and will flow to good ends if we don't get impatient. When change comes, we should prepare for it to be rapid and rather unpredictable.

An ethic of wealth needn't be complicated. When my son Sid learns to read well enough—he's five years old as of this writing—he should be able to understand the five tenets above. What can I leave the boy I dearly love? Something I believe is more valuable than money.

Max Borders, 2012

ACKNOWLEDGEMENTS

First, I have to thank Carly and Sid Borders who put up with hours of Daddy with his head down in a laptop. Without their patience and support, *Superwealth* would have been as good as smoke trails swirling around in my head.

Then there are those who, along the path, pointed the way:

Rick Borders—Taught me to tell stories since I was old enough to talk.

Ann Hord-Heatherley—Created the conditions. Channeled my intensity.

Brad Bostian—Gave up dozens of afternoons coaching me as a young writer, after teaching middle school English all day.

Orson Scott Card—Told me when I was bad that I was terrible; when I was good, I was unstoppable.

Greg Baxter, Adam Knapp, Ed Gottsman, John Schrock, Scott Cook and Mike Fenner—Used red ink and high praise – both as I needed it. They all helped me learn to write for food.

Nick Schulz—Found me in obscurity, made me his second-in-command and taught how me to ask tough questions.

Don Boudreaux—Guided me, chapter by chapter, through the process of writing Superwealth and helped me better apply the economic way of thinking.

This book and this writer were made possible thanks to these mentors.

Superwealth as an undertaking would not have been possible without: Tom Phillips, John Farley, David Donadio and the rest of the fine people associated with the Phillips Foundation. The Robert Novak Fellowship allowed me to support my family while writing a book. John Farley's and David Donadio's feedback on key chapters made the book far stronger.

I also received tremendous financial and moral support from "Team Superwealth" to get the book to market. These are the folks who funded the Kickstarter campaign, which allowed me to get this into book form and promote it – all while circumventing traditional publishing. I want to thank all who backed me, but some who deserve special recognition are:

Barry and Laura Rand

Ann and Trish Hord-Heatherley

Ron Muhlenkamp

Rusty Reese

Carl Hankins

Doug Stafford

Surse Pierpoint

Jon Henke

Emma and Andrew Chisholm

G.K. Gerig

Gabe Dellinger

Robert M. Metcalfe

Joe Coletti

Maurice Hord

Greg Carroll

James and An Dreea Monnat

Jackson Kuhl

Ed Hord

Jim Tusty

Thomas Brand

Peter Pakalnis

Mary Stout

Carl Oberg

Bob Coli, MD

Jerry Adkins

The folks at Throne Publishing have been consummate professionals – putting up with my imperfections even as I demanded perfection from them. Jeremy Brown, Christine Whitmarsh, Matt Arps, Nathan Orme and Kandi Miller to name a few.

I owe Bob Chitester huge a debt of gratitude both in introducing me to so many of these inspiring characters, but in being a flexible boss as I ran with the project. He also reinforced the importance of balancing "show" with "tell," and sticky stories with exposition.

Chris Rufer gave me the story of his life and career for a whole chapter and I owe him tremendous thanks. Chris has fundamentally changed the way I think and act in ways he might not have anticipated.

John X gave me tremendous insights in another chapter, which he practically wrote. John's humility and brilliance stand juxtaposed in happy paradox. He is one of those rare people who makes the world a better place without the need for recognition. In short, he helped me understand how wealth works.

Max Krasnow and Thomas Sparks gave their time for extensive interviews and their contributions added color, dimension and credibility.

Adrian Bejan has been generous with his time. Thanks to Professor Bejan, I can see how things flow.

Mike Rypka gave valuable time, as well. His tacos continue to feed our family while his entrepreneurial lessons inspire us.

Ed, Ann, Ellen, and Jean offered deeper insights about their father, my grandfather, Whitey Hord. My dad, Rick, and grandmother Bebe gave me critical information about Mama Borders, my great grandmother.

Those who know me know that I am scatterbrained. If there is anyone who belongs in these acknowledgements I failed to mention, please contact me and I will put their name in subsequent editions. All who helped me with this project deserve my sincerest appreciation.

Max Borders, 2012

Notes

[1] Schulz, Nick. "Steve Jobs: America's Greatest Failure," *National Review Online* (Aug. 25, 2011), http://www.nationalreview.com/articles/275528/steve-jobs-america-s-greatest-failure-nick-schulz

[2] Cash, W. J. *The Mind of the South*. Vintage; 1991
http://www.amazon.com/The-Mind-South-W-J-Cash/dp/067973647

[3] Cash, W. J. *The Mind of the South*. Vintage; 1991
http://www.amazon.com/The-Mind-South-W-J-Cash/dp/067973647

[4] Schmidt, Ronald and Janice Willett. "Slamming Economic Inequality -Not A Slam Dunk," Kudlow's Money Politic$ (Dec. 6, 20111), http://kudlowsmoneypolitics.blogspot.com/2011/12/slamming-economic-inequality-not-slam.html

[5] Foresman, Chris. "Wireless survey: 91% of Americans use cell phones," *Ars Technica* (March 24, 2010), http://arstechnica.com/telecom/news/2010/03/wireless-survey-91-of-americans-have-cell-phones.ars

[6] Strong, Michael. "Forget the World Bank, Try Wal-Mart," *Ideas in Action With Jim Glassman* (Aug. 22, 2006), http://www.ideasinactiontv.com/tcs_daily/2006/08/forget-the-world-bank-try-wal-mart.html

[7] http://marketplace.publicradio.org/display/web/2009/11/23/pm-walmart/

[8] Bunce, Victoria and J.P. Wieske. "Health Insurance Mandates in the States 2010: Executive Summary," Council for Affordable Health Insurance. http://www.cahi.org/cahi_contents/resources/pdf/MandatesintheStates2010ExecSummary.pdf

[9] Peele, Stanton. "Why Do Low-Income People Smoke More and Drink More Soda, but Drink Less Alcohol?" *The Huffington Post* (June 29, 2010), http://www.huffingtonpost.com/stanton-peele/why-do-poor-people-smoke_b_627057.html

[10] Cox, W. Michael and Richard Alm. "Myths of Rich & Poor: Why We're Better off than We Think," (New York: Basic, 1999)

[11] Diane Alter. "Study: Violent video games reduce real violence," Gant Daily, September 30, 2011, http://gantdaily.com/2011/09/30/study-violent-video-games-reduce-real-violence/

[12] Freeman, Bob. "Researchers Examine Video Gaming's Benefits." January 25, 2010. http://www.defense.gov/news/newsarticlc.aspx?id=57695

[13] http://www.amazon.com/The-Bourgeois-Virtues-Commerce-ebook/dp/B003QHYIXY/ref=sr_1_1?s=digital-text&ie=UTF8&qid=1346772330&sr=1-1&keywords=bourgeois+virtue

[14] Dimitri, Carolyn, Anne Efland, and Neilson Conklin. "The 20th Century Transformation of U.S. Agriculture and Farm Policy." United States Department of Agriculture Economic Information

Bulletin No. 3 (June 2005). http://www.ers.usda.gov/publications/eib3/eib3.htm#changes

[15] G. Warren Nutter. "Freedom in a Revolutionary Economy," in *Nutter, Political Economy and Freedom*. (Indianapolis: Liberty Press, 1983), 3-19; the quotation is on pp. 15-16.

[16] Folsom, Burton W. "Billy Durant and the Founding of General Motors." The Mackinac Center for Public Policy (September 8, 1998). SKU: V1998-28. http://www.mackinac.org/article.aspx?ID=651

[17] http://www.sloan.org/pages/18/who-was-alfred-p-sloan-jr

[18] Goswami, Bijoy with David K. Wolpert. *The Human Fabric: Unleashing the Power of Core Energy in Everyone* (Austin, Texas: Aviri Publishing, 2004). http://www.bijoygoswami.com/book/TheHumanFabric.pdf.

[19] The Self-Management Institute, http://self-managementinstitute.org/

[20] Hamil, Gary. "First Let's Fire All the Managers," Harvard Business Review, December 2011, http://www.uky.edu/Centers/iwin/RTOCT12/GreenHBRarticle.pdf

[21] *Concise Encyclopedia of Economics*, 1st ed., s.v. "Free Market" by Murray N. Rothbard. http://www.econlib.org/library/Enc1/FreeMarket.html

[22] Burrows, Sara. "Street Food: Raleigh Says No to Entry-Level Culinary Spots," Carolina Journal, September 15, 2010, http://www.carolinajournal.com/exclusives/display_exclusive.html?id=6852

[23] *Concise Encyclopedia of Economics*, 2nd ed., s.v. "Fascism" by Sheldon Richman. http://www.econlib.org/library/Enc/Fascism.html

[24] *Concise Encyclopedia of Economics*, 1st ed., s.v. "Free Market"

[25] Yandle, Bruce. "Bootleggers and Baptists in Retrospect," *Regulation* magazine of Cato Institute, Vol. 22, No. 3, http://www.cato.org/pubs/regulation/regv22n3/bootleggers.pdf

[26] Rauch, Jonathan. *Government's End: Why Washington Stopped Working*. Public Affairs; December 1999

[27] *Ibid.*

[28] "Durant Versus Sloan – Part 1," posted October 1, 2009, http://steveblank.com/2009/10/01/durant-versus-sloan-part-1/

[29] Loomis, Carol J. "The $600 Billion Challenge," *CNN Money*, posted June 16, 2010, http://features.blogs.fortune.cnn.com/2010/06/16/gates-buffett-600-billion-dollar-philanthropy-challenge/

[30] Kawamoto, Dawn. "Buffett donates his billions to Gates Foundation," CNET News, posted June 26, 2006, http://news.cnet.com/Buffett-donates-his-billions-to-Gates-foundation/2100-1022_3-6087682.html

[31] Buffet, Warren. "Stop Coddling the Super-Rich," *New York Times* op-ed, August 14, 2011, http://www.nytimes.com/2011/08/15/opinion/stop-coddling-the-super-rich.html?_r=1

[32] Bernstein, Jared. "Don't worry, rich people will keep making money despite higher taxes," On the Economy, *Christian Science Monitor*, September 1, 2011, http://www.csmonitor.com/Business/On-the- Economy/2011/0901/Don-t-worry-rich-people-will-keep-making-money-despite-higher-taxes

[33] Noah, Timothy. "The United States of Inequality," *Slate*, Sept. 3, 2010, http://www.slate.com/articles/news_and_politics/the_great_divergence/features/2010/the_united_states_of_inequality/introducing_the_great_divergence.html

[34] Boudreaux, Donald J. "Don't Curse the Oil Speculators," *Newsday*, April 5, 2012, http://www.newsday.com/opinion/oped/boudreaux-don-t-curse-the-oil-speculators-1.3645329

[35] *The New Palgrave: A Dictionary of Economics* (London: Macmillan Press Ltd., 1987), pp. 609-614, http://www.auburn.edu/~garriro/e4hayek.htm

[36] From an interview with Thomas Sparks.

[37] http://hamiltonsocietyofwallstreet.com/2012/03/25/thecustomer/

[38] http://hamiltonsocietyofwallstreet.com/wp-content/uploads/2012/03/Merrill-Lynch-Leslies-Weekly-Article-1911.jpg

[39] Wallison, Peter. "Hey, Barney Frank: The Government Did Cause the Housing Crisis," The Atlantic, December 13, 2011, http://www.theatlantic.com/business/archive/2011/12/hey-barney-frank-the-government-did-cause-the-housing-crisis/249903/

[40] Online newsroom of Bernie Sanders, U.S. senator for Vermont, July 21, 2011, http://www.sanders.senate.gov/newsroom/news/?id=9e2a4ea8-6e73-4be2-a753-62060dcbb3c3

[41] Bejan, Adrian and J. Peder Zane. *Design in Nature: How the Constructal Law Governs Evolution in Biology, Physics, Technology, and Social Organization.* Doubleday, January 24, 2012

[42] Lorenz quoted in James Gleick's *Chaos.*

[43] Bejan and Zane, *Design in Nature.*

[44] *Ibid.*

[45] Adrian Bejan, S. Lorente, S., and L. Lee, L. "Unifying constructal theory of tree roots, canopies and forests," *Journal of Theoretical Biology* (forthcoming).

[46] Bejan and Zane, *Design in Nature.*

[47] Bejan and Zane, *Design in Nature.*

[48] John Mackey, "Conscious Capitalism: Creating a New Paradigm for Business," blog for Whole Foods Market, http://www.wholefoodsmarket.com/blog/john-mackeys-blog/conscious-capitalism-creating-new-paradigm-for%C2%

[49] http://www.taxfoundation.org/news/printer/250.html

[50] Higgs, Robert. "Nineteen Neglected Consequences of Income Redistribution," The Freeman, December 1994, Volume 44, Issue 12, http://www.thefreemanonline.org/columns/nineteen-neglected-consequences-of-income-redistribution/

[51] Winship, Scott. "Mobility Impaired," National Review Online, November 7, 2011, http://www.nationalreview.com/articles/282292/mobility-impaired-scott-winship?pg=3

[52] Sowell, Thomas. "The Poverty Empire," uploaded October 15, 2010 by FreeToChooseNetwork, http://www.youtube.com/watch?feature=player_embedded&v=IwauhPzdnlc#!

[53] Biggs, Andrew and Richwine, Jason. "Comparing Federal and Private Sector Compensation," American Enterprise Institute Economic Policy Working Paper 2011-02 (revised June 2011), http://www.aei.org/files/2011/06/08/AEI-Working-Paper-on-Federal-Pay-May-2011.pdf

[54] Walzer, Michael. "'Spheres of Justice': An Exchange," *The New York Review of Books*, in response to the review "To Each His Own" (published April 14, 1983) http://www.nybooks.com/articles/archives/1983/jul/21/spheres-of-justice-an-exchange/?pagination=false

[55] Boudreaux, Donald. "Quotation of the Day," CafeHayek.com, March 5, 2012, responding to a line from "Robust Political Economy" by Mark Pennington, http://cafehayek.com/2012/03/quotation-of-the-day-224.html

[56] Will, George F. "Government: The redistributionist behemoth," Washington Post, January 6, 2012, http://www.washingtonpost.com/opinions/government-the-redistributionist-behemoth/2012/01/05/gIQAFqqpfP_story.html

[57] Novack, Janet. "Tax Waste: $6.1 Billion Hours Spent Complying With Federal Tax Code," Personal Finance, *Forbes* online, January 5, 2011, http://www.forbes.com/sites/janetnovack/2011/01/05/

tax-waste-6-1-billion-hours-spent-complying-with-federal-tax-code/

[58] Muhlenkamp, Ron. *Ron's Road to Wealth: Insights for the Curious Investor*, Wiley, November 2007.

[59] Meyerson, Harold. "A Different Recession," *The Washington Post*, January 16, 2008

[60] Boudreaux, Don. "The Real 'Truth About the Economy': Have Wages Stagnated?" YouTube video posted January 31, 2012, by LearnLiberty.org, http://www.youtube.com/watch?v=s6FmhXQ32Wo

[61] Boudreaux, Don. "The Real 'Truth About the Economy': Have Wages Stagnated?" http://mungowitzend.blogspot.com/2012/01/d-bood-deals.html

[62] Krugman, Paul. "Progress or Regress?" *New York Times*, September 15, 2006, http://www.nytimes.com/2006/09/15/opinion/15krugman.html?_r=2

[63] Sowell, Thomas. *Economic Facts and Fallacies*. Basic Books, 2008. pg. 125.

[64] Freddoso, David. "The Myth of Household Wage Stagnation," *National Review Online*, March 11, 2008, http://www.nationalreview.com/corner/160157/myth-household-wage-stagnation/david-freddoso

[65] The Equality Trust, http://www.equalitytrust.org.uk/why

[66] Joyner, James. "U.S. Life Expectancy: We're Number 1," *Outside the Beltway*, July 31, 2009, http://www.outsidethebeltway.com/us_life_expectancy_were_number_1/

[67] http://www.biggovhealth.org/resource/myths-facts/infant-mortality-and-premature-birth/

[68] Grady, Denise. "Premature Births Are Fueling Higher Rates of Infant Mortality in U.S., Report Says," *New York Times*, November 3, 2009, http://www.nytimes.com/2009/11/04/health/04infant.html

[69] Gordon, John Steele. "Blowing the Statistics," *Commentary*, February 27, 2011, http://www.commentarymagazine.com/2011/02/27/blowing-the-statistics/

[70] Simon, Julian. "Julian Simon on Resources, Growth and Human Progress," posted on YouTube by FreeToChooseNetwork, October 1, 2010, http://www.youtube.com/watch?v=mV_38mQ1iG4&feature=player_embedded#!

[71] Putnam, Robert. "E Pluribus Unum: Diversity and Community in the Twenty-first Century -- The 2006 Johan Skytte Prize Lecture." Scandinavian Political Studies 30 (2): 137–174. doi:10.1111/j.1467-9477.2007.00176.x.

[72] *Ibid.*

[73] Transparency International, "Corruption perceptions index 2011," http://cpi.transparency.org/cpi2011/results/

[74] KIing, Arnold. "Should You Trust the Government," *Ideas in Action With Jim Glassman*, July 3, 2007, http://www.ideasinactiontv.com/tcs_daily/2007/07/should-you-trust-the-government.html

[75] http://www.edelmanhttp://cafehayek.com/2008/01/not-stagnant.html.com/trust/2011/uploads/Edelman%20Trust%20Barometer%20Global%20Deck.pdf

[76] Zakaria, Fareed. "The downward path of upward mobility," Opinions, *WashingtonPost.com*, November 9, 2011, http://www.washingtonpost.com/opinions/the-downward-path-of-upward-mobility/2011/11/09/gIQAegpS6M_story.html

[77] Sanandaji, Tino. "American mobility is high and increasing," *Super Economy: Kurdish-Swedish perspectives on the American economy*, November 2, 2011, http://super-economy.blogspot.com/2011/11/income-mobility-is-high-and-increasing.html

[78] http://www.economicmobility.org/

[79] de Rugy, Veronique. "De Rugy vs. Chait: Round 2," The Corner, *National Review Online*, February

10, 2012, http://www.nationalreview.com/corner/290693/de-rugy-vs-chait-round-2-veronique-de-rugy

80 *Ibid.*

81 Nye, John V.C. "Economic Growth. Part I. Economic Growth and True Inequality," *Library of Economics and Liberty,* January 28, 2002, http://www.econlib.org/library/Columns/Nyegrowth.html

82 "Forbes 400 Richest Americans," September 2012, http://www.forbes.com/profile/bill-gates/

83 Meltzer, Allen. "Defending Capitalism." (Oxford University Press, 2012)

84 Caplan, Bryan. "The 4 Boneheaded Biases of Stupid Voters (And We're All Stupid Voters)," *Reason.com,* October 2007, http://reason.com/archives/2007/09/26/the-4-boneheaded-biases-of-stu/singlepage

85 Huemer, Michael, "The Irrationality of Politics," TedX video, http://www.youtube.com/watch?v=4JYL5VUe5NQ

86 Becker, Gary. "Market Failure Compared to Government Failure," *The Becker-Posner Blog,* September 8, 2011, http://www.becker-posner-blog.com/2011/09/market-failure-compared-to-government-failure-becker.html

87 McChesney, Fred S. and William F. Shughart II. *The Causes and Consequences of Antitrust: The Public-Choice Perspective.* (University of Chicago Press, March 15, 1995) http://books.google.com/books/about/The_causes_and_consequences_of_antitrust.html?id=hb6K5tqjUPMC

88 Meltzer, Allan H. "Why Capitalism?" (Oxford University Press, February 20, 2012)

89 Tullock, Gordon. "Voting Schmoting," film by Chris Metzler and Josh Kurz, posted August 22, 2008, http://www.youtube.com/watch?v=21uJUZuIcEo

90 Reed, Lawrence. "The Golden Calf of Democracy: Democracy May Be the World's Most Oversold Concept of Political Governance," Ideas and Consequences, *The Freeman,* December 2004, http://www.thefreemanonline.org/columns/ideas-and-consequences/ideas-and-consequences-the-golden- calf-of-democracy/

91 Mencken, H.L. "Prejudices: Fourth Series." http://www.unz.org/Pub/MenckenHL-1924

92 Brooks, Michael. "Born believers: How your brain creates God," Science in Society, *New Scientist,* February 4, 2009, http://www.newscientist.com/article/mg20126941.700-born-believers-how-your-brain-creates-god.html

93 Plummer, Brad. "Ezra Klein's Wonkblog," *Washington Post,* September 9, 2011.

94 Roberts, Russell. "More scientism from the defenders of stimulus," *Café Hayek,* September 13, 2011 http://cafehayek.com/2011/09/more-scientism-from-the-defenders-of-stimulus.html

95 Dyson, Freeman. "Heretical Thoughts about Science and Society," *Edge,* August 8, 2007, http://www.edge.org/3rd_culture/dysonf07/dysonf07_index.html

96 Kling, Arnold. "The soothsayers of macroeconomics," The American, September 19, 2011, http://www.american.com/archive/2011/september/the-soothsayers-of-macroeconometrics

97 Tetlock, Philip E. "Expert Political Judgment: How Good Is It? How Can We Know?" (Princeton University Press. July 5, 2005)

98 From Plato's Euthyphro, http://en.wikipedia.org/wiki/Euthyphro_dilemma

99 Hammermesh, Daniel S. "Ugly? You May Have a Case," Sunday Review, *The New York Times,* August 28, 2011, http://www.nytimes.com/2011/08/28/opinion/sunday/ugly-you-may-have-a-case.html

100 Cohen, Patricia. "Professor Is a Label That Leans to the Left," Arts, *New York Times,* January 17, 2010, http://www.nytimes.com/2010/01/18/arts/18liberal.html

[101] The University of Chicago Law Review (The University of Chicago Press, 1949), pp. 417-433.

[102] Cardiff, Christopher F. and Klein, Daniel B. "Faculty Partisan Affiliations in all Disciplines: A Voter-Registration Study," *Critical Review*, Vol. 17, Nos. 3–4 (2005), http://www.criticalreview.com/2004/pdfs/cardiff_klein.pdf

[103] Nozick, Robert. "Why Do Intellectuals Oppose Capitalism?" Cato Policy Report, January/February 1998, http://www.cato.org/pubs/policy_report/cpr-20n1-1.html

[104] *Ibid.*

[105] Feser, Edward. "Why are universities dominated by the Left?" *Tech Central Station*, 2004

[106] California Postsecondary Education Commission, "Faculty Salaries at California's Public Universities, 2007-08," http://www.cpec.ca.gov/completereports/2007reports/07-15.pdf

[107] http://dailycaller.com/2012/05/15/rot-at-potemkin-u/

[108] Feser, Edward. "Why are universities dominated by the Left?" *Tech Central Station*, 2004

[109] Tierney, John. "Social psychologists detect liberal bias within," *The New York Times*, February 7, 2011, http://www.nytimes.com/2011/02/08/science/08tier.html?_r=0

[110] http://www.simplypsychology.org/social-identity-theory.html

[111] Toyama, Kentaro. "The case for happiness-based economics," *The Atlantic*, March 21, 2011, http://www.theatlantic.com/business/archive/2011/03/the-case-for-happiness-based-economics/72764/

[112] *Ibid.*

[113] *Ibid.*

[114] *Ibid.*

[115] Cohen, Roger. "The happynomics of life," *The New York Times*, March 12, 2011, http://www.nytimes.com/2011/03/13/opinion/13cohen.html

[116] Mill, John Stuart. *On Liberty*, 1869.

[117] Michael I. Norton and Dan Ariely. "Spreading the wealth," Los Angeles Times, November 8, 2010, http://articles.latimes.com/2010/nov/08/opinion/la-oe-norton-wealth-inequality-20101108

[118] Norton, Michael I. and Dan Ariely. "Building a Better America—One Wealth Quintile at a Time," *Perspectives on Psychological Science* (2011, 6:9). doi: 10.1177/1745691610393524

[119] Sowell, Thomas. "Intellectuals and society," *Creators Syndicate*, January 2010, http://www.creators.com/opinion/thomas-sowell/intellectuals-and-society.html

[120] Sowell, Thomas. *A Conflict of Visions* (New York: Basic Books, 2002), 71.

[121] Weaver, Richard M. *Ideas Have Consequences*, Chicago: University of Chicago Press, September 1984.

[122] Sowell, Thomas. *The Vision of the Anointed: Self-Congratulation as a Basis for Social Policy*. Basic Books, June 1996.

[123] Henderson, David. "How I fought envy," Econlog, August 16, 2011, http://econlog.econlib.org/archives/2011/08/how_i_fought_en.html

[124] Matthew Yglesias. "The Money is the Scandal," *Think Progress*, April 26, 2010, http://thinkprogress.org/yglesias/2010/04/26/197004/the-money-is-the-scandal/?mobile=nc

[125] Mencken, H. L. *A Mencken Chrestomathy*, Vintage, April 1982

[126] Aquinas, Thomas. *Summa Theologica*.

[127] Cosmides, Leda and Tooby, John. "The multi modular nature of human intelligence," *Origin and*

Evolution of Intelligence, Los Angeles, Center for the Study of Evolution and Origin of Life, 1997.

[128] Tooby, J., Cosmides, Leda and Barrett, H. Clark. "Resolving the Debate on Innate Ideas," last modified August 5, 2011, http://www.psych.ucsb.edu/research/cep/papers/innate05.pdf

[129] From an interview with Max Krasnow.

[130] Ridley, Matt. *The Origins of Virtue*, Penguin Books, 1998

[131] From an interview with Max Krasnow.

[132] Charlie L. Hardy and Mark Van Vugt. "Nice Guys Finish First: The Competitive Altruism Hypothesis," *Personality and Social Psychology Bulletin*, Vol. 32, No. 10 (October 2006), doi: 10.1177/0146167206291006

[133] John Cloud. "Competitive Altruism: Being Green in Public," *Science, Time*, June 3, 2009, http://www.time.com/time/health/article/0,8599,1902361,00.html

[134] Wilson, Bart. "Experimental economist on the meaning of 'fair'," Reason.tv video, July 30, 2010, http://youtu.be/HaFpB7z5y3Y

[135] *Ibid.*

[136] Pinker, Steven. *The Blank Slate: The Modern Denial of Human Nature*, Viking, September 2002

[137] Gladwell, Malcolm. *The Tipping Point*, Back Bay Books, January 2002

[138] McCloskey, Deidre. "Bourgeois Virtues?" *Cato Policy Report*, May/June 2006, http://www.cato.org/research/articles/cpr28n3-1.html

[139] Ariely, Dan. "Wealth Inequality in America," http://danariely.com/2010/09/30/wealth-inequality/

[140] Caplan, Bryan. "Hard-Wired Envy," *Library of Economics and Liberty*, http://econlog.econlib.org/archives/2011/08/hard-wired_envy.html

[141] Pinker, Steven, *The Blank Slate: The Modern Denial of Human Nature*, Viking, September 2002

[142] Choi, Young Back. "Misunderstanding distribution." Paul, E.F., Miller, F.D. , Paul, J. (eds.) *Should Differences in Income and Wealth Matter?* Cambridge University Press, January 2002

[143] Angier, Natalie. "The pathological altruist gives until someone hurts," *The New York Times*, October 3, 2011

[144] This chapter was first published in *The American* magazine under the same title.

[145] Bragg, Rick. "Oseola McCarty: Washerwoman with a Heart of Gold," *The New York Times*, September 28, 1999.

[146] Schultz, Ron. "Adjacent Opportunities: Engaged Emergence—Part 2," *E:CO*, Vol. 11 No. 3, 2009 pp. 85-86.

[147] Beito, David. *The Voluntary City*, University of Michigan Press, May 2002

[148] *Ibid.*

[149] *The Voluntary City*, pg. 194.

[150] *The Voluntary City*, pg. 196.

[151] Haidt, Jonathan. *The Righteous Mind*, pg 101-102.

[153] Congressional Budget Office, "A 125-Year Picture of the Federal Government's Share of the Economy, 1950 to 2075," June 4, 2002. http://www.cbo.gov/doc.cfm?index=3521&type=0.

[154] Wasley, Paula. "Charitable Donations Fell by Nearly 6% in 2008, the Sharpest Drop in 53 Years," *The Chronicle of Philanthropy*, June 10, 2009, pg. 194, http://philanthropy.com/article/Charita-

ble-Donations-Fell-by/63106/.

[155] Part of this chapter appeared in the journal *Conversations on Philanthropy*, published by The Philanthropic Enterprise.

[156] Shirky, Clay. *Here Comes Everybody: The Power of Organizing Without Organization*. Penguin Press: 2008.

[157] Meltzer, Allan. *Why Capitalism?* Oxford University Press, February 2012

[158] http://www.omidyar.com/investment_areas/access-capital/microfinance

[159] Stutz, Terrence. "Spending per student drops sharply in Texas public schools," *The Dallas Morning News*, February 22, 2012, http://trailblazersblog.dallasnews.com/archives/2012/02/spending-on-public-school-stud.html

[160] Mackey, John. "Creating a new paradigm for business," *Be the Solution* (Michael Strong), Wiley, March 2009

[161] Strong, Michael. *Be the Solution*, Wiley, March 2009

[162] Hayek, F.A. "The meaning of competition," *Individualism and Economic Order*, Mises Institute Books, 2009

[163] Borders, Max. "The Plan to Replace the Welfare State," *Ideas in Action With Jim Glassman*, March 28, 2006, http://www.ideasinactiontv.com/tcs_daily/2006/03/the-plan-to-replace-the-welfare-state.html

[164] Murray, Charles. "In Our Hands: A Plan To Replace the Welfare State," (Aei Press: February 21, 2006)

[165] Borders, Max. "The Plan to Replace the Welfare State"

[166] Ebeling, Richard. "No buts about freedom," *The Freeman*, July 2005, http://www.thefreemanonline.org/columns/from-the-president/no-buts-about-freedom/